The Rise of Cities

For more than fifty years, since the works on the rise of cities in north-west Europe by Fernand Vercauteren, François-Louis Ganshof and Hans Van Werveke were published, no synthesis which systematically examines the growth and development of cities in north-west Europe has been written. Adriaan Verhulst takes as his subject the history of urban settlements and towns in the region between the rivers Somme and Meuse from the late Roman period (fourth century) to the end of the twelfth century. This region comprises Flanders and Liège, two of the most urbanized areas not only in the southern Netherlands but in north-west Europe as a whole until the twelfth century. Fifteen towns are studied in all, and Professor Verhulst provides rich details of the impact of political, military and ecclesiastical as well as social and economic factors on the developing towns, as they were transformed from regional markets to centres of industry and international commerce.

ADRIAAN VERHULST is Professor Emeritus at the University of Ghent. He has written many books, including *Rural and Urban Aspects of Early Medieval Northwest Europe* (1992), and has contributed articles to journals such as the *Journal of Medieval History*, *Past and Present* and the *Economic History Review*.

Themes in International Urban History

Series Editors
PETER CLARK
DAVID REEDER

The Centre for Urban History, University of Leicester

This series examines from an international perspective key themes in the historic development of cities and societies. The series is principally, although not exclusively, concerned with the European city, with an emphasis on the early modern and modern periods, and it will consider urban systems, structures and processes. Individual volumes will bring together and present in an accessible form the best work of the wide variety of scholars from different disciplines and nations currently engaged in research on urban history. The series is published by Cambridge University Press and Editions de la Maison des Sciences de l'Homme in association with the Centre for Urban History, University of Leicester. The first volumes in the series include collections of commissioned pieces organized around certain key themes that lend themselves to comparative analysis. They have a substantive introduction by the volume editor/s, making explicit linkages between individual essays and setting out the overall significance and context of the work. *Themes in International Urban History* will interest scholars and students in a variety of sub-disciplines within social and economic history, geography, sociology and urban planning. It rides on the wave of important and exciting new developments in the study of cities and their history, and reflects the growing internationalization of the area of study.

Titles already published

1 Edited by Ronald K. Goodenow and William E. Marsden *The City and Education in Four Nations*
2 Bernard Lepetit *The Pre-industrial Urban System: France 1740–1840*
3 Edited by Peter Clark *Small Towns in Early Modern Europe*
4 Adriaan Verhulst *The Rise of Cities in North-West Europe*

The Rise of Cities in
North-West Europe

Adriaan Verhulst

CAMBRIDGE
UNIVERSITY PRESS

Editions de la Maison des Sciences de l'Homme

PUBLISHED BY THE PRESS SYNDICATE OF THE UNIVERSITY OF CAMBRIDGE
The Pitt Building, Trumpington Street, Cambridge CB2 1RP, United Kingdom

CAMBRIDGE UNIVERSITY PRESS
The Edinburgh Building, Cambridge, CB2 2RU, UK http://www.cup.cam.ac.uk
40 West 20th Street, New York, NY 10011–4211, USA http://www.cup.org
10 Stamford Road, Oakleigh, Melbourne 3166, Australia

and Editions de la Maison des Sciences de l'Homme
54 Boulevard Raspail, 75270 Paris Cedex 06

© Maison des Sciences de l'Homme 1999
and Cambridge University Press

First published 1999

Printed in the United Kingdom at the University Press, Cambridge

Typeset in Plantin 10/12pt [VN]

A catalogue record for this book is available from the British Library

Library of Congress Cataloguing in Publication data

Vershulst, Adriaan E.
The rise of cities in north-west Europe/Adriaan Verhulst.
  p. cm. – (Themes in international urban history)
Includes bibliographical references.
ISBN 0 521 46491 9 (hb). – ISBN 0 521 46909 0 (pb)
1. Cities and towns – Europe, northern – History – To 1500
2. Urbanization – Europe, northern – History – To 1500. I. Title.
II. Series.
HT131.V467 1999
307.76'0948–dc21 98–43641 CIP

ISBN 0 521 46491 9 hardback
ISBN 0 521 46909 0 paperback
ISBN 2-7351-0817-1 hardback (France only)
ISBN 2-7351-0818-X paperback (France only)

Contents

Maps

Editor's preface

Written by one of the most distinguished historians of medieval Europe, this volume is important for four reasons. First, it brings together and presents in a coherent, wide-ranging argument a great deal of the recent research on the southern Netherlands by French, Dutch, Belgian and German scholars; some of this work has been hidden in local or regional publications. Secondly, the book mobilizes the discoveries and insights not just of a diversity of historians (political, religious and agrarian as well as urban), but of archaeologists and numismatists. This gives a methodological richness to the study and puts it at the forefront of writing in the field. Thirdly, Professor Verhulst offers a powerful critique of much of the earlier writing on the rise of European cities in the high Middle Ages. In particular, the influential views of Henri Pirenne, a previous professor at Ghent, are finally given a decent funeral. Rather than being the flagship of European long-distance trade, as Pirenne argued, the major towns of the southern Low Countries had a much more complex evolution. Enjoying only limited continuity from the Roman era, their upsurge from the ninth century owed much to the patronage of increasingly buoyant abbeys and churches. In the next century there was the further stimulus provided by the backing of the Count of Flanders and by the breakdown of the manorial system. Growing regional market activity and the drift of industrial crafts to towns provided a springboard for the surge of long-distance trade.

The fourth reason for the importance of this book is that it focuses on one of the two most developed and successful urban networks in medieval Europe – along with that of northern Italy. Though more explicit comparison with the Mediterranean urban system might have been ventured, we get a clear sense of that complex interaction of political, locational, agrarian and other factors which contributed to the virtual invention of a new urban world in the southern Low Countries, one which, unlike in Italy, owed little to the infrastructure and urban design (if more to the urban concepts) of the Roman past. It was a dynamic urban system that despite regional shifts of power (from Flanders to Brabant) proved amazingly resilient, not only through the upheavals of the late Middle Ages, but over subsequent centuries.

Peter Clark

Preface

This book was prompted by the publication in 1991 of *Towns in the Viking Age* by Helen Clarke and Björn Ambrosiani. The fact that that book scarcely mentions the towns in the southern Low Countries and is chronologically restricted to the Viking Age – however broadly based, from the seventh to the ninth centuries – led to the realization that, apart from a number of valuable contributions in the old (1950) and new (1981/2) *Algemene Geschidenis der Nederlanden*, there is no recent work which provides a clear view of the urban history of the southern Low Countries from the late Roman period to the first burgeoning of the towns in the twelfth century.

Though they still have the capacity to fascinate, the works of Pirenne in this area are outdated, as is the work of Edith Ennen, *Frühgeschichte der europäischen Stadt* (1953), which deals with the southern Low Countries at some considerable length. Since then, and especially since the major overview in the form of an article by Franz Petri, *Die Anfänge des mittelalterlichen Städtewesens in den Niederlanden und dem angrenzenden Frankreich* (1958), much research has been carried out into the urban history of the whole of the southern Netherlands and into the emergence and earliest history of many individual towns in this area. I recently compiled and reprinted a collection of the most important of these studies in *Anfänge des Städtewesens an Schelde, Maas und Rhein bis zum Jahre 1000*, which appeared in the series Städteforschung, vol. A/40, produced by the Institut für vergleichende Städtegeschichte in Münster (1996). It can serve as a sort of reader for the work under consideration here. However, this book is based not purely on the studies dating from 1958–86 which were reprinted in the above-mentioned compilation, but also and in particular on studies which have since been published by myself and others, historians and archaeologists, about the history of numerous individual towns or groups of towns between the late Roman period and the end of the twelfth century.

Geographically, I have chosen the area between the River Somme and the River Meuse as a framework because this area comprises both the county of Flanders, which reached almost to the Somme, and the prince-bishopric of Liège, whose leading medieval cities lay on the banks of the Meuse. The two areas were among the most urbanized regions not only in the southern Netherlands, but in north-west Europe as a whole, until into the twelfth century. The twelfth century has been chosen as the chronological cutoff point because that was when the cities under consideration really flourished for the first time, while in the second half and especially at the end of that century new developments began, from both a socio-economic and a politico-institutional point of view which would come to fruition in the thirteenth century. I have taken the end of the third and the beginning of the fourth century as the chronological starting point for the work, i.e. the commencement of the late Roman Empire, which signified a break in the urban history of the Roman period larger and more consequential than the migration of the Germanic peoples and the fall of the Roman Empire. The book has a chronological structure, and each of the five main chapters corresponds, I believe, to a specific period in the urban history of the southern Low Countries.

I am greatly indebted to my former collaborators at Ghent University, Dr Frans Verhaeghe and Dr Georges Declercq, now professors at the Vrije Universiteit Brussels, for the help they offered in a number of areas in the preparation of this work. Dr Arent Pol of the Koninklijk Penningkabinet in Leiden provided valuable information about the monetary history of a few places along the Meuse in the sixth–seventh centuries and kindly made corrections to what I thought I knew. I had an interesting and fruitful exchange of ideas on various aspects of the subject with Dr Derek Keene, Director of the Centre for Metropolitan History in London.

I wish to thank Professor Peter Clark of Leicester University for encouraging and making a critical assessment of my initial plans for this book and for introducing my definitive proposal at Cambridge University Press. I would also like to thank Richard Fisher, Publishing Development Director at Cambridge University Press, and his collaborators and referees for their interest in and commitment to the publication of this book, and to thank more especially Frances Brown for her accurate copy editing and her remarks, corrections and suggestions. Alison Mouthaan-Gwillim provided a careful rendering of my Dutch text into English and I am indebted to her for her work. Hans Rombaut was of great help in drawing up the maps. Luc Pareyn, Director of the Liberaal Archief in Ghent, allowed me to use a whole range of facilities that enabled me to prepare my manuscript for publication. I am also most grateful to Nancy Criel, a staff member at the Liberaal Archief, for all her typing work. Finally, my thanks must go to the Belgian National Fund for Scientific Research

(NFWO, now FWO-Flanders) which awarded us the funds for the project 'Historical, archaeological and topographical research into the emergence and the earliest development of the Flemish Cities (late Roman period–twelfth century)', thereby facilitating the realization of this work and making the English version possible.

A Note on place-names

Names of Flemish cities are given in their official Dutch form and names of French and French-speaking cities in their French form, except where a generally accepted English form exists, e.g., Antwerp, Ghent, Bruges, Brussels.

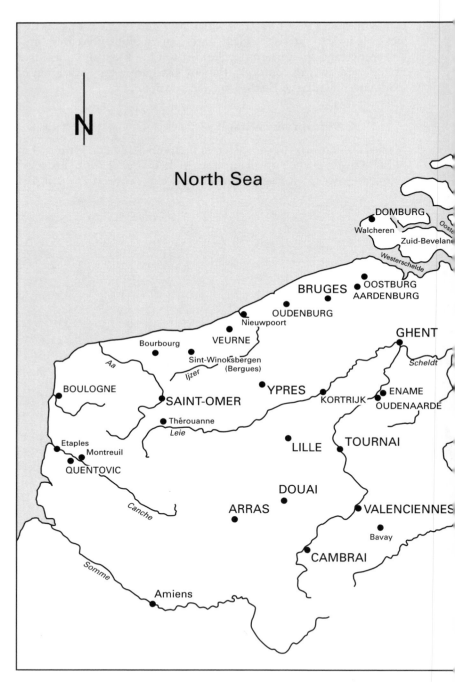

Map 1　Cities and towns between the Somme and the Meuse/Rhine delta up to the twelfth century. *Legend*: big capitals – cities individually treated at length; small capitals – cities treated briefly; big roman – geographical reference only; small roman – cities and places mentioned briefly

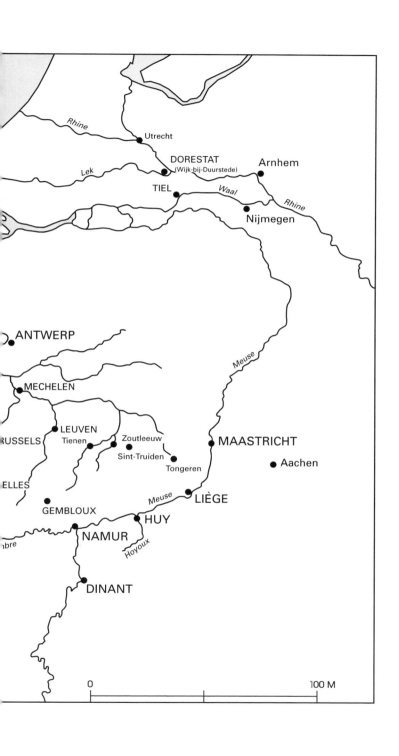

1 The transformation of the Roman towns

A history of the origin of the medieval cities between the Meuse, the Somme and the North Sea must begin in Roman times, even though there is no immediately apparent direct link between the emergence of urban centres in the eighth–ninth centuries and possible Roman antecedents.

The Romans did indeed introduce the city as a geographical phenomenon in the area under consideration here.[1] The real question we must ask, however, is whether the location of the Roman urban agglomerations determined the location of important medieval cities, and first and foremost of the oldest group of cities in the area in question, namely those which emerged in the eighth–ninth centuries. This does not necessarily mean, in our opinion, that the existence of an urban agglomeration in Roman times had any influence on or significance for the topography of most of these cities. This is only the case – and then still to a limited extent – further south than the area under consideration here, to the south of the Somme and Seine and even to the south of the Loire. In the regions between the Meuse, the Somme and the North Sea, probably only the location of the Roman city or agglomeration – and then usually not even in a micro-topographical, but in a general-geographical sense – affected the location of the oldest group of medieval cities.

On the other hand, medieval cities did not always emerge as early as in the eighth–ninth centuries on or near the place where a Roman city or agglomeration had existed. Sometimes this happened much later, in the eleventh–twelfth centuries, as for example in Tongeren, Kortrijk and Aardenburg; sometimes it did not happen at all, as in Oudenburg and Bavay. Moreover four phases are distinguishable in urban development in our area during the four to five centuries of Roman domination, and of these only the last, that of the Late Empire (260/84 to mid-fifth century), is of importance in the limited sense that we have indicated. A few cities, like Cassel and Bavay, which had been administrative capitals of the

---

[1] E. M. Wightman, *Gallia Belgica*, London, 1985, pp. 75–100.

civitas Menapiorum and the *civitas Nerviorum* respectively, lost this status at the beginning of the Late Empire, and with it their importance, to the advantage of earlier *vici* such as Tournai (*civitas Turnacensium*) and Cambrai (*civitas Cameracensium*).[2] Located on a waterway, the Scheldt, and no longer on a land route, in the ninth–tenth centuries these earlier *vici* – unlike Cassel and Bavay – would become centres not only of ecclesiastical administration but also of trade and industry. Above all, however, walls were built around large and small urban agglomerations at the end of the third century, enclosing a much smaller expanse than the earlier urban area (Amiens: 25 ha; Tournai: 13 ha; Bavay and Maastricht: 2 ha).[3] The walled centre was made into a sort of fortified citadel, which in some cities, such as Cambrai, would play the role of pre-urban nucleus in the emergence of the medieval city.

The Meuse Valley

Tongeren (Tongres), with a second, smaller wall – but 2,650 m in length nevertheless – dating from the late third century, and still one of the largest cities in the northern provinces of the Roman Empire at that time, is an exception to this, even if here too the surface area was reduced from 72 to 43 ha.[4] But it was Tongeren that was to founder as a city in the fifth–sixth centuries. It did not play an urban role again until the twelfth century, long after the episcopal see, which had been based there since the middle of the fourth century, was eventually transferred at the beginning of the sixth century to Maastricht where the first bishop of Tongeren, Servaas (d. 384), was buried.[5] Also interesting in this respect is the shift of a centre served exclusively by land routes, like Tongeren, to a place on a river, like Maastricht on the Meuse, though in this case at a later time and in a context different from the shift from Cassel to Tournai and from Bavay to Cambrai.

In **Maastricht**, as in many other places, the nature of the settlement in the fourth century is completely different from that before its destruction during one of the great invasions by Germanic tribes in the seventies of the third century.[6] A fortification was built on the ruins of the earlier *vicus* in the fourth century, around 333, a small fort measuring 170 by 90 m, the longest side being the one running along the (western) left bank of the

[2] *Ibid.*, pp. 204–5.   [3] *Ibid.*, pp. 222–7.

[4] J. Mertens, 'La destinée des centres urbains gallo-romains à la lumière de l'archéologie et des textes', in *La genèse et les premiers siècles des villes médiévales dans les Pays-Bas méridionaux*, Brussels, 1990 (Crédit Communal, Collection Histoire in–8°, no. 83), pp. 68–9.

[5] T. Panhuysen and P. H. Leupen, 'Maastricht in het eerste millennium', in *La genèse et les premiers siècles*, pp. 429–30, 432–3.   [6] *Ibid.*, pp. 411–49.

Meuse (Map 2). Like many similarly small fortified settlements, it is usually called *castellum* or *castrum*, though this word does not appear to have been used with reference to Maastricht in the Roman period.

The walls were probably provided with ten round turrets and two massive rectangular gatehouses. A wide moat was dug around the walls. The old bridge over the Meuse must have been repaired at about the time the fortification was built. The road from Cologne to Tongeren ran over the bridge and straight through the *castellum* in an east–west direction. Within the fortification there was a 30×15 m grain store or *horreum*, which was wrongly thought to have been the oldest bishop's church and the forerunner of the nearby Church of Our Lady. Another storehouse or barracks, built on the ruins of a former temple, stood against the inside of the bulwark near the west gate. So far insufficient archaeological proof has been found to ascribe a purely military function or population to the *castellum* of Maastricht, even though it is obvious that the fortification was built for military and strategic purposes. The development of a large cemetery on the road to Tongeren, 400 to 500 m to the west of the fortification near the later Vrijthof, gave the settlement an added dimension. This could be an indication of population growth during the fourth century. The first bishop of Tongeren, St Servaas (d. 384) was buried here. Later, shortly after 550, a cemeterial church was built over his grave. This church and the grave were both archaeologically identified under the crossing of the actual Church of St Servaas.[7] Under the successors of St Servaas, in the fifth or at the latest at the beginning of the sixth century, Maastricht became the centre of the bishopric, ousting Tongeren from that position. It is far from certain whether the bishop of Maastricht took up residence in the *castellum*, for no layers of waste dating from the sixth and seventh centuries have been found in the southern part. Traces of habitation from the fourth and fifth centuries have been found outside the walls of the *castellum*. They indicate the presence of a predominantly Roman population. Many typical fifth-century shards have been found, often with Christian motifs, while graves from the fifth century, unaccompanied by gifts and so undoubtedly Christian, have been found in the western cemetery near and under the Church of St Servaas. These signs of growth in Maastricht between the middle of the fourth and the end of the fifth centuries cannot be dissociated from the decline of Tongeren, perhaps as early as the fifth century. Indeed, finds from that century and later are extremely rare in Tongeren.

So, unlike Tongeren, in Maastricht there is clearly continuity through

[7] T. Panhuysen, 'Wat weten we over de continuïteit van Maastricht?', in C. G. De Dijn (ed.), *Sint-Servatius, Bisschop van Tongeren-Maastricht: het vroegste christendom in het Maasland*. Borgloon and Rijkel, 1986, pp. 125–46.

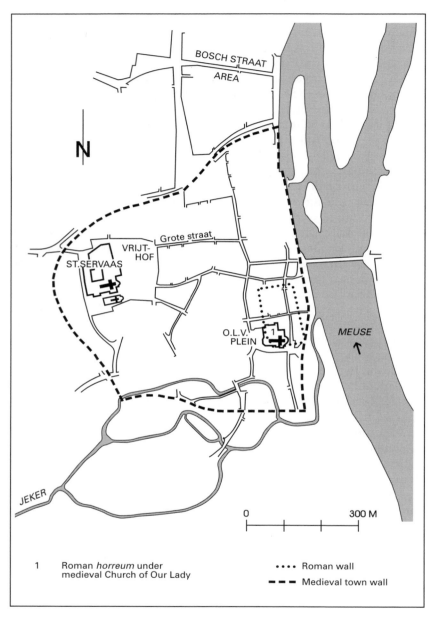

Map 2   Maastricht

the fifth century to the sixth, and not only topographical continuity with regard to location and structure but also continuity of habitation. The latter, unlike topographical continuity, is fairly rare in the area between the Meuse and the North Sea, at least as regards the furnishing of proof.

Upriver from Maastricht, in **Huy**,[8] there are traces not only of continuity of habitation but even of functional continuity. This however does *not* apply to the place where we would expect to find the oldest centre, that is to say the medieval Huy, between the right bank of the Meuse and the left bank of the Hoyoux, in the corner formed by the confluence of the two rivers, where the Church of Notre Dame has stood since the second quarter of the seventh century and possibly longer (Map 3). Owing to a lack of archaeological data, the siting of the oldest centre is based on evidence of a topographical nature like the debouchment of the Hoyoux into the Meuse, the jutting promontory between the two rivers close to this debouchment, the easily defensible site on that spot and the location of the oldest bridge over the Meuse. Furthermore, arguments of an ecclesiastical nature favour the siting of the oldest medieval centre of Huy and a certain continuity with the fifth century, namely the location of the Church of Notre Dame at the foot of the promontory, close to the confluence of the Meuse and the Hoyoux, and the fact that it had been the religious centre of the whole district, at least since the second quarter of the seventh century and perhaps since the fifth century. The traces of a Christian presence in Huy in the fifth century (see below) and the cult there of St Domitian, bishop of Tongeren-Maastricht between 535 and 549, who was buried in the Church of Notre Dame and whose relics were dated at between 535 and 640 using the radiocarbon method, serve to substantiate this early dating.

The parish of Notre Dame originally extended over both banks of the River Meuse. This fact is important because on the left bank of the Meuse, in the Batta area, close to the bridge over the river, archaeological evidence is said to have been found of a more than purely topographical continuity between the late Roman period and the early Middle Ages.[9] Five pottery kilns dating from the fourth–fifth centuries were excavated there, together with shards of late *terra sigillata* (fourth–fifth centuries) with Christian motifs. Furthermore, the discovery of pottery kilns, two of which date from *c.* 700, and of bone and metal workshops, with vestiges from the second half of the sixth century or from around 600, in the Batta and Outre-Meuse areas and on the right bank of the Hoyoux (rue des Augustins and rue St Séverin), led to the conclusion that there was continuity in the production of ceramics in Huy from the fifth to the

[8] A. Dierkens, 'La ville de Huy avant l'an mil', in *La genèse et les premiers siècles*, pp. 391–409.
[9] Bibliography of the numerous archaeological reports by J. Willems, *ibid.*, p. 393, note 9.

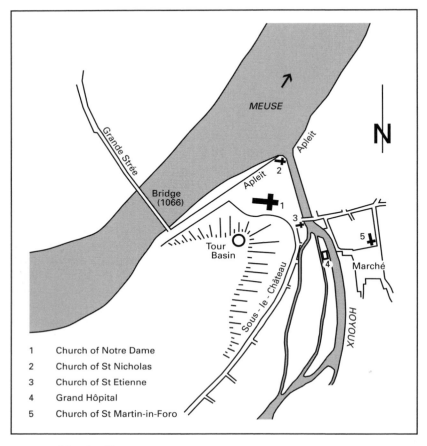

Map 3   Huy

eighth centuries and so a functional continuity. This is extremely rare. Traces of habitation on the left bank of the Meuse and the right bank of the Hoyoux since the beginning of the fifth century and the continuous subsequent use through the sixth and seventh centuries of some cemeteries on the left bank of the Meuse, to the west of the Batta area (St Hilaire and St Victor), could be further confirmation of the continuity of habitation on and in the area around these places. The question remains, in the light of all these facts, whether the name *castrum*, which was given to Huy on a seventh-century coin, relates to a possible reinforcement of the promontory at the confluence of Meuse and Hoyoux and if that reinforcement dates back to the late third or the fourth century, or whether it denotes a hypothetical fortification on Mont Falize on the left bank of the Meuse, a recent stratigraphic section of which appears to suggest dates from the fourth century. These questions have not been answered with any certainty, but this does not detract from the importance of the other arguments for continuity in Huy, as regards both occupation and function, between the late Roman period and the early Middle Ages.

In many ways the topographical situation in **Namur** is very similar to that of Huy.[10] Here, too, a promontory dominates between Sambre and Meuse: on top of it stands the modern citadel; below it the two rivers meet. However, as in Huy, it is difficult to furnish archaeological proof of the fortification of this promontory in the late Roman period, for information relating to an excavation carried out in 1885 is incomplete and not very accurate and some of it has even been lost. Yet a fortification is believed to have existed and a link is even made with a medieval fortification to which the oldest reference as *castrum* dates from the late seventh century. There is greater certainty, based on archaeological data, about the habitation at the foot of the promontory. This grew during the Late Empire by comparison with the left bank of the Sambre, where habitation was substantial during the first centuries of the Christian era but declined in the late Roman period. Growth can be identified from the end of the fourth and during the fifth century in the habitation between Sambre and Meuse, at the foot of the promontory which may have been fortified as a *castrum*, so that its continuity is almost certain until after the end of Roman domination.[11]

Clues about the Roman history of **Dinant**, upstream from Namur on the Meuse, are scant.[12] A Roman road led from Bavay to the Meuse near Dinant and bifurcated on the right bank in an easterly direction, with one road leading to Cologne and the other to Trier. However, we do not know exactly where it crossed the Meuse and whether it was through a ford or over a bridge. There is mention in 824 of a *pons publicus* in Dinant, located near the later Church of Notre Dame and thought to be of Roman origin. Likewise, the existence of a *vicus*, a little further upstream in the southern part of the city between rue St Martin and rue des Fossés, is still hypothetical, as is its conversion into a *castrum*, a term first applied to Dinant in 744.

[10] A. Dasnoy, A. Dierkens, G. Despy *et al.* (eds.), *Namur: le site, les hommes, de l'époque romaine au XVIIIe siècle*, Brussels, 1988 (Crédit Communal, Collection Histoire, in−4°, no. 15).

[11] A. Dasnoy, 'Les origines romaines et mérovingiennes', in Dasnoy *et al.* (eds.) *Namur: le site, les hommes*, pp. 9–32.

[12] J. Gaier-Lhoest, *L'évolution topographique de la ville de Dinant au moyen âge*, Brussels, 1964 (Crédit Communal, Collection Histoire in−8°, no. 4).

The Scheldt Valley

The arterial importance of the River Scheldt increased in the late Roman period to the disadvantage of the earlier road network. Likewise urban settlements along the Scheldt, which had hitherto been small *vici*, like Cambrai, Bavay's successor as capital of a *civitas*, and Tournai, Cassel's successor as capital of a *civitas*, also gained in importance.

All we know of **Valenciennes**, also situated on the Scheldt between Cambrai and Tournai, is that the name *Valentinianas* (manor belonging to Valentinus) is of Roman origin.[13] However, 5 km south of Valenciennes – not right on the Scheldt though only a few kilometres to the east of the river – lay the Roman *vicus* Famars (*Fanum Martis*). The fact that for the first centuries of the Middle Ages Famars continued to give its name to the *Pagus Fanomartensis*, whose name was only finally changed to *Pagus Hainoensis* after 900, together with the military importance of Famars around 400 AD, where a high-ranking general, prefect of the Nervic *laeti* (Germanic auxiliary troops) was stationed, may have played a role in the evolution of the *fiscus* Valenciennes to an urban settlement in the ninth century, after the relatively late decline of Famars.[14] In addition to a temple, hypothetically devoted to Mars, and *thermae*, which were converted into a *castellum* in the fourth century (after 333), this *vicus*, located on a byway of the Bavay–Cambrai road, probably had a *diversorium*, an inn for travellers. Here it was that at the end of the sixth century or the beginning of the seventh Gaugericus (St Géry, bishop of Cambrai 584/90–623/6), met a slave trader whose slaves, possibly from Central Europe, he released while the slave trader was asleep at the inn.[15]

An absence of archaeological excavations means that little or nothing is known about **Cambrai** during the Late Empire, except that in the third and fourth centuries it was an important textile centre whose products were traded as far afield as the eastern basin of the Mediterranean.[16] A wall was probably built around Cambrai in the course of the fourth century, as was the case with many other places in the north of the Roman Empire. This belief is indirectly derived from late sixth-century information which tells us that the wall was still in a good state of repair and provided protection. We can also deduce from this information that there was a building inside the walls which could still be used as a royal

---

[13] F. Deisser-Nagels, 'Valenciennes. Ville carolingienne', *Le Moyen Age* 68 (1962), pp. 53–6; H. Platelle, 'Du "domaine de Valentinus" au comté de Valenciennes (début du XIe siècle)', in *La genèse et les premiers siècles*, pp. 159–68.

[14] H. Platelle, 'Du "Domaine de Valentinus"', pp. 160–2.

[15] F. Vercauteren, *Etude sur les civitates de la Belgique Seconde*, Brussels, 1934, pp. 213–14.

[16] *Ibid.*, pp. 205–14; M. Rouche, 'Topographie historique de Cambrai durant le haut moyen âge', *Revue du Nord* 58 (1976), pp. 339–47.

residence and which was probably also of Roman origin. It would appear from a rather uncertain hypothesis regarding the location of the fourth-century wall that the fortified area was not much larger than 4 ha, which is relatively small compared with the 13 to 14 ha inside the Roman wall of Tournai and the 10 ha in Arras. In any case, the Frankish conquest of Cambrai and, from the middle of the fifth century, the sojourn there of a rival of Clovis, who defeated and killed him in 509, heralded a period of decline for the city which came to an end with the arrival of Bishop Géry in Cambrai at the end of the sixth century. Christians had certainly lived in Cambrai before the middle of the fifth century, possibly under the authority of a bishop. It is doubtful whether Christianity survived the seizure of Cambrai by the heathen Franks around the middle of the fifth century. At any rate, there is no mention of a bishop in Cambrai before the end of the sixth century, when Géry took up residence there as such. To suppose any form of continuity with the second half of the fifth and the beginning of the sixth centuries is therefore questionable.

Arras is situated on the Scarpe, a tributary of the River Scheldt, less than 40 km west of Cambrai, to which it was linked by a Roman road. Consequently, as one of the southernmost cities in the area in question, we are treating it here immediately after Cambrai and in the group of the Scheldt cities.[17] And yet so long as the Scarpe was unnavigable until the tenth–eleventh centuries, it was primarily important as an intersection of land routes: north-west via Thérouanne to Boulogne, north-east to Tournai, south-east to Cambrai and from there to Bavay and Cologne, and south to Amiens. In the third and fourth centuries it was the most important textile centre in the north of the Roman Empire. Its reputation in this respect had given rise to a major export trade with Italy and the Mediterranean world and continued into the sixth century. Arras' strategic location on the road to Boulogne made it an important transit centre for troop movements between England and the Rhineland. *Laeti* (Germanic auxiliary troops) were also garrisoned there around 400 AD. So it is not surprising that at the end of the third or the beginning of the fourth century the city was surrounded by walls. A section of those walls was discovered archaeologically not so long ago and is still being studied. The area fortified in this way more or less corresponds to the present-day park of the Préfecture, of which the east side is formed by rue Baudimont, where recent excavations have been carried out (Map 6). An area of 9 to 10 ha was enclosed, which is more than in Cambrai (4 ha), yet less than in Tournai (13 to 14 ha). Apart from the *castrum*, the urban settlement

[17] Vercauteren, *Civitates*, pp. 181–204; C. Brühl, *Palatium und Civitas*, I, *Gallien*, Cologne and Vienna, 1975, pp. 91–9; L. Kéry, *Die Errichtung des Bistums Arras 1093/1094*, Sigmaringen, 1994, pp. 211–24, 255–76.

dating from the High Empire (second–third centuries) was abandoned during the fourth century. The walls of the *castrum*, which was called the *civitas* (Fr. cité) in later centuries, still existed in the seventh century. By the second half of the ninth century, however, they were so dilapidated that they no longer offered any protection against the Vikings, when the latter destroyed the Church of Our Lady in the south-east corner of the *civitas* in 883. It is not known if this edifice and the later episcopal palace inside the walls of the *civitas*, which is now the seat of the Préfecture, stand on the site of earlier Roman buildings such as a *praetorium*. The recent excavations next to the eastern wall of the *castrum* have revealed two layers of a barracks dating from the late fourth and early fifth centuries. We know of the early presence of Christians in Arras in the fourth and fifth centuries only through later traditions. It is not even certain that Arras was ever the seat of a bishopric prior to 1094, when it became a bishopric independent of Cambrai. St Vaast, who lived at the beginning of the sixth century (d. 540) and is the only bishop of Arras known with any certainty to have existed before 1094, must have been a travelling bishop without a permanent residence.

There was, it seems, no continuity in Arras between the late Roman period and the early Middle Ages, more specifically with the second half of the seventh century when, in addition to the aforementioned Church of Our Lady inside the *civitas*, St Vaast Abbey also existed. The abbey was located outside the *civitas*, close to where the medieval city was to develop. At best the late Roman fortification provided some continuity in terms of location, but that can only be described as relative.

During the High Empire (second and third centuries) **Tournai** spanned both banks of the River Scheldt, which were linked by a bridge whose arches also carried an aqueduct.[18] The right bank was little more than an intersection for traffic on the main road from Boulogne to Cologne, and the most important edifices were located on the left bank: a building which has been identified as a *praetorium*; a second building which may have the ground plan of a basilica and *thermae* (Map 7). On the right bank there were probably storehouses belonging to the imperial *fiscus*, where stone, which was quarried in great quantities around Tournai and exported down the River Scheldt, may have been piled up. Little remained of all these constructions after the devastation unleashed during the second half of the third century. At the beginning of the fourth century, a stone wall was constructed on the left bank, enclosing an area of some 13 to 14 ha. This is quite a size compared to other cities fortified at that time. This bulwark still existed at the end of the ninth century,

---

[18] Vercauteren, *Civitates*, pp. 233–53; *La genèse et les premiers siècles*, pp. 169–233 (chapters by M. Amand, R. Brulet, J. Pycke).

when it was restored. Around 400 AD the walls probably encompassed a state-run workshop, a *gynaeceum*, where under the authority of a *procurator* women made kit, possibly mainly of wool, for the Roman army. There may also have been a military garrison stationed there to defend the Bavay–Tournai–Kortrijk road. There were several cemeteries outside the walls: in 1653 the grave of Childeric, father of Clovis, who had died in 481, was discovered in one of them on the right bank of the Scheldt in the vicinity of the later St Brice Church. Both Childeric and Clovis had stayed in a residence inside the walls which was inhabited by members of the Merovingian royal dynasty and still existed around 575. The oldest trace of a Christian presence in Tournai probably dates from the second half of the fourth century, and less disputable proof was found of the presence of Christians in Childeric's heathen burial place dating from the second half of the fifth century. The cemetery was still used from the sixth century until into the eighth century. Together these various details point to continuous habitation in Tournai through the fourth, fifth and sixth centuries and to the relative importance of the city as a political and administrative centre.

Kortrijk (*Cortoriacum*, Fr. Courtrai), on the same latitude as Tournai but located on the River Leie some 25 km to the west, was an important intersection in the first and second centuries AD.[19] Several roads ran from west to east close to the river along the northern and southern banks of the Leie (from Cassel and from Arras to Tongeren and Cologne). Not all of these roads have been identified with certainty as being Roman. On the south bank, a road from Tournai joined one of these roads. At that time Kortrijk was a large *vicus* covering an area of more than 40 ha on both banks of the Leie. As a result of the Germanic invasions in the second half of the third century, the *vicus* was largely abandoned by the beginning of the last quarter of the third century. Only a small part of it – 7 ha at the most – on the south bank of the Leie, between the medieval St Martin's Church, the marketplace and the Leie, was still inhabited in the fourth and the first half of the fifth centuries, as appears from the recent discovery of several shards of cooking utensils. It is far from certain that this area was fortified by a wall or bulwark. Likewise, it is equally uncertain whether the *Cortoriacenses* cavalry unit, which is mentioned in the *Notitia dignitatum* around the year 400, was quartered in Kortrijk itself, or if it consisted of cavalrymen from Kortrijk who were quartered elsewhere.

[19] N. Maddens (ed.), *De geschiedenis van Kortrijk*, Tielt, 1990, pp. 13–28; P. Despriet, *2000 jaar Kortrijk*, Kortrijk, 1990, pp. 9–17; A. Verhulst, 'An Aspect of the Question of Continuity between Antiquity and Middle Ages: The Origin of the Flemish Cities between the North Sea and the Scheldt', *Journal of Medieval History* 3 (1977), pp. 186–8 (reprinted in A. Verhulst, *Rural and Urban Aspects of Early Medieval Northwest Europe*, Aldershot, 1992).

There was a complete absence of information about Kortrijk after the middle of the fifth century until a few fragments of Merovingian earthenware were found inside the zone of the late Roman settlement. While difficult to date, they do suggest habitation in the sixth or seventh century. Continuity between then and habitation during the first half of the fifth century seems doubtful, however. Bearing in mind the lack of information about the late fifth, the sixth and the seventh centuries and the absence of any trace of urban life in Kortrijk in the ninth, tenth and eleventh centuries, it is difficult to interpret the reference to Kortrijk as a *municipium*, i.e. with the role of capital of a *gouw* (district or *pagus*), in the early eighth-century *Vita Eligii* as absolute proof of the existence of an urban settlement, which is permissible for the other *municipia* (Ghent and Bruges) mentioned at the same time.

Ghent lies on the Scheldt downriver from Tournai and some 60 km to the north of that city, at the point where the Leie enters the Scheldt, i.e. a very favourable location in terms of traffic.[20] So it is hardly surprising that the most important Roman settlement in the territory of the later city of Ghent was located at this very confluence, on a slightly higher (8–9 m) sand ridge along the (eastern) left bank of Scheldt and Leie (Map 5). This is the only favourable location for a settlement on either river in the immediate vicinity of the confluence. Directly opposite this spot, the right bank of the Leie and the left bank of the Scheldt where the rivers meet consist of low-lying, wet terrain (called 'meers' and 'briel' in Dutch; *mariscus* and *broilum* in Latin). In the seventh century the missionary Amand built a church at the higher place on the left bank, called *Ganda*, which means 'mouth'. Before the end of that century, the church became an abbey and was later called Sint-Baafs or St Bavo. A huge amount of Roman building material has been found, particularly in the abbey church which was demolished in 1540: fragments of roof tiles (*tegulae* and *imbrices*) and above all large blocks of tuff and sand-lime bricks. These materials may have come from one of the Roman public buildings in the immediate vicinity. *Ganda* is also important because this site stands out from all the other Roman centres of habitation in the territory of the later city of Ghent, not only because of the concentration of the finds, but also and above all because of their date, which runs uninterrupted into the late fourth century. This dating may indicate a late third- or a fourth-century military fortification, as are known to have existed in other cities. As well as being a toponymic relic, the use of the word *castrum* in the ninth–tenth centuries to refer to *Ganda* and St Bavo's Abbey should serve to strengthen this assumption. The facts that Amand founded a church there

[20] J. Decavele (ed.) *Ghent: In Defence of a Rebellious City*, Antwerp, 1989, pp. 28–59 (chapters by M.-C. Laleman with H. Thoen and by A. Verhulst with G. Declercq).

around 630 and that *Ganda* is the first and only place on Ghent territory where a commercial settlement grew up in the third quarter of the ninth century point to the importance of *Ganda* in the development of this first medieval commercial settlement in Ghent. This importance can perhaps be explained by the assumed continuity of habitation on that spot from the late fourth to the early seventh century. Continuity of habitation, however, is not in the least certain, although continuity in terms of location is beyond all doubt.

The other traces of Roman life in Ghent outside *Ganda* are much less relevant to the emergence of the medieval city. In the medieval centre of Ghent, which – as will be illustrated in a different context – was no longer located on the *Ganda* site after the ninth century, traces of Roman habitation and burial places were identified by means of finds from graves, concentrations of shards and random discoveries, partly in the vicinity of the oldest medieval urban church (the present-day St Bavo's Cathedral) and partly on the site of the medieval castle, the Gravensteen. Their location shows that when the centre of the medieval trade settlement was moved there after the ninth century, the area between the Leie and the Scheldt had already been inhabited for a long time. This may still have played a role in the location factor in the late ninth and tenth centuries without necessarily suggesting continuity of habitation from the Roman period. The dating of the Roman finds in the historical centre of Ghent is in any case fairly vague; in particular, it is unclear whether they carry on through into the fourth century.

To the north of Ghent, **Antwerp** lies some 60 km downstream, on the right bank of the Scheldt. Excavations in the 1950s and 1970s revealed traces of a totally unsuspected Roman presence.[21] These were single finds dating from the second and third centuries AD, mainly concentrated inside and just outside the medieval semicircular fortification alongside the Scheldt, of which the present-day Steen is a remnant and which was known by the name of *Burg* (Map 12: 'Burcht'; only the name 'Burcht-gracht' survived). The items discovered inside the *Burg* were Roman in origin and brought here from the surrounding area, whereas traces of a real settlement were found just outside the *Burg* when the present-day municipal car park was being laid. Its urban character, however, is very doubtful. On the other hand, there have been no Roman finds to date 1,000 m to the south along the same right bank of the Scheldt, i.e. on the site of the medieval St Michael's Abbey, where we can deduce from texts

[21] Verhulst, 'An Aspect of the Question of Continuity', pp. 195–9; A. Verhulst, 'The Origins and Early History of Antwerp' in Verhulst, *Rural and Urban Aspects*, XIV; T. Oost and R. Van Uytven, 'Een historisch-archeologisch overzicht van het vroegste Antwerpen', in *La genèse et les premiers siècles*, pp. 331–45.

that a fortification (*castrum*) stood in the seventh century. Since new Merovingian castles are rather rare, it may have been a Roman fortification. Yet, as is evident from its eccentric position, it played no role in the creation and location of the medieval urban settlement in Antwerp, perhaps because it was destroyed by the Vikings in 836 when they set fire to the *civitas* of Antwerp, a term which may refer to this castle. The commercial settlement (*vicus*) which grew up in Antwerp in the ninth–tenth centuries, as we will see later, lay 1,000 m to the north, in and/or outside the above-mentioned *Burg*, though there is no demonstrable link with the Roman vestiges excavated there.

If one follows the Scheldt downriver from Antwerp, i.e. in the late Roman and early medieval period along the Eastern Scheldt because the Western Scheldt did not exist at that time, then one comes to the sea on the north coast of the island of Walcheren. Just to the west of this estuary, on the north-west coast of Walcheren on the North Sea, near **Domburg** and a few hundred metres seawards of the present coastline in the then so-called 'Old' (Roman) dunes, which were engulfed by the advancing sea during a phase of transgression in the fourth–fifth centuries, there stood a Roman sanctuary with a temple dedicated to the goddess Nehalennia and probably also a commercial settlement.[22] One day in 1647, when the sea retreated far from the present-day coastline, remains of buildings, altars, votive stones and coins were found: proof of occupation in the second and third centuries AD, which ended fairly suddenly between 260 and 279, probably as a result of Germanic attacks from the sea. The advance of the sea in the fourth–fifth centuries, which is known as the Dunkirk-II transgression phase, meant that the site lay abandoned and eventually disappeared. Three centuries later, however, in the late sixth century, people must have begun to repopulate the area around the Roman site. Another commercial settlement began to emerge in the late sixth century approximately 1,000 m to the north-east, in the dunes – before they disappeared into the sea – and a couple of hundred metres beyond the present-day coastline. That settlement achieved its peak in the eighth century and at the beginning of the ninth. An account

---

[22] H. Jankuhn, 'Die frühmittelalterlichen Seehandelsplätze im Nord- und Ostseeraum' in T. Mayer (ed.), *Studien zu den Anfängen des europäischen Städtewesens*, Lindau and Konstanz, 1958 (Vorträge und Forschungen 4), pp. 464–72; P. A. Henderikx, 'The Lower Delta of the Rhine and the Maas: Landscape and Habitation from the Roman Period to c. 1000', *Berichten van de Rijksdienst voor het Oudheidkundig Bodemonderzoek* 36 (1986), pp. 445–599; Henderikx, 'Walcheren van de 6e tot de 12e eeuw' in *Archief van het Koninklijk Zeeuws Genootschap der Wetenschappen*, 1993, p. 115 note 2; S. Lebecq, *Marchands et navigateurs frisons du haut moyen âge*, I, Lille, 1983, pp. 142–4; Lebecq, 'L'emporium proto-médiéval de Walcheren-Domburg: une mise en perspective', in J.-M. Duvosquel and E. Thoen (eds.), *Peasants and Townsmen in Medieval Europe: Studia in honorem Adriaan Verhulst*, Ghent, 1995, pp. 73–89.

of this will follow in another connection. In the context of this chapter about the late Roman period, it is interesting to note that the location has remained practically unaltered, give or take 1,000 m. This is all the more remarkable because there is a gap of three centuries between the two occupations and very probably nothing remained of the Roman site in the sixth–seventh centuries. Perhaps in this case the explanation for the continuity of the location is not the Roman antecedent, but the favourable location at the Scheldt estuary.

The North Sea coast

If one follows the North Sea coast from the (Eastern) Scheldt estuary near Domburg to the south-west, bearing in mind that the estuary of the present-day Western Scheldt to the south of Walcheren did not exist in Roman times, then the first Roman urban settlement one encounters is the small modern-day town of **Aardenburg**.[23] It must have had access to the sea via one of the creeks which penetrated inland from the then coastline as a result of the flooding allied to the Dunkirk-I transgression in the last centuries before the beginning of the Christian era. The *Rudanna* watercourse, from which Aardenburg derives the first part of its Germanic name (original form *Rodenburgh*, *Rodenburg*), may have been the remnant of one such Roman creek in the ninth–tenth centuries. It was reactivated by the inundations of the Dunkirk-II transgression (fourth–sixth centuries). The *-burg* element of the name indicates that in the ninth–tenth centuries the Germanic-speaking inhabitants from the area knew the place via oral tradition, or perhaps from their own observation, as a fortification, probably as a dilapidated Roman one, which had lost its original name. Indeed it is very uncertain that Aardenburg was fortified again in the ninth century, as was the case in Domburg where a round fortification was built in that century. As in Domburg, at the end of the ninth century a round stronghold was also constructed in Oostburg, some 7 km to the north of Aardenburg, as part of the coastal defence against the Vikings. The late Roman fort of Oudenburg, to the west of Bruges, which shows a certain analogy with Aardenburg and will be discussed later, was not restored in the ninth century as a fortification against the Vikings either, but used as a stone quarry. Aardenburg was in fact a Roman camp dating from 170–225 AD which developed into an important civil settle-

---

[23] D. De Vries, 'The Early History of Aardenburg to 1200', *Berichten van de Rijksdienst voor het Oudheidkundig Bodemonderzoek* 18 (1968), pp. 227–60; Verhulst, 'An Aspect of the Question of Continuity', pp. 182–3, 194–5; R. Brulet, 'Le Litus Saxonicum continental', in V. A. Maxfield and M. J. Dobson (eds.), *Roman Frontier Studies 1989*, Exeter, 1991, pp. 163–4.

ment between 225 and 275 AD with (among other things) a large stone building, which could have been a temple, and turreted walls surrounded by a moat. Two coin hoards hidden around 271–3 AD confirm that the site was abandoned shortly after that. Unlike Oudenburg, Aardenburg played no role in the *Litus Saxonicum* coastal defence line during the fourth century, perhaps because it had become uninhabitable as a result of flooding during the Dunkirk-II transgression. Despite the fact that the site was uninhabited for a fairly long period, a new settlement started to emerge in the ninth–tenth centuries on the ruins of the Roman settlement in Aardenburg. It became a small town of more than regional importance in the eleventh–twelfth centuries.

Aardenburg was linked to **Bruges** in a westerly direction and further westwards to Oudenburg by what is generally regarded as a Roman road. This road crossed the Reie, i.e. the main watercourse in Bruges, at the very site of the castle built there during the ninth century, now in the centre of the modern-day city (Map 9). Roman archaeological remains have been found there *in situ* in recent years, as well as further westwards along the road.[24] Consequently it was believed that the medieval castle in Bruges might have been built on the remains of a Roman fortification, yet absolutely no trace of a Roman edifice has been found there to date, just a few single shards, such as have been discovered in several other places in Bruges. On the other hand, a real settlement was discovered in 1899 on the northern edge of the modern-day city, in the area called Fort Lapin, during excavation work for the port of Zeebrugge. This was a commercial settlement which developed fairly late, around 200 AD, but it was destroyed in the third quarter of the third century and shortly after this was flooded during the Dunkirk-II transgression. The floods reached the settlement from the sea via the creek on which it was located, thereby creating a favourable link with the North Sea. In the light of the recent Roman finds in the centre of Bruges itself, it is now believed that there must have been a link between the centre and the commercial settlement some 2,000 m to the north. The nature of this link is, however, far from clear. Moreover, it is not certain if some rare discoveries from the late third century and from the fourth century in the centre of the medieval city indicate a continuation of the Roman presence, more specifically a military one as indicated above. We are feeling our way in total darkness as regards habitation in Bruges in the fifth, sixth and seventh centuries. Yet it is interesting to note that the earliest provable medieval habitation in Bruges, as in a number of other places, was established in the area around and

---

[24] Verhulst, 'An Aspect of the Question of Continuity', pp. 178–80, 192–4; H. Thoen, *De Belgische kustvlakte in de romeinse tijd*, Brussels, 1978, pp. 107, 147; H. De Witte (ed.), *Brugge onder-zocht*, Bruges, 1988, pp. 16–19, 64–70.

partly on the very site of the Roman presence, despite a possible absence of habitation in the fifth, sixth and seventh centuries. As observed elsewhere, however, this choice of location could have been the result of the continued existence or even the improvement of a favourable geographic location on the edge of the Pleistocene sand bed and the polder plain which had been covered with clay during flooding. As we will see in another chapter, the link between Bruges and the sea was in fact maintained by the Roman creek to the north of the city which was widened by flooding during the Dunkirk-II transgression in the fourth–fifth centuries and perhaps even extended in the direction of the medieval centre.

The small town of **Oudenburg** lies some 15 km to the north-west of Bruges. Though an important fortified base on the coast in Roman times, in the Middle Ages Oudenburg did not become a town, of secondary importance, until the twelfth century.[25] It nevertheless deserves a mention here, not so much because of the important excavations carried out there over a period of many years, but because of certain comparisons (for example, with Aardenburg and Boulogne) and because of the fact that the Roman fort was used as a stone quarry in the tenth–eleventh centuries, partly for the construction of the castle in Bruges. This fort represents a third phase in the Roman presence in Oudenburg, when in the second half of the fourth century a larger fortification measuring 146 × 163 m (2.4 ha) was built in stone on the square ground plan of a clay fortification which was perhaps half a century older (Oudenburg II). Surrounded by a 20 m moat, this stone fortification consisted of a stone wall 1.3 m thick with round towers at the four corners and octagonal towers near the four gates. A main feature of the *Litus Saxonicum* was that the regular troops who had been stationed there were withdrawn after the year 400. This happened as part of the general strategic movement inland, but in Oudenburg more specifically also because the rising ground- and seawater caused by the Dunkirk-II transgression made use of the fort and its surroundings, including a camp village (*canaba*) and two cemeteries, increasingly difficult, despite the fact that they were located on a Pleistocene sand bed which formed a small peninsula surrounded on three sides by the rising seawater. The northern wall of the fort was even directly exposed to the seawater. According to a description in an eleventh-century chronicle from the Abbey of Oudenburg, which archaeology has confirmed, the foundations of the wall consisted of large square stones, probably from the Boulogne region, secured to each other by iron and lead.

We have no record of the Roman name of this important fort, which

[25] J. Mertens, 'Oudenburg and the Northern Sector of the Continental Litus Saxonicum', in D. E. Johnston (ed.), *The Saxon Shore*, London, 1977, pp. 51–62; Verhulst, 'An Aspect of the Question of Continuity', pp. 180–2, 190–1; Brulet, 'Litus Saxonicum', pp. 161–3.

suggests that the place lay abandoned for a long time, perhaps because flooding during the Dunkirk-II transgression in the fifth and sixth centuries rendered it uninhabitable and it became difficult to reach from the Pleistocene mainland, where rural Merovingian settlements have recently been excavated. The Abbey of Lobbes had a cattle pasture (*vaccaritia*) there in the ninth century. The Germanic name Oudenburg (*Aldenborg*), which appeared for the first time during the ninth century, leaves little or no doubt that no new castle was built there against the Vikings, as in Domburg, and that the name referred to the abandoned Roman fort. Only after the establishment of a chapter of canons, which was turned into a Benedictine abbey in 1090, did Oudenburg become a small town of secondary importance.

The Roman settlement in the 'Old Dunes' of **De Panne**, in what is now a nature reserve a few hundred metres to the east of the French–Belgian border, would not be mentioned here were it not for the recently launched hypothesis that there had been a trading settlement on the same spot since the end of the seventh century and during the eighth–ninth centuries and that its establishment was comparable with that of Domburg.[26] This hypothesis is based on the discovery there of a substantial quantity of *sceattas* dating from 680–750 AD and on the possible existence of one or two cemeteries. Moreover, the author of this hypothesis identifies the trading settlement in the dunes of De Panne with the *Iserae portus* where a fleet of Vikings moored in 860 and which has been difficult to locate. In the next chapter we will contest this hypothesis, showing that in this case the various data are too fragile for the problem of continuity even to be posed.

In reality there are no archaeological or historical indications of a Roman settlement of any significance between Oudenburg and Boulogne on or near the coast where a (trading) settlement might have grown up during the early Middle Ages and developed into a medieval city. Saint-Omer is a case in point. Lying close to the mouth of the River Aa between Dunkirk and Calais, it was to become an important city in the eleventh–twelfth centuries but had no Roman antecedent.

Boulogne, on the other hand, was an important Roman city, but, despite the very remarkable and exceptional continuity of its habitation in the fifth and at the beginning of the sixth centuries, its development into a medieval city did not take place during the early Middle Ages but had to wait until the tenth century.[27] The Roman name *Bononia* was used to

---

[26] J. Termote (ed.), *Tussen Land en Zee: het duingebied van Nieuwpoort tot De Panne*, Tielt, 1992, pp. 54–60.

[27] A. Lottin (ed.), *Histoire de Boulogne-sur-Mer*, Lille, 1983; Brulet, 'Litus Saxonicum', pp. 158–61.

refer to the upper town. At the beginning of the second century the troops of the *classis Britannica* were stationed there at an army camp with barracks surrounded by a stone wall. The camp was temporarily and partially abandoned soon after 270 AD, but shortly after that, at the end of the third century, a new turreted wall was built in the ditch around the earlier wall. In the thirteenth century this provided the basis for the city wall and enclosed an area of 320 × 400 m or 12 to 13 ha. The city owes its survival and that of its name to this fortification. We have no information about its military role as a possible part of the *Litus Saxonicum* in the fourth century. Boulogne is *not* mentioned in the *Notitia dignitatum* (*c.* 400 AD), though there are references to other places along the coast as moorings for the fleet, to the north of Boulogne (possibly Marck and/or Marquise) and to the south of that (possibly Etaples, on the right bank of the Canche, opposite Quentovic). This can probably be explained by the theory that the lower town, where the port was situated and whose name, *Gesoriacum*, disappeared for good at the beginning of the fourth century apart from a mention in Beda Venerabilis, could no longer be used as a naval base because the Dunkirk-II transgression had caused the sea level to rise. According to some, the port was moved upstream to Audisque on the River Liane. Attempts have been made to identify Audisque as the *portu Aepatiaci* referred to in the *Notitia dignitatum,* but others associate this mysterious name with the above-mentioned Etaples not far from the mouth of the Canche, 29 km south of Boulogne. Whatever the case, only the upper town of Boulogne continued to be of any significance after the fourth century: around the middle of the fifth century, the Roman troops there were replaced by Saxons from overseas who made cemeteries inside the Roman walls in the fifth and sixth centuries, a serious degeneration of the habitation though one that did nothing to interrupt its continuity. The occupation of the upper town by the Franks around the middle of the seventh century and the temporary resumption of minting in the second half of that century did not prevent Boulogne's further decline. Thérouanne and not Boulogne was chosen as the seat of a bishop in the second quarter of the seventh century, despite the fact that there was a church in Boulogne even at the beginning of that century which, according to some, dated back to a brief evangelization of the region by Vitricus, bishop of Rouen, around the year 400, though this is also doubtful. The resistance of the heathen Saxons, who were fairly numerous in Boulogne and especially around the city, would also explain the choice of Thérouanne rather than Boulogne as a bishopric. After the introduction of Christianity at the end of the seventh and the beginning of the eighth centuries, nothing is known about Boulogne in the eighth century. Even the fact that Charlemagne had a fleet built there in 810–11 as defence against the Viking threat and had the ancient fire tower restored says little about the economic importance of Boulogne at that time. One might well deduce from this that the port in the lower town was usable again, which is quite well possible after the end of the Dunkirk-II transgression, though its end must be dated earlier, at the latest in the sixth–seventh centuries. Consequently, it seems more likely that Boulogne never managed to recover as a port in the sixth–seventh centuries after being out of use for some three centuries.

In the meantime the traffic with England went through **Quentovic**, which began to emerge as the most important crossing place to England around the year 600 AD.[28] The explanation for this development should not in our opinion be sought in the fact that the port of Boulogne was unusable as a result of the rise in the sea level between *c.* 300 and *c.* 600. This probably affected the mouth of the Canche to the same extent, but Quentovic lay some 10 km upstream from there. Much later, in the eighth–ninth centuries, the site of Quentovic, which was situated on the very low left bank of the river, was having to cope with the problem of flooding, as the latest archaeological prospecting shows.[29] The question is why, despite being a generally less favourable site – though one which did offer some advantages (protection as a result of being 10 km from the mouth) – Quentovic grew up here.

There is scope within the limitations of this chapter only to pose the question – and it applies to other early medieval urban settlements too – of whether Roman antecedents played a role in the siting of Quentovic. The question can be answered positively, even though only one Roman kiln has been discovered a little less than 1 km south of the place where large quantities of Merovingian and Carolingian remains were found. This was between Visemarest and La Calotterie where, for this reason, Quentovic is currently thought to have been sited. Etaples, some 7–8 km downriver from Quentovic, on the other and higher right bank of the Canche and close to the estuary, was, as we have said, probably a Roman naval base and still served as a port in the ninth century. These Roman antecedents in the area around Quentovic currently seem to us too weak to be attributed the most important role in the siting of Quentovic. Moreover, the Roman roads in the area were directed at Boulogne and not at Quentovic.

[28] J. Dhondt, 'Les problèmes de Quentovic', in *Studi in onore di Amintore Fanfani*, I, Milan, 1962, pp. 181–248; D. Hill, D. Barrett, K. Maude *et al.*, 'Quentovic defined', *Antiquity* 64 (1990), pp. 51–8; S. Lebecq, 'Quentovic: un état de la question', *Studien zur Sachsenforschung* 8 (1993), pp. 73–82; H. Clarke and B. Ambrosiani, *Towns in the Viking Age*, London, 1995, pp. 16–18.

[29] D. Hill, 'The Siting of the Early Medieval Port of Quentovic', in *Rotterdam Papers* 7, Rotterdam, 1992, pp. 17–23.

Conclusion

We must now take stock of the significance of the Roman substratum in urban development during the early Middle Ages for all the cities and urban settlements with such a substratum that we have so far dealt with in the area between the Somme and the Meuse.[30]

Though a Roman substratum of some significance is often present on the site or in the area where a medieval city grew up in the seventh–eighth centuries or only in the tenth century, in most cases this has not been of decisive significance for the establishment and rise of the medieval city, as we will see in the next chapter. In only a few cases did the substratum consist of what is regarded as an actual Roman 'city', for example at Tongeren and Tournai. Even then Tongeren did not become a town of some importance until long after the beginning of the Middle Ages, in the eleventh–twelfth centuries, and then one which remained of secondary importance after it had lost all urban significance during the early Middle Ages. Tournai, on the other hand, achieved more than regional economic significance even as early as the ninth century. In most cases these Roman settlements were relatively small ones whose non-agrarian character is not always certain: either *vici*, whose structure was less strict than that of a real city (Huy, Kortrijk), or, more often late Roman (third–fourth-century) fortifications around an earlier civil settlement (Maastricht, Aardenburg) or established from the outset as fortified military camps (Oudenburg, Boulogne).

Apart from the possible presence of a Roman substratum, there is the question of the continuity of the settlements, particularly through the fifth and sixth centuries to the seventh, when in a number of cases urban life began again. Indications supporting the actual continuity of habitation through these centuries are very rare, though real in the case of Maastricht, Huy, Tournai and Boulogne. Functional continuity, more specifically of certain artisanal activities, is probable only in Huy, namely with regard to the production of ceramics. With the exception of Boulogne, which would only later – as of the tenth century – become a town of some (albeit secondary) importance again, this continuity of habitation probably played a limited role in the revival of these urban settlements in the seventh, eighth and ninth centuries, which – as we shall see in the next chapter – may be attributed in the main to totally different factors. On the other hand, it is interesting to note that in practically all the cases where urban life picked up again in the course of these centuries, it was in or near places where there had been Roman habitation. This link with the past

[30] F. Verhaeghe, 'Continuity and Change: Links between Medieval Towns and the Roman Substratum in Belgium', in *Studia Varia Bruxellensia* 2 (1990), pp. 229–53.

has taken various forms which can help to explain this general geographical and in some cases even topographical continuity. The geographic location and/or certain elements of the topography of the settlement in question may in itself have been favourable and have served as a draw. A location on a higher point alongside a river, and particularly on the confluence of two rivers, certainly played a role in the transition from antiquity to Middle Ages, as in Maastricht, Huy, Namur and Ghent, when the Roman land routes fell into a state of disrepair and diminished in importance.

The existence of a Roman fortification, or – in rare cases as in Huy and in Namur – of a natural protection like a high rock, was an attractive element. This element usually consisted of thick, high walls built at the end of the third or in the fourth century around a civil or military settlement greatly reduced in size, such as in Tongeren, Maastricht, Cambrai, Arras, Tournai, Aardenburg, Oudenburg and Boulogne. Even when these walls still existed in the seventh century, as they usually did, or were wholly or partially visible even much later (for example, in the tenth century in Oudenburg), or were used as foundations for the medieval city wall (as in Boulogne in the thirteenth century), then this still did not necessarily encourage continuity of habitation. Continuity is only more or less certain in Maastricht, Tournai and Boulogne, while in places like Tongeren, Aardenburg and Oudenburg the neglected walls became ruins in the sixth–seventh centuries. Indeed, in the last two cases, there was absolutely no continuity of habitation: the walls of Oudenburg even served as a stone quarry in the tenth–eleventh centuries. In fact, the existence and the preservation of walls were no guarantee *per se* of an early revival of the urban settlement, as Tongeren, Aardenburg, Oudenburg and Boulogne prove. However, in a number of cases (Maastricht, Cambrai, Arras, Tournai) these walls did serve as a geographical magnet which fulfilled a certain topographical role in determining the location, inside or outside the Roman walls, of settlements which for totally different reasons acquired an urban character early in the Middle Ages. These causes or conditions for urban development must take into account the role of these centres as a central place with regard to the surrounding area, particularly in the last four cases mentioned: for example, from the sixth century, as a bishopric, as in Maastricht and Cambrai (Arras and Tournai had no resident bishop before the eleventh–twelfth centuries); or as a residence of the Merovingian king or members of his family (as in Tournai and Cambrai in the fifth–sixth centuries) – even if that role was only temporary – because it nevertheless lent a degree of prestige to the place. Moreover, places which had not been actual cities in the Roman period, but settlements which were more urban than rural in character, owe their survival or their revival to their role as a central place in the new Merovingian administration of the sixth–seventh centuries. Specifically, this was the case for Ghent and Bruges, which were labelled *municipium* in the life of St Eloy written at the beginning of the eighth century, in the context of places with a Roman substratum designated as *civitas*. They were in fact capitals of a *pagus*, which was frequently even the continuation of a subdivision of a Roman *civitas* as an administrative district.

With these considerations and suppositions we are, however, anticipating the difficult problem of urban settlements in the Merovingian period which will be treated in the next chapter. As far as the Roman period itself is concerned, the urban decline was so marked from the second half of the third century that the Roman substratum which in a fairly large number of places dates from the late third and the fourth centuries was of secondary importance to urban development in the successive centuries and particularly to the revival which becomes visible in various places in the seventh century, after the gap of the fifth and sixth centuries. The dearth of contemporaneous written sources from these two centuries and the scanty archaeological information for that period – in terms of both quantity and quality – make it look as if the period constituted an all-time low. In only a few cases is a weak continuity of habitation demonstrable or probable; in only a single case a functional continuity (Huy). In practice only the functions of a few sites as central places in ecclesiastical and administrative terms ensured the survival of a number of late-ancient urban settlements and their role as a factor in the location of places with similar or new functions during the sixth–seventh centuries. The economic factor, which was of marginal importance in the Roman cities compared with their administrative and military role, played little or no part in this. These cities were already living – and increasingly so in the late Roman period – as parasites of the surrounding countryside. That countryside, however, yielded less in general, and certainly less for the landowning aristocracy which had remained in the cities since political and military events had brought about the collapse of the *villa* system and, as a result of the arrival of Germanic landowners in the countryside, the corrosion of the Roman tax system and the reduction of slavery. All this led to the collapse of Roman urban life. This situation was to continue until the late sixth and the seventh centuries when changes of a political-institutional and of an economic nature made themselves felt and had major consequences for urban development.

2   The nadir of urban life (sixth–seventh centuries)

The sixth and seventh centuries constitute a low point in our knowledge of most of the places which may be considered to have had urban or semi-urban characteristics in Roman times. This impression is first and foremost the result of the almost complete absence of written sources dating from that period and of the dearth of archaeological finds and the difficulty of identifying them. Moreover, in many cases the written information we do have about the sixth and seventh centuries relates only to members of the Merovingian aristocracy, to members of the royal house, and in particular to bishops taking up residence or staying in a city of Roman origin with the rank of *civitas*. Nothing is known about their exact place of residence, save that this was not necessarily always inside the Roman walls. Their presence may have had some economic significance owing to their wealth and their need for luxury and other goods. Centres other than the *civitates*, probably also with some urban functions, are only mentioned in the context of the activities of missionaries, such as those of St Amand in Ghent and in Antwerp in the second quarter of the seventh century. Even though seventh-century sources, and particularly the numismatic sources, are more numerous, the latter still pose major problems of interpretation. In particular, this applies to their generally accepted but questionable economic significance. Moreover, the accident of archaeological discoveries plays a large role, so that it is very difficult to gauge the importance, and especially the economic importance, of particular places, or of particular regions with a certain concentration of urban centres, within the area under consideration here or indeed within Western Europe as a whole.

In twentieth-century historical literature, then, two specialists in the urban history of the Meuse Valley, Felix Rousseau and Fernand Vercauteren, and other scholars such as Jan Dhondt and Franz Petri, credited that region with a huge chronological advantage in terms of the economic significance of the urban centres located there during the seventh century compared to more westerly-lying areas such as the

Scheldt Valley, and even to more easterly areas such as the Rhineland.[1]

On the basis of mainly numismatic sources[2] these scholars believed that in the seventh century the Meuse Valley was part of an international trade route which must have linked the ports of Marseilles and Fos on the coast of Provence, via the Rhône and Saône, with the delta of the Scheldt, Meuse and Rhine, a region that belonged to what was then called Friesland (Lat. *Frisia*). These scholars contended that, even after the decline of the Provençal ports early in the eighth century, Dinant, Namur, Huy and Maastricht would have continued to build on their earlier role and to maintain their economic importance as trading places during the eighth century. This view was strongly opposed by Georges Despy and his successor J.-P. Devroey.[3] The latter, in particular, has since contested the value of the numismatic sources as an indicator of the importance particularly of international trade, referring to the authority of Philip Grierson.[4] According to Devroey, trade was not the only and not even the principal driving force behind the circulation of coins: coins could be struck, used and collected for fiscal purposes, given as presents or used as payment for services rendered. Their quantity, the number of *monetarii* or moneyers and the continuity of mintage, which are generally used as criteria in addition to circulation, should be just as important, if not more so than this last criterion and be linked more to the political and adminis-

[1] F. Rousseau, *La Meuse et le pays mosan en Belgique: leur importance historique avant le XIIIe siècle*, Namur, 1930 (Annales de la Société archéologique de Namur 39); F. Vercauteren, 'La vie urbaine entre Meuse et Loire du VIe au IXe siècle', in *La città nell'alto medioevo*, Spoleto, 1959 (Settimane di studio del Centro italiano di studi sull'alto medioevo, 6), pp. 453–84; J. Dhondt, 'L'essor urbain entre Meuse et Mer du Nord à l'époque mérovingienne', in *Studi in onore di A. Sapori*, Milan, 1957, pp. 57–78; F. Petri, 'Merowingerzeitliche Voraussetzungen für die Entwicklung des Städtewesens zwischen Maas und Nordsee', *Bonner Jahrbücher* 158 (1958), pp. 233–45.

[2] P. Berghaus, 'Wirtschaft, Handel und Verkehr der Merowingerzeit im Licht numismatischer Quellen', in K. Düwel, H. Jankuhn, H. Siems and D. Timpe (eds.), *Untersuchungen zu Handel und Verkehr der vor- und frühgeschichtlichen Zeit in Mittel- und Nordeuropa*, III, *Der Handel des frühen Mittelalters*, Göttingen, 1985 (Abhandlungen der Akademie der Wissenschaften in Göttingen, Philologisch-historische Klasse, 3rd Series, no. 150), pp. 193–213; P. Grierson and M. Blackburn, *Medieval European Coinage*, I, *The Early Middle Ages, 5th–10th Centuries*, Cambridge, 1986; M. Blackburn, 'Money and Coinage', in R. McKitterick (ed.), *The New Cambridge Medieval History*, II, *c. 700–c. 900*, Cambridge, 1995, pp. 538–59; A.Pol, 'Les monétaires à Huy et Maastricht. Production et distribution des monnaies mérovingiennes mosanes', *Bulletin de l'Institut Archéologique Liégeois*, 107 (1995), pp. 185–200.

[3] G. Despy, 'Villes et Campagnes aux IXe et Xe siècles: l'exemple du pays mosan', *Revue du Nord* 50 (1968), pp. 145–68; J.-P. Devroey and C. Zoller, 'Villes, campagnes, croissance agraire dans le pays mosan avant l'an mil', in J.-M. Duvosquel and A. Dierkens (eds.), *Villes et campagnes au moyen âge: Mélanges Georges Despy*, Liège, 1991, pp. 223–60.

[4] P. Grierson, 'Commerce in the Dark Ages: A Critique of the Evidence', *Transactions of the Royal Historical Society*, 5th Series, 9 (1959), pp. 123–40; Devroey and Zoller, 'Villes, campagnes', p. 245.

trative significance – also in ecclesiastical matters – of the place where these moneyers worked than to the intensity of trade.

If we are to be able to judge this proposition, we need to examine aspects other than the purely numismatic, namely data about the political, administrative and ecclesiastical history of the places in question, as well as their geographic character, so as to link them to the numismatic data and to evaluate both groups of indicators from an economic viewpoint.

We will endeavour to do this for Maastricht, Huy, Namur and Dinant in turn, focusing on the seventh century.

The Meuse Valley

All the possible sources, written, archaeological and numismatic, are the most plentiful for **Maastricht**, which was in various respects the most important urban centre along the middle reaches of the Meuse throughout the period under consideration.[5]

When Maastricht was first called *urbs treiectensis* or *traiectum ad Mosam* by Gregory of Tours at the end of the sixth century, the bishop of Tongeren had been residing there since the beginning of the century. Bishop Monulf built a great tomb house above the grave of the first bishop of Tongeren, St Servaas, who had lain buried in a cemetery along the south side of the military highway to Tongeren, to the west of the late Roman *castellum* on the Meuse, since the late fourth century (384). The foundations of that tomb house were discovered under the present-day basilica between 1981 and 1990, together with the grave of St Servaas (Map 2). A community of *clerici* had probably served this church even in the sixth or seventh century, and in the first half of the eighth century it was designated a *monasterium*. The church was used by Bishop Monulf as an episcopal church, while a church within the fourth-century *castellum* probably served as a parish church. In 691/2 that parish church, dedicated to Our Lady, was granted immunity so that we can assume that the latter, and no longer St Servaas, was the episcopal church of Maastricht at that time. This can perhaps be explained by the hypothesis that the Merovingian king, who owned the Church of St Servaas, had made it and the annex buildings his place of residence, which meant that the bishop had had to move to the Church of Our Lady. At any rate, in 668/70 King Childeric II resided in Maastricht, because it was there that he conferred a charter on the Abbey of Stavelot. There is, however, no archaeological proof that he had a royal residence of his own, either

---

[5] Panhuysen, 'Continuïteit van Maastricht'; Panhuysen and Leupen, 'Maastricht in het eerste millenium', pp. 411–19; Devroey and Zoller, 'Villes, campagnes', pp. 234–6.

within the walls of the *castellum* where a Merovingian palace is generally sought, or in the vicinity of St Servaas.

Apart from the cemetery where St Servaas lay buried, which seems to have been intended mainly for the Germanic elite but which apparently had no settlements in its vicinity, two other cemeteries dating from the sixth and seventh centuries were discovered which did belong to nearby settlements. There are strong suspicions that more cemeteries existed, including one in the centre of the later city. Here, on the south side of the present-day Onze Lieve Vrouw-plein, i.e. south-west of the *castellum*, on ground that became habitable after the fifth century with the silting up of the Valley of the Jeker, the stone substructure of sixth- and seventh-century houses was uncovered. Near the cemetery on the Boschstraat, some 500 m to the north of the *castellum*, and also elsewhere, parts of narrow paved streets and ditches demarcating the borders of parcels of land were discovered. Numerous traces of sixth- and seventh-century artisanal activity were also found, namely bone workshops, a foundry that produced bronze buckles and ornaments, a pottery and even the remnants left behind by a sixth-century glass bead maker.

All this undoubtedly indicates a city in the making, consisting of various separate and perhaps still partly rural residential nuclei which were fairly densely populated. Moreover it still had the Roman bridge over the Meuse and perhaps also a mooring place on the river. No details about Maastricht's economic significance are available, however, other than the numerous gold tremisses which were struck there in the seventh century. Yet, as already noted at the beginning of this chapter, the interpretation of these coins raises great problems. They supply us with the names of no fewer than twelve moneyers (Lat. *monetarii*). These may have had a public function, though it is currently thought that they were private and rich persons working for the king and using the services of a travelling engraver, when they were not engravers themselves, which must sometimes have been the case, as indeed it was with St Eloy. Among the numerous moneyers working in Maastricht there were two, Madelinus and Rimoaldus, who also minted in Dorestat. The inscriptions on their coins from Dorestat closely resemble those of their Maastricht period. This particularity is currently explained by the hypothesis of the existence of a workshop in the two places, where both moneyers struck coins. It is also possible that Madelinus moved from Maastricht to Dorestat, because his Maastricht coins show a typological evolution and the Dorestat type fits in with the latest Maastricht coins. The large circulation of the Madelinus coins in early medieval Friesland, i.e. mainly in the river areas of the central Netherlands, their counterfeiting on a large scale in Friesland and the existence of numerous coins from

Maastricht in Frisian coin hoards point to a link between Maastricht and Dorestat in the first half of the seventh century.

However, Dorestat was not yet the Frankish kingdom's important gateway to the world around the North Sea that it was to become in the eighth century. It was first and foremost a military base for the Frankish king to the south-east of Utrecht on the Rhine, which formed the border with the independent kingdom of the Frisians.[6] As such it was captured from the Frisians by King Dagobert I (623–39), yet was lost again by the Franks probably around 650. It was not until 690/5 that Dorestat came under Frankish rule again, as a result of Pippin II's defeat of the Frisian King Radbod, before being definitively annexed to the Frankish kingdom by Charles Martel between 715 and 720. So the rise of Dorestat as an international trading centre began only at the end of the seventh century. During the period of the first Frankish dominion over Dorestat (*c.* 625–*c.* 650), when we know the names of only two moneyers in Dorestat, which is very few compared to the number in Maastricht (12) and in Huy (8), the sparsely populated settlement may have consisted mainly of a rural manor of the Merovingian kings. This argues against a purely economic interpretation of the linked mintage in Maastricht and Dorestat between 625 and 650. It seems equally acceptable to interpret the monetary connection between Maastricht and Dorestat at that time as the result of the military and political expansion of the Franks and more specifically of the Pippinids from the Central Meuse to the Lower Rhine under and after King Dagobert.[7] This does not necessarily mean that the position of power of the Pippinids in the area around Maastricht and the Central Meuse, and contemporaneously but only temporarily in Dorestat, had no favourable economic consequences, particularly for Maastricht. In our opinion the conditions for this were not in place before the end of the seventh century, or were insufficiently so. With the definitive establishment of the Frankish royal dominion over Dorestat and its economic rise beginning in the eighth century, these conditions were to provide the commercial stimuli from Dorestat which we believe offer an important explanation for the growing role of Maastricht in the flourishing international trade during the eighth century.

At first sight there are two arguments against this hypothesis concerning Maastricht: the significance in the seventh century of Huy, located on

---

[6] Clarke and Ambrosiani, *Towns in the Viking Age*, pp. 18–19; W. A. van Es, 'Dorestad centred', in J. C. Besteman, J. M. Bos and H. A. Heidinga (eds.), *Medieval Archaeology in the Netherlands*, Assen and Maastricht, 1990, pp. 151–82.

[7] F. C. W. J. Theuws, 'Centre and Periphery in Northern Austrasia (6th–8th Centuries)', in Besteman *et al.*, *Medieval Archaeology*, pp. 41–69; I. Wood, 'Teutsind, Witlaic and the History of Merovingian *Precaria*', in W. Davies and P. Fouracre, *Property and Power in the Early Middle Ages*, Cambridge, 1995, pp. 31–4.

the Meuse a few score kilometres upstream from Maastricht, and the shift of the bishopric from Maastricht to Liège around 720.

As regards the shift of the bishopric from Maastricht to Liège, the history of the evolution of Liège as a city shows that this was a purely religious matter which had nothing to do with a partial decline of Maastricht.[8] Lambert, Bishop of Tongeren-Maastricht, whose murder in Liège around 700 AD occasioned the religious and ecclesiastical rise of the place, was buried in Maastricht; his relics were only transferred to Liège around 715. Bishop Hubert (d. 727), who was responsible for their transfer, was invested as bishop in Maastricht around the year 700 and did not make Liège his main residence until much later, so that Liège eventually became a bishopric during the second half of the eighth century. At the same time Maastricht began to flourish as an international trade centre.

During the same period as in Maastricht, where twelve moneyers are known by name, no fewer than eight moneyers were working in **Huy**. Some sixty gold tremisses which bear the name of Huy (*Choe*), and also one coin on which Huy is even called *castrum*,[9] could sow doubts about the political explanation outlined above concerning the importance of Maastricht as a place where large quantities of coins were struck between approximately 620 and 650 and could suggest an economic explanation for this instead.

Yet recent studies attribute this great monetary activity in Huy, as in Maastricht, chiefly to the importance of Huy as a centre of power rather than to commercial activity. This explanation is supported by the following facts: Huy was very probably the centre of a Merovingian crown estate; it was a *castrum*, and above all Domitian, bishop of Tongeren-Maastricht between the years 535 and 549, was buried in Huy in the Church of Notre Dame at the foot of the rock between the rivers Meuse and Hoyoux.[10] This has been interpreted as proof of some sort of link between Huy and Maastricht, but it is not possible to define this further without Huy being regarded as a second residence of the bishops of Tongeren-Maastricht, which is difficult to accept. Huy may at most be considered a base offering support for episcopal power and influence.

Nevertheless it is not impossible that Huy, like Maastricht, had either political or economic links with Dorestat. If this was the case, its importance might also be associated with the Frankish expansion along the Meuse in a northerly direction, to Dorestat. From there, or so it is

[8] J.-L. Kupper, 'Archéologie et histoire: aux origines de la cité de Liège (VIIIe–XIe siècle)', in *La genèse et les premiers siècles*, pp. 377–89.   [9] Dierkens, 'Huy'.
[10] Devroey and Zoller, 'Villes, campagnes', p. 238; Dierkens, 'Huy', pp. 400–9; A. Joris, *La ville de Huy au moyen âge*, Paris, 1959, p. 81.

thought, stimuli for urban life, also on an economic level, must have followed the Meuse upstream[11] to Maastricht and Huy, and later, after the commercial rise of Dorestat in the eighth century, further upstream to Namur and Dinant. This hypothesis is precisely the opposite of earlier views which, wrongly it is now thought, saw mainly economic impulses from the south – from Marseilles and Fos along the Rhône and Saône – as activating the Meuse area upstream from Verdun, which would have provided it with an economic edge over other regions in our area of study.

Monetary activity in Huy in the seventh century (from *c.* 595 to *c.* 660 AD) and its position as a centre of power may have contributed to the urbanization of the various nuclei, perhaps still partly rural residential and artisanal, from which Huy and also Maastricht grew in the sixth and seventh centuries. Kilns, two of which must date from *c.* 700 AD, and bone and metal workshops (the latter with objects belonging typologically to the second half of the the sixth century or around 600 AD) have been discovered in Huy, both on the left bank of the Meuse, in the areas 'Batta' and 'Outre-Meuse', and on the right bank (rue des Augustins) and throughout the area on the right bank of the Hoyoux close to where it debouches into the Meuse (St Séverin quarter) (Map 3). We referred in the first chapter to their possible continuity as regards fifth-century activity. This continuity also applies to the largest of the cemeteries which were discovered on the left bank of the Meuse, to the west of 'Batta' (St Victor and St Hilaire). It was used without interruption from the middle of the fifth century and the number of graves there increased in the sixth and seventh centuries. However, we are still unfamiliar archaeologically with what is considered to have been the centre of Huy both before and during the Middle Ages: the place at the foot of the promontory near the confluence of Meuse and Hoyoux, which possibly identifies with the *castrum* on one of the seventh-century coins from Huy. Below it stands the Church of Notre Dame, mother church of Huy, and until the thirteenth century the only parish church, closely linked to Maastricht by the grave of Domitian, bishop of Maastricht (535–49).

To the relief of the poor registered for help in this church (*matricula*), the Austrasian landowner Adalgisel Grimo, deacon of Verdun, left a manor on the Ourthe in his famous will of 634 AD.[12] The existence of an institution like the *matricula* suggests a fairly well-developed administration of Huy church property. It could also say something about the urban character of church and surroundings, though Huy, like Maastricht, appears to have developed from various sixth–seventh-century

[11] Devroey and Zoller, 'Villes, campagnes', p. 246.
[12] W. Levison, 'Das Testament des Diakens Adalgisel-Grimo (634)', *Trierer Zeitschrift* 7 (1932), pp. 69–85; Joris, *Huy*, p. 85; Dierkens, 'Huy', pp. 399–400.

residential and artisanal nuclei, which were not necessarily urban in character. Only in the course of the eighth and ninth centuries is there certainty about the urban character of church and surroundings, as well as about Huy's commercial role.

Though there were striking similarities and various links between Maastricht and Huy, the data about the two places in the sixth–seventh centuries may not of course be automatically applied through generalization, and on the basis of these similarities or by interpretation from later data, to **Namur** (located on the Meuse some 30 km upstream from Huy) and **Dinant** (30 km upstream from Namur). Yet we know of four moneyers in Namur and six in Dinant in the seventh century. A purely economic interpretation of such data cannot be given here, any more than it can for Maastricht and Huy. In the past this has led to the Meuse being presented as one great coherent trade route in the international movement of goods in the seventh century, where cities prospered simultaneously. This is dismissed outright by Despy and Devroey, not only on grounds of a different interpretation of the phenomenon of the moneyers but also because of the difficulty of navigating the Meuse, of the importance of the land routes and of the fact that these crossed the Meuse in the above-mentioned places.[13] Moreover, Namur, unlike the other urban centres along this river, is a city not of the Meuse ('ville mosane'), but of the Sambre. It was originally located on both banks of the Sambre and on the left bank of the Meuse, but never extended along the right bank as well, as did the other Meuse cities.[14]

The first written mention of **Namur** dates from the seventh century when, around 675, the anonymous so-called Cosmographer of Ravenna includes Namur (*Namon* in the writer's rather corrupted style) in a list of places along the Meuse, all of which, without exception, he calls *civitates*. The qualification *civitas* is not very relevant partly because a purely rural locality, which is not located on the Meuse anyway, appears in this list of *civitates*. In contrast to older opinions, nothing can be deduced from it, neither with regard to the urban character of Namur at that time, nor with regard to an interpretation of *civitas* as an episcopal city, though the qualification C[IVITAS] also appears on a few of the gold tremisses which were struck in Namur between *c.* 620 and *c.* 660. At the very most, *civitas* could be interpreted as an indication of a fortification, were it not that this meaning is only attested in the ninth century. It is perhaps not without significance in this connection that an anonymous chronicle of about fifty years later calls Namur a *castrum* in relation to an event that

---

[13] See note 3 above.
[14] G. Despy, 'L'agglomération urbaine pendant le haut moyen âge', in *Namur: le site, les hommes*, pp. 63–78.

took place around 680. In the light of ninth-century qualifications of Namur as an *oppidum* and *castellum*, this is thought to refer to the promontory at the confluence of the Sambre and the Meuse, where there was a fortification which may go right back to the late Roman period. This may have been the occasional place of residence of the Merovingian king who issued a charter in Namur in 692, without further qualification of the place. It could also have been the place where coins were struck in the seventh century. Unfortunately none of this tells us anything about the urban character of the banks of the Sambre and the Meuse in Namur, let alone about their economic significance.

We do know the names of six moneyers who struck coins in **Dinant** in the seventh century, i.e. two more than in Namur, but otherwise even less is known about Dinant as a location in the sixth and seventh centuries than about Namur, apart from a reference to it as *civitas* by the anonymous Cosmographer of Ravenna, to which the same objections apply as those made above with regard to his reference to Namur.[15] Other written data relating to Dinant in the sixth–seventh centuries appear in tenth–eleventh-century sources and are not reliable, because they were intended to legitimize the claims of the prince-bishopric of Liège over Dinant. Archaeological discoveries dating from the sixth–seventh centuries were made in Leffe, just to the north of the medieval city, but their link with Dinant is not immediately clear.

Given that the moneyers who were active during the seventh century, and particularly during the second quarter of that century, worked in Maastricht (12), Huy (8), Namur (4) and Dinant (6), yet whose presence could have had a political rather than an economic significance in relation to the position of power of the Austrasian nobility and in particular of the Pippinids in the Meuse Valley and their expansion in a northerly direction along this river to Dorestat, indications supporting older views about the importance of the role of this river as an international trade route in the seventh century have proved unfounded. These views were in fact based exclusively on the interpretation of numismatic sources as economic indicators, which, since the studies of Grierson, Despy, Devroey and others, is no longer the most obvious interpretation. Yet there are signs, particularly in Maastricht and to a slightly lesser extent in Huy, of rudimentary urban life in the sixth–seventh centuries. Both places appear to be cities in the making, consisting of several separate nuclei, possibly still rural and/or artisanal in character. In terms of character and function some of them very probably date back to the late Roman period; others are new and fairly dynamic. It is highly questionable whether this is

---

[15] Gaier-Lhoest, *Evolution topographique de Dinant*, pp. 17–21; Devroey and Zoller, 'Villes, campagnes', p. 240.

sufficient for us to speak of the Meuse Valley having an urban and particularly an economic advantage, at least in the seventh century, over, for example, the Scheldt Valley. This seems rather to have been a historiographic myth of the first half of the twentieth century.

The Scheldt Valley

The arrival in **Cambrai**, the most southern city on the Scheldt, of Bishop Géry, who, according to a much later tradition, moved the episcopal seat from Arras to Cambrai between 584 and 590, throws some light on the history of this city in the sixth century when it is otherwise a total mystery.[16] According to St Géry's biographer, who wrote some seventy years after the bishop's death (624/7), he had a church built outside the walls of the late Roman city. He was later buried in that church and it was named after him. Shortly after the church was built, a monastic community must have been formed nearby, the later Abbey of St Géry (Map 8). According to a later tradition (eleventh–twelfth centuries), a church must already have existed inside the Roman walls in the sixth century. The same tradition has it that two more churches were built in Cambrai in the seventh century.

We learn from the late seventh-century biography of St Géry that a count administered the *pagus Cameracensis*, which is first mentioned in 662, and that he had a *tribunus* as his subordinate who kept guard over the prison. Around the year 600, a succession of at least four moneyers, whose names are known, began striking gold tremisses in Cambrai. Seven or eight of these coins have been preserved; one was found near Antwerp and one in Domburg – both, like Cambrai, located on the River Scheldt.[17]

This information, of an administrative and ecclesiastical nature, does suggest some form of urban life in Cambrai in the seventh century and yet, as we saw in the discussion about the cities along the Meuse, even the coins from Cambrai, struck between *c.* 600 and *c.* 675, cannot be interpreted as absolute proof of significant commercial activity at that time. Any traffic along the Scheldt, suggested by the coins from Cambrai found near Antwerp and Domburg, was not necessarily commercial traffic in the seventh century, as we shall see later from St Amand's missionary travels along this river.

There is nevertheless one famous text which refers to Cambrai as a place where costly goods, often of Eastern origin, could be purchased.[18] There is just some doubt about its date. It was found in a Paris

---

[16] See chapter 1, notes 15 and 16.
[17] J. Lafaurie, 'Les monnaies émises à Cambrai aux VIe–IXe siècles', *Revue du Nord* 69 (1986), pp. 393–404.

manuscript dating from shortly after 986. After a copy of the famous so-called 'Statutes' of Abbot Adalhard of Corbie dating from 822, there is a list of quantities of goods, mainly spices of Eastern origin to be purchased in Cambrai, 'if there is money available'. Pirenne was of the opinion that this text had nothing to do with the Statutes of Adalhard, which we believe is disputable. Likewise, according to Pirenne, its place in the manuscript after the Statutes does not mean that it should be dated between 822 and 986. In fact, Pirenne dated the list much earlier, in the Merovingian period, because it speaks of papyrus. Pirenne mistakenly thought that this papyrus was obtained in Cambrai like the spices, and believed, also wrongly,[19] that papyrus had completely disappeared from Western trade in the ninth century. Furthermore, Pirenne believed that there is not a single text from the Carolingian period summarizing so many different sorts of spices. On the contrary, they do appear, together with, for instance, papyrus, in texts from the Merovingian period, namely in Chilperic II's charter of 716 for the Abbey of Corbie, which confirms two toll exemptions in Fos for this abbey from the seventh century, and also in a model for a *tractoria* letter in Marculf's formulary from the second half of the seventh century. This reference of Pirenne's to the toll exemption for Corbie is unconvincing and indeed contradictory: it is hard to see why the Abbey of Corbie should purchase exotic Mediterranean products in Cambrai when it had a toll exemption for such products in Fos, where, moreover, it received large quantities of these products as presents from the king.[20] Pirenne's analysis of the content of the text regarding the purchases in Cambrai is also superficial. The text merits an in-depth study which has not yet been undertaken, not even by those who rejected Pirenne's dating of it and his arguments. In the light of current views about international trade in the Carolingian period in general, and about the growing importance in the ninth–tenth centuries of the trade route along the Po and over the Alps to Western Europe, including along the Rhine, the date of 822–986 can nevertheless be retained and it can be used to support the importance of the Scheldt as a trade route in that period with Cambrai as a case in point.

A passage from the biography of St Géry dating from the late seventh century (which we cited in chapter 1 to underline the importance of the

---

[18] *Polyptyque de l'abbé Irminon de Saint-Germain-des-Prés*, ed. B. Guérard, I, 2 (vol. 3), Paris, 1844, p. 336; H. Pirenne, 'Le commerce du papyrus dans la Gaule mérovingienne', in *Comptes-rendus de l'Académie des Inscriptions et Belles-Lettres*, Paris, 1928, reprinted in H. Pirenne, *Histoire économique de l'Occident médiéval*, [Bruges], 1951, pp. 96–9; Vercauteren, *Civitates*, p. 211.

[19] D. Claude, *Der Handel im westlichen Mittelmeer während des Frühmittelalters*, Göttingen, 1985 (Abhandlungen der Akademie der Wissenschaften in Göttingen, Philologisch-Historische Klasse, 3rd Series, no. 144), p. 143.   [20] *Ibid.*

late Roman *vicus* of Famars, 5 km to the south of Valenciennes, in the development of the latter locality into a trading place on the Scheldt in the ninth century) is related by Vercauteren to Cambrai, 24 km further south.[21] He wants to show that in the seventh century Cambrai was a city which slave traders passed through with their bevies of slaves. Though we do not wish to deny this possibility, we still believe that the passage in question shows first and foremost that Famars, a late Roman military base, still had some significance in the seventh century. The text teaches us nothing about possible slave trading in Cambrai at that time.

Moving on from Cambrai, there are reasons of an ecclesiastical-historical nature to devote a few lines to **Arras** in the Merovingian period, even if this city was not located on the Scheldt, like Cambrai, but approximately 40 km to the west of Cambrai on a tributary of the Scheldt, the Scarpe. Indeed, the traditional view[22] has it that St Vaast (*c.* 500–540) must have administered the two bishoprics of Arras and Cambrai together and that, after him, St Géry, as explained above, must have transferred the seat of this double bishopric to Cambrai, where it remained until Arras became an independent bishopric in 1093. Recent studies have rejected this view.[23] They regard St Vaast as an itinerant bishop who had no clearly defined bishopric, while the story of the shift of the seat of the bishopric to Cambrai by St Géry or a predecessor does not appear in the sources until towards the end of the twelfth century. So Arras would never have been the seat of a bishop before 1093. This explains the great power wielded by the Abbey of St Vaast in Arras during the early Middle Ages. It is very likely that at the end of the seventh century a church devoted to Notre Dame existed within the walls of the late Roman *civitas* which later, after the bishopric of Arras was founded in 1093, became a bishop's church and where St Vaast must originally have been buried. But St Aubert, bishop of Cambrai (633–69) probably built another church quite a distance from there on the right bank of the Crinchon river, to which he must have had St Vaast's relics transferred and which he dedicated to this saint (Map 6). This we believe was the origin of the Abbey of St Vaast, which St Aubert himself probably founded as a cloister or which at any rate certainly existed towards the end of the seventh century and which was completed and invested by St Aubert's successor Bishop Vinditian and King Theuderic III.[24] It was to play a major role in the emergence of the city of Arras from the ninth–tenth centuries, unlike the old Roman *civitas*

---

[21] Vercauteren, *Civitates*, pp. 212–14.   [22] *Ibid.*, pp. 186–7.
[23] Kéry, *Errichtung des Bistums Arras*, pp. 213–17; B. Delmaire, *Le diocèse d'Arras de 1093 au milieu du XIVe siècle*, I, Arras, 1994, pp. 41–3.
[24] Vercauteren, *Civitates*, p. 188; Kéry, *Errichtung des Bistums Arras*, p. 255–7.

with its Church of Notre Dame, which remained unimportant in this respect because of the absence of a bishop until the foundation of the bishopric of Arras in 1093.

Despite the importance of Arras as a late Roman textile centre whose reputation lived on until the sixth century, nothing tangible of this remained in the sixth–seventh centuries. We may well wonder if there was any continuity in the technical knowledge and tradition of wool manufacture from the late Roman period, particularly in the Carolingian period, as some historians suppose.[25] Regulations in connection with the sale of slaves and of gold which appear in two toll tariffs for Arras dating from the eleventh and twelfth centuries, which may relate to pre-1100 situations, are interpreted by various historians as dating from the Merovingian period.[26] New views on slavery in the early Middle Ages, however,[27] make this line of reasoning less convincing. Moreover, we refer to the above remarks relating to a text about exotic products at the market in Cambrai in the early Middle Ages.

There are no known data for the sixth–seventh centuries relating to **Valenciennes,** located on the Scheldt between Cambrai and Tournai, that would suggest the emergence of an economically important urban settlement on the royal manor there as early as the ninth century.

The information we have about **Tournai** in the sixth–seventh centuries reflects only information about the administrative and ecclesiastical significance of this place, which had at least partially preserved its late Roman urban character.[28] Documents once interpreted as evidence of economic significance are now suspect: first, what was thought to be a genuine Chilperic II charter dating from 716 in which this king granted the toll payable within the city to the church of Tournai is as spurious as Chilperic I's charter of 562 on which it is based;[29] and second, the data about the sale of gold and slaves which appear in the cathedral's oldest toll tariff of *c.* 1160 should not necessarily be interpreted as archaic relics from the Merovingian period, by analogy with what was said above about similar data relating to Cambrai and Arras.[30] The only fairly isolated indication of economic activity in Tournai in the sixth century relates to the export and tooling of the well-known local stone, which

---

[25] F. Vercauteren, 'Un exemple de peuplement urbain au XIIe siècle. Le cas d'Arras', in *Annales de la Faculté de la Faculté des Lettre et Sciences Humaines de Nice* 9–10 (1969), p. 24; Kéry, *Errichtung des Bistums Arras,* p. 276.   [26] Kéry, *Errichtung des Bistums Arras,* p. 277.

[27] A. Verhulst, 'The Decline of Slavery and the Economic Expansion of the Early Middle Ages', *Past and Present* 133 (1991), pp. 195–203.

[28] Vercauteren, *Civitates,* pp. 236–41.

[29] J. Pycke, 'Urbs fuerat quondam quod adhuc vestigia monstrant. Réflexions sur l'histoire de Tournai pendant le haut moyen âge (Ve–Xe siècle)', in *La genèse et les premiers siècles,* p. 219.   [30] *Ibid.,* p. 227.

carried on an ancient tradition that remained important throughout the Middle Ages.

For the rest, a number of cemeteries have been discovered in Tournai which were used during the sixth and seventh centuries, two of which date back to the late fifth century and one to even before that.[31] It has, however, not been possible to establish whether the population lived in the late Roman city area or on its rural edge.

At the beginning of the sixth century Bishop Eleutherus (died *c.* 531) was head of the bishopric of Tournai the foundation of which may date from before the end of the fifth century. From an important Gallo-Roman family of local landowners, he was count of Tournai, which was the centre of a *pagus*, before becoming bishop. He may have held this position as *defensor civitatis* even after becoming bishop. We can assume the same about one of the bishops who succeeded him around the middle of the sixth century. At the end of that century, around 575, Sigebert of Austrasia, one of the four sons of Chlotarius and a grandson of Clovis, laid siege to his brother Chilperic I who had taken cover inside the late Roman walls of Tournai. During the siege a son was born to Chilperic and that son was christened by the bishop. This is the last mention of a bishop in Tournai, for between 626/7 and 637/8 Bishop Acharius of Noyon united the two bishoprics, making Noyon the main seat.[32] Yet, around 590, important members of the royal family were still living in Tournai, where they had a vast manor, a *fiscus*, whose centre (*caput fisci, curtis indominicata*) was still in the *civitas* in the ninth century, i.e. within the late Roman walls. The royal residence of the Merovingians, from where Chilperic and Clovis had once reigned, may also have been located there.[33]

The foundation of no fewer than four churches in Tournai (St Piat, St Quentin, St Martin and St Brice), located at the four gates of the *civitas*, was attributed without conclusive evidence to St Eloy, who became bishop of Noyon-Tournai in 640. In that way he would have sanctified (among other things) several cemeteries. These churches could also be evidence of a sizeable population and perhaps even of its growth in the seventh century.[34] But none of this is at all certain, because at least three of these churches were rebuilt in the tenth–eleventh centuries.

Upstream from Tournai on the River Scheldt, **Ghent** and **Antwerp** are places we do know something about in the seventh century, thanks to

---

[31] R. Brulet, 'Reflexions sur la recherche archéologique à Tournai', in *La genèse et les premiers siècles*, pp. 209–10.   [32] Pycke, 'Urbs fuerat quondam', pp. 212–21.

[33] H. Pirenne, 'Le fisc royal de Tournai', in *Mélanges d'histoire affects à Ferdinand Lot*, Paris, 1925 reprinted in Pirenne, *Histoire économique*, pp. 83–9.

[34] Pycke, 'Urbs fuerat quondam', p. 221.

the missionary activities of St Amand. He operated from his monastery Elnone (today Saint-Amand) on the River Scarpe, whence he reached the River Scheldt, which he navigated downstream. He was active in Ghent[35] around 630 and, after being bishop of Tongeren-Maastricht between 647 and 649, in Antwerp.[36]

St Amand's evangelization in **Ghent** was made possible by the support of King Dagobert (d. 639), who put a rural manor at his disposal. That manor was located on the hill known as *Blandinium*, on the edge of the later city, and there it was that St Amand and several followers founded a small monastic community (*cellula*) with a chapel (*cubiculum*), the later St Peter's Abbey, also called *Blandinium* (Map 5). From there, still following the Scheldt, St Amand reached the place called *Ganda* , about 1.5 km downriver, on the left bank of the confluence of the Scheldt and the Leie. There, shortly before the year 639, he founded a church which became an abbey even before the year 700, because it was there that the relics of St Bavo, who as a follower of St Amand died a hermit somewhere near Ghent, were taken. *Ganda* had been the most important Roman settlement in the area at least until the fourth century. Even in the seventh century it must have had a sizeable population, because St Amand found it necessary to build a church there, even though he had already founded a monastery on the nearby *Blandinium* hill. The foundation of the church in *Ganda* was apparently so important for St Amand that, even before 639, he bought a large part of Slote manor to the north-east of and adjoining the settlement, with money made available to him by King Dagobert, who apparently owned no land in this area. After 639 other parts of Slote manor were purchased from the same family for sizable sums – the equivalent, probably largely in gold bullion, of around 4,000 tremisses – so one may well wonder what became of the former owners and of the money. Perhaps they went to the nearby *Ganda*, and the gold the members of the Slote family took with them may have provided an economic injection for the place, about which, however, nothing more is known.[37] Only in the ninth century are there indications of imports of Badorf ceramics in *Ganda*, probably the result of trade activity. Though indicating a settlement with urban characteristics, the term *municipium*, by which *Ganda* was qualified shortly after the beginning of the eighth century, has no economic but only an administrative connotation. *Ganda*

[35] A. Verhulst and G. Declercq, 'Early Medieval Ghent between Two Abbeys and the Count's Castle', in Decavele, *Ghent: In Defence of a Rebellious City*, pp. 37–44, reprinted in Verhulst, *Rural and Urban Aspects*, XII, pp. 1–17.

[36] Verhulst, 'Origins of Antwerp', pp. 5–16.

[37] H. C. Van Bostraeten, *De nederzetting Sloten en de merovingische begraafplaats te Gent–Port Arthur*, Brussels, 1972 (Crédit Communal, Collection Histoire in–8°, no. 25) (with a summary in French).

had after all been the capital of a *pagus*, at the head of which was a count, almost a century earlier. Though Merovingian archaeological discoveries over the area of the later medieval city as a whole are rare, there are two zones where the finds are slightly more numerous. The first is *Ganda* itself, where excavations have been carried out under difficult conditions next to the vanished medieval abbey church. A Merovingian well was found, and also traces of a wooden church which may date from the time of St Amand. The second is a zone on the left bank of the Scheldt, 500 m upriver from *Ganda*, to the south of the oldest city church, the present-day St Bavo's Cathedral. There a few odd Merovingian shards were found in an area which, as we will postulate in the next chapter, may in the late ninth century have been the successor of the ninth-century commercial settlement near St Bavo's Abbey in *Ganda*, after it was destroyed by the Vikings in 879. A few scattered Roman finds have been made in this zone, as explained in the previous chapter. So in Ghent, apart from in *Ganda* at the confluence of Leie and Scheldt, there must have been other scattered nuclei of habitation in the Merovingian and even in the Carolingian period, which in some cases date back to the Roman period, without there having been continuity as we can assume was the case for *Ganda*.

Antwerp must have been an important enough population centre in the seventh century for two missionaries to believe it worthwhile to undertake conversion work there: St Eloy shortly after 640 and St Amand after 647–9. While no traces of St Eloy's work remain, Amand founded a church there in honour of St Peter and St Paul which is mentioned at the beginning of the eighth century. It was given by a large landowner or high-ranking civil servant, called Rauchingus, to St Willibrord in 726. St Willibrord's conversion work in Taxandria, to the north-east of Antwerp, must have extended as far as Antwerp. After that the church came into the possession of the Abbey of Echternach via St Willibrord. Texts from the abbey dating from the beginning of the eighth century locate the church in the *castrum* (of) Antwerp. This *castrum*, which may be of Roman origin, can, we believe, be identified as the *civitas* Antwerp, the term used by the ninth-century *Annales Fuldenses* to refer to a fortification which the Vikings set fire to in 836. Probably little remained either of the church or of the fortification. Though perhaps an indirect consequence, the fact remains that the later St Michael's Abbey which was built on this site in the late ninth or the tenth century, though eccentrically located 1,000 m south of the later medieval city centre and of the Church of Our Lady, was the mother church of Antwerp until the beginning of the twelfth century (Map 12). The explanation for this rather singular location of Antwerp's mother church should in our opinion be sought in the supposition that St Michael's was the successor of the Church of St Peter and St Paul from St

Amand's time which was destroyed in 836. Consequently, that church, and the *castrum* in which it was located, must have stood on the site of the later St Michael's Abbey which was still located 500 m outside the city walls in *c.* 1200.

So after the Viking invasion in 836, the pre-urban centre of the Merovingian and early Carolingian period must have shifted to the place where it was in the late Carolingian and post-Carolingian period, i.e. almost 1,000 m further north, inside and outside the semicircular fortification which Emperor Otto II built there on the River Scheldt shortly before 980. Oddly enough the only traces of a Roman settlement in Antwerp are found just outside this settlement, as we saw in chapter 1. On the other hand, neither Roman nor Merovingian material has been found at the place where the centre of Merovingian Antwerp is thought to have been. No Merovingian layer has been found between the Roman layer and the ninth–tenth-century layers inside Otto II's fortification either, so that the explanation may lie in an insufficient knowledge of Merovingian archaeology and in problems of identification, in Antwerp in particular. Pending a solution to the problem, we believe it is not inconceivable that during the Roman period and the early Middle Ages there were several population centres in Antwerp along the Scheldt, of which perhaps only the one near the Merovingian *castrum* and the Church of St Peter and St Paul showed a few urban traits.

There is no trace of any economic activity in Antwerp in the sixth–seventh centuries, save the mention of a toll which Rauchingus must have donated to St Willibrord in 726 together with the Church of St Peter and St Paul. This appears to be a later interpolation in the Echternach texts. Even the gold tremissis struck between 620 and 650 and bearing the inscription *Anderpus*, which was found alongside the Scheldt not far downstream from Antwerp, is irrelevant from an economic standpoint.

The North Sea coast

Within the area under consideration here, the often incipient signs of urbanism in the sixth–seventh population centres are mainly along the two rivers Meuse and Scheldt, whereas along the coast between the mouth of the Somme and the delta of the great rivers in the Netherlands, even in the seventh century, we can only point to Quentovic and the trading place, since vanished, off the north-west coast of Walcheren, near Domburg, as well as to Dorestat.[38] Yet in the course of the eighth century these became international gateways of the Frankish kingdom, although

[38] See chapter 1, notes 22 (Domburg), 28–9 (Quentovic), and in this chapter, note 6 (Dorestat).

at the beginning of this chapter we found Dorestat in the seventh century, both in its own right and in relation to Maastricht, to be more important politically than economically.

Quentovic, which is known mainly as a crossing place to and from England in the seventh century, had – like Dorestat – none of the economic significance it was to acquire in the two centuries that followed.[39] Moreover, it was located on the edge of the area under consideration here and its links were directed mainly towards the south-east, to Amiens and Paris (Saint-Denis) and not, or to a lesser extent, towards the valleys of the Scheldt and Meuse.

Boulogne, as we saw in the previous chapter, continued to decline as a port in the seventh century, despite the Frankish occupation of the late Roman upper town and a temporary resumption of mintage. Furthermore, it was quite isolated from the interior because of a fairly large Saxon population in the area. For this reason not Boulogne but **Thérouanne** was chosen as the seat for a bishopric in the second quarter of the seventh century, though this did not contribute to the development of Thérouanne as a city despite a temporary mintage there as well.[40]

As regards **Bruges** in the seventh century, we can only presume that it was already an administrative centre for the immediate area, the later *pagus Flandrensis*, on the basis of its qualification as a *municipium (Flandrense)* at the beginning of the eighth century. That Bruges could not foist its name on the surrounding *pagus*, as for example Tournai and Ghent did, suggests it was of limited importance and that the place had little by way of an urban character.[41]

Consequently, the only place on the coast which could exercise some influence over the burgeoning urban centres along the Scheldt in particular was the now lost settlement off the north-west coast of Walcheren, near **Domburg**. As far as the seventh century is concerned, we know that numerous (approximately 100 to 200) gold tremisses were found, of which a few were struck in Cambrai and Tournai, but others in Maastricht and other centres in the Meuse Valley and in the region of Trier and Metz. Though they are less numerous than the 500 to 800 eighth-century *sceattas* found there on the beach in the course of the last three centuries, the economic significance of this place in the seventh century can be deduced from the number of tremisses. Whether this had an influence on places along the Scheldt such as Ghent and Antwerp becoming trade centres is a question which certainly cannot be answered for the seventh

[39] P. Johanek, 'Der "Aussenhandel" des Frankenreiches der Merowingerzeit nach Norden und Osten im Spiegel der Schriftquellen', in Düwel *et al.*, *Untersuchungen zu Handel und Verkehr*, III, pp. 237–8.   [40] Vercauteren, *Civitates*, pp. 318–23.
[41] Verhulst, 'An Aspect of the Question of Continuity', pp. 191–4.

century, and only with great reservation and rather negatively for the eighth–ninth centuries. It is also very unlikely that Domburg carried any political weight with regard to Antwerp and Ghent on the Lower Scheldt, as was the case with Dorestat in relation to Maastricht and Huy in the seventh century.

Conclusion

As regards the last two places, we must not lose sight of the fact that the Valley of the Meuse between Maastricht and Huy was the centre of the Pippinids' estates and the road along which Frankish power extended towards Friesland in the seventh century. In our opinion, it is these circumstances, and the military and political significance of Dorestat, that were largely responsible for the leading edge which at least this part of the Valley of the Meuse had over the Scheldt Valley, for example from a monetary standpoint. For the rest, the differences between the two river areas in terms of urban development are not very great. In Maastricht and Huy as well as in Cambrai and Tournai the presence of a bishop, who often performed secular functions such as those of a count, was a significant factor in the preservation or development of urban traits and in the role of these urban agglomerations as central places in a political and administrative sense. The economic consequences of this remain unknown as far as the sixth–seventh centuries are concerned because they cannot automatically be deduced from the numismatic data. In a topographic respect there is one great similarity between most of the places examined in this chapter. Each consisted of several nuclei, at least one of which dated back to the late Roman period and often, but not always, continued to be important in the sixth–seventh centuries, sometimes as a fortified area with a political, administrative and military function. Such was, however, no longer the case in Maastricht and in Arras, where new nuclei with a central function had already developed in the seventh century, more specifically around an abbey. The changes which had taken place in this and in other respects during the seventh century were important conditions for the development of commercial settlements in the eighth–ninth centuries. In particular the increasing role and influence of the Frankish and especially the Austrasian aristocracy who owned manors around the Meuse Valley, and of the newly founded abbeys, impacted on trade, and especially on international trade, in the seventh–eighth centuries. Their power and wealth increased substantially in the seventh–eighth centuries as they acquired more and more land and utilized it more intensively in a bipartite exploitation system. The income derived from the manors increasingly enabled the landowners, laymen as well as bishops and abbots, to acquire luxury goods via international trade. Moreover, that trade, which until then had been of minor importance in the area between the Somme and the Meuse under consideration here, was stimulated by this demand.

Whereas, in the sixth century, cities like Paris, Orléans, Soissons and Reims had been royal abodes *par excellence*, in the eighth–ninth centuries it was the more northerly, rural manors along the Meuse and the Scheldt (which, originally royal manors, were now often in the hands of the aristocracy), the episcopal residences and above all the great abbeys founded during the seventh century that became centres of power and wealth under the Carolingians. In the course of the eighth–ninth centuries, they stimulated the development of the seventh-century administrative and political centres in their vicinity into trading centres and after that into cities.

3 New urban beginnings and the Viking raids (eighth–ninth centuries)

The emporia on the southern North Sea and Channel coast

As of the last quarter and perhaps even the middle of the seventh century, there was a considerable amount of traffic – and seemingly increasing commercial traffic – between the coasts of southern and south-east England and of the Continent from the mouth of the Seine to the mouth of the Scheldt, Meuse and Rhine.[1] On the Continent that traffic emanated from several ports often located some distance from the coast in the estuaries of large or smaller streams: from south to north those ports were Rouen on the Seine, Amiens on the Somme, Quentovic on the Canche, Domburg at the Scheldt estuary on the north-west coast of Walcheren, *Witla* on a connecting watercourse between Scheldt and Meuse in their estuary area, and Dorestat at the bifurcation of Rhine and Lek.[2] This development in the late seventh century was new and contrasts with the lack of written information about this area in the sixth and a large part of the seventh centuries. It is, however, unrelated to the development of urban agglomerations or non-rural centres along the rivers in the interior into centres of supra-local or supra-regional trade, signs of which did not begin to appear in the sources until three-quarters of a century or a

---

[1] Ian Wood, *The Merovingian North Sea*, Alingsås, 1983; R. Hodges, 'North Sea Trade before the Vikings', in K. Biddick (ed.), *Archeological Approaches to Medieval Europe*, Kalamazoo, 1984 (Studies in Medieval Culture 18, Western Michigan University), pp. 192–201; P. Johanek, 'Der "Aussenhandel" des Frankenreiches der Merowingerzeit nach Norden und Osten im Spiegel der Schriftsquellen', in Düwel *et al.* (eds.), *Untersuchungen zu Handel und Verkehr*, III, pp. 234–44; S. Lebecq, 'La Neustrie et la Mer', in H. Atsma (ed.) *La Neustrie: les pays au nord de la Loire de 650 à 850*, I, Sigmaringen, 1989 (Beihefte der Francia 16/1), pp. 405–40.

[2] R. Hodges, *Dark Age Economics: The Origins of Towns and Trade AD 600–1000*, London, 1982, pp. 46–86; H. Steuer, 'Die Handelsstätten des frühen Mittelalters im Nord- und Ostsee-Raum', in *La genèse et les premiers siècles*, pp. 75–116; Clarke and Ambrosiani, *Towns in the Viking Age*, pp. 24–45.

century later.[3] The above-mentioned coastal ports, with the exception of Rouen and Amiens which were in fact *civitates* of Roman origin, did not develop into medieval cities. The question is whether their existence and their activity had any influence on the inland places along the rivers, primarily the Meuse and Scheldt, which did develop into centres of trade in the eighth–ninth centuries. In chapter 2 we answered this question with cautious positiveness only for Maastricht and Huy, on the basis of the links that existed, at least on a monetary level, between Maastricht and Dorestat in the second quarter of the seventh century and between Huy and Maastricht. And yet there is a gap of half to three-quarters of a century between Dorestat's definitive start as an international mercantile port at the beginning of the eighth century and the first mention of a toll in Huy and in Dinant in 743/7 and of a toll in Maastricht in 779. The reference to a toll in Huy and in Dinant at that time is, moreover, not entirely reliable and, certainly as far as Dinant is concerned, is fairly isolated in the urban development of the two places.[4] Only the toll in Maastricht, from which the Abbey of St Germain-des-Près in Paris was granted exemption for its *negociantes* in 779 as a confirmation of a privilege from Pippin III, was put on the same footing as the tolls in Rouen, Amiens, Quentovic and Dorestat in the relevant charter of Charlemagne.[5] At that time these were ports located on the maritime borders of the Frankish kingdom along the North Sea and the Channel, whose main traffic was with England, though in the case of Dorestat also with Scandinavia. They were so-called 'gateways' and the site of customs offices and tolls which fed the royal coffers. They enjoyed special protection from the king, who had a *procurator* or *prefectus emporii* (858/68) at least in Quentovic, who also supervised other ports in the area, such as Rouen.[6] Their burgeoning and perhaps even, in the case of Quentovic

---

[3] S. Lebecq, 'Entre les invasions et le grand essor du XIe siècle: vrai ou faux départ de la croissance urbaine dans l'espace rhéno-mosan', in *Les petites villes en Lotharingie. Actes des 6e journées lotharingiennes,* Luxembourg, 1992 (Publications de la Section Historique de l'Institut G.-D. de Luxembourg 108), pp. 21–40.

[4] Joris, *Huy,* p. 84 note 49; F. L. Ganshof, 'A propos du tonlieu sous les Mérovingiens', in *Studi in onore di Amintore Fanfani,* I, Milan, 1962, p. 307 note 63 and p. 308 note 69; M.-L. Fanchamps, 'Etude sur les tonlieux de la Meuse Moyenne du VIIe au milieu du XIVe siècle', *Le Moyen Age* 70 (1964), p. 207 note 7.

[5] E. Muehlbacher, *Diplomata Karolinorum,* I, MGH in-4°, Hanover, 1906, no. 122, pp. 170–1; new edition by H. Atsma and J. Vezin, *Chartae Latinae Antiquiores,* XVI, France IV, Zurich, 1986, no. 625, pp. 38–41. See F. L. Ganshof, 'A propos du tonlieu à l'époque carolingienne', in *La città nell'alto medioevo,* p. 494 note 19. In the extended version in Dutch of this article (*Het tolwezen in het Frankisch rijk onder de Karolingen,* Brussels, 1959 (Mededelingen van de Koninklijke Vlaamse Academie voor Wetenschappen. Klasse der Letteren 21 (1959), no. 1)) Ganshof (p. 14) identified '*in Treiecto*' with Utrecht, but this identification is now generally rejected in favour of Maastricht: see Johanek, 'Aussenhandel', p. 222 note 33.   [6] See chapter 1, note 28.

and Dorestat, their very existence seem to have been closely linked to royal power, so closely in fact that the decline of the most important of them, Quentovic and Dorestat, as of the second quarter and through the second half of the ninth century, is attributed chiefly to the diminution of royal power. This does not apply to Rouen, Amiens or Maastricht, perhaps because as cities of Roman origin and as bishoprics (at least until the beginning of the eighth century in the case of Maastricht), they had deeper roots than the ephemeral 'villes-champignons' ('mushroom towns'), as Dhondt aptly called Quentovic and Dorestat, a term which might equally be applied to the trade settlement on the beach at **Domburg**.

The latter settlement, known only from archaeological sources and currently believed to be identifiable with what post-*c.* 790 written sources call *Walichrum (villa)*,[7] must have had its heyday between 670 and 750 but had barely any influence on urban development in its immediate hinterland, which was formed by the Scheldt Valley and the Flemish coastal region. Domburg-*Walichrum* has also been described – though perhaps not with total justification – as just a transit or transshipment port on the seaway between England and the Rhineland. We do, however, need to consider it in this overview of urban development between Somme and Meuse, for Domburg-*Walichrum* was the only early medieval trading place on the coast within this area. Quentovic lay right at the southern edge of that area and the traffic from England which passed through the port was directed southwards to Amiens and Paris. Dorestat was located on the northern border of the area under consideration and was really only of indirect importance to it through its links with Maastricht and Huy, for which it served as a gateway and through which it certainly exerted an influence on Maastricht, partly thanks to the Pippinids' sphere of influence to which all three belonged.

Of the coins found on the beach in Domburg, the Merovingian gold trientes from the first half and the middle of the seventh century originated mainly from the known mints along the Meuse and the Mosel and only a few rare pieces from mints in *civitates* along the upper reaches of the Scheldt (Cambrai and Tournai). Not a single one of the not very numerous Carolingian *denarii* found in Domburg and dating from the time of Charlemagne and Louis the Pious comes from the Scheldt Valley, though there are a few from the Rhineland and from Dorestat. The *denarii* from the middle and the third quarter of the ninth century, on the other hand, derive almost exclusively from mints along the Scheldt and the Flemish

---

[7] See ch. I, note 22 above and R. M. van Heeringen, P. Henderikx and A. Mars, *Vroeg-Middeleeuwse ringwalburgen in Zeeland*, Goes and Amersfoort, 1995, pp. 42–8; Lebecq, 'L'emporium proto-médiéval de Walcheren-Domburg', pp. 73–89.

coastal region (Bruges). It was during the latter period, which was also Domburg's period of decline, that commercial settlements emerged along the Scheldt in Valenciennes, Tournai and Ghent and perhaps also along the coast in Bruges. These did not exist as such in the eighth century during Domburg-*Walichrum*'s heyday. These numismatic data are sufficient for us to argue that the prestige of Domburg-*Walichrum* at the height of its prosperity (last quarter of seventh to first half of eighth century) was not directed at its immediate hinterland, the Scheldt Valley. Perhaps it was directed via the delta of the Meuse and Rhine and via Dorestat – to which Domburg-*Walichrum* may have been subordinated like Rouen to Quentovic – to the river area of the Meuse and Rhine.

The conclusion we must draw from all this is that the generation of international trade activity to which the continental ports along the North Sea and the Channel testify in the course of the eighth century may have had some influence on urban development in the area between Somme and Meuse only in Maastricht, where a royal toll of international significance was established around the middle of the eighth century at the latest.

The Meuse Valley

As far as the Meuse area is concerned, this conclusion is borne out by the observation that, again with the exception of Maastricht, traces of significant trade activity in Huy, Namur and Dinant, accompanied by consistent urbanization, only become evident, indisputable and numerous from the middle of the ninth century onwards. According to Despy, these places must have been essentially centres of regional trade at that time and only gained a foothold in international traffic towards the end of the tenth century.[8]

By contrast, the observation made by Einhard, Charlemagne's advisor and lay abbot of St Servaas in **Maastricht**, about that city – whose toll clearly had an international character in 779 – in his *Translatio SS. Marcellini et Petri* (c. 830) is well known. Einhard described the city – as Maastricht may now be called, and which is twice referred to as *vicus* in this source – as being densely populated, especially with merchants who apparently also had a permanent home there (*estque habitantium et praecipue negotiatorum multitudine frequentissimus*).[9] There are almost no topographical data or clues about the urbanization of Maastricht before

[8] Despy, 'Villes et campagnes'.
[9] Einhard, *Translatio et miracula SS. Marcellini et Petri*, ed. G. Waitz, in MGH. SS. XV, Hanover, 1887, p. 261. For the correct translation and interpretation of this passage see Despy, 'Villes et campagnes', p. 152.

the tenth century. While the city as a whole was usually called *vicus* in the ninth century – it was referred to once (*c.* 735) as *oppidum* and *civitas* (and *civitas* again in 772) and as *municipium* (847, and again in 871) – the term *portus* was used of Maastricht *c.* 735 in its limited sense of mooring place for ships, and only on late ninth-century coins in the general sense of trade settlement as had become customary during the second half of that century. Finally, the term *castrum* is used once, around 833–40, in connection with the Abbey of St Servaas, which, partly for that reason, is regarded as a fortified abbey, and once (in 908) in connection with the devastation of Liège, Maastricht and Tongeren by the Vikings in 881, about which more will follow.[10] These terminological indications are particularly useful in the case of places for which there is no other information to determine their urban and commercial character.

This applies to **Huy**, **Namur** and **Dinant**, as well as to Liège, whose evolution to city commenced in the second half of the eighth century and is discussed here for the first time. *Castrum*, the only surviving technical term for Huy and Namur in the seventh century, may refer to the fortified promontory which in both Huy and Namur is situated between the Meuse and the place where the Hoyoux and the Sambre respectively debouch into it, rather than to the scattered nuclei of settlements in the area, whose urban character is far from certain. The term is again used for both places in the eighth century and for Huy in the ninth century, while Dinant, about which practically nothing is known in the seventh century, is also called *castrum* for the first time in the eighth century (743/7), though it has not been established whether this refers to one element of the settlement or to the whole settlement. If it refers to the whole settlement, then its non-rural character would be firmly established. With greater certainty than for the word *castrum*, this is the case for *vicus*, a qualification which, apart from Maastricht *c.* 830, is attested in Dinant in 824 and in Huy on coins dating from the beginning and the first half of the ninth century, and becomes very frequent in written texts for both places from the middle of that century and from then on also in Namur.[11]

However, the rural familial manor (*villa*) in **Liège**, where Bishop Lambert was murdered and a church with his relics was built shortly before 714, and which had become the residence of the bishop of Tongeren-Maastricht, was called *vicus publicus* as early as the second half of the eighth century.[12] At best, only the predominantly non-rural character

---

[10] H. R. Van Ommeren, 'Bronnen voor de geschiedenis van Maastricht (359–1204)', part I (359–923), *Publications de la Société Historique et Archéologique dans le Limbourg* 127 (1991), pp. 5–48.

[11] See the items cited in chapter 1, notes 8, 10, 12 and in chapter 2, notes 1, 3, 10.

[12] Kupper, 'Origines de Liège'; Devroey and Zoller, 'Villes, campagnes', pp. 254–6.

of a settlement in the ninth century can be deduced from the isolated use of the term *vicus*, if there is no other indication of trade activity such as we have for Maastricht. Any trade activity of more than local significance can be deduced only from the use of the term *portus*, when this is referring not just to one element of the settlement, namely the mooring place on a river. The term *portus*, used in the general sense of commercial settlement on a river, appears for the first time in the context of the Meuse Valley with reference to Huy in 862, to Maastricht at the end of the ninth century, and to Namur and Dinant only shortly after the middle and at the end of the tenth century respectively.[13] *Sedilia* or *sessi* are mentioned at various intervals during the second half of the ninth century with reference to Huy, simultaneously with the term *portus*, and to Dinant without further qualification of the settlement; with reference to Namur together with *portus*, but then only in 960. This was the technical term for small plots of land on which just one house could be built. Though the word is also used in the agrarian sector – for example, with reference to vineyards as in Huy *c.* 900 – the enforced division of land into lots to which the term refers is essentially an urban phenomenon. Used in combination with *portus*, as in Huy, but even without this connection, as in Dinant, *sedile-sessus* suggests that the settlement in question was already highly urbanized.[14]

None of this alters the fact that we have no more direct proof of the possible role played by Huy, Namur and Dinant in supra-regional trade in the eighth–ninth centuries than we do for the more recent Liège, apart from the toll exemption which the majordomo Carloman granted, together with immunity, to the Abbey of Stavelot in Dinant (on that occasion called *castrum*) and in Huy in the name of Childeric III in 743/7. The text of this charter has come down to us in a much later and highly corrupted version. Yet F. L. Ganshof, an expert on toll regulations under the Merovingians and Carolingians, refused to regard the passage in it about the toll as an interpolation, but without stating his arguments.[15] If, on Ganshof's authority, we accept the existence of a royal toll in Huy and in Dinant at such an early period, then two considerations are raised which reduce its significance in international trade or even cast doubt on it. In the first place the reference to a toll in Huy and in Dinant, as mentioned above, is fairly isolated compared to other references to the trading character of the two places, which for Huy are more than a hundred years later and for Dinant date only from the end of the tenth century, i.e. 250 years later. If we were nevertheless to accept the existence of a toll in both places at such an early date – mid-eighth century –

---

[13] See note 11 above.
[14] Despy, 'Villes et campagnes', pp. 150–1; Devroey and Zoller, 'Villes, campagnes', pp. 254–6.   [15] See note 4 above.

then we do not believe that substantial royal tolls, for instance, would have been levied at such a short distance from each other (approximately 60 km). So, in our opinion, they were tolls of at best regional significance. This interpretation fits in very well with an explanation of the development of these places into commercial centres which was given by Despy and which has found wide acceptance.[16]

The Abbey of Stavelot's ownership in 862 of small plots of land (*sedilia*) in Huy, which was then called *portus*, and in Dinant, which is given no such qualification in the same charter, also fits in with this explanation. Like many other abbeys in other centres of regional and even of international trade, the Abbey of Stavelot was keen to have a presence in those two places with a view to obtaining supplies. It is interesting to note in this connection that the toll exemption for Stavelot of a hundred years earlier (743/7) is not repeated in these ninth-century texts about Stavelot.

The conclusion, then, about the development of urban life and trade along the Meuse in the eighth–ninth centuries is that this river was not yet the great international trade route it was long thought to have been on the basis of Rousseau's and Vercauteren's theories in particular.[17] It is therefore hardly surprising that absolutely no trace has been found along this route of the Frisians who conducted the international trade in the eighth–ninth-century commercial settlements on the coast of north-west Europe and along the Rhine. Their presence along the Rhine is in striking contrast to their absence along the Meuse during that same period.[18] Maastricht, the only place on the Meuse where merchants are expressly mentioned in the ninth century, was perhaps an exception to this. This is hardly surprising, given the long-standing connections (since the seventh century) between Maastricht and Dorestat, the centre of Frisian trade. In the eighth, ninth and even a good part of the tenth centuries, the Meuse owed its importance to the waterways (Hoyoux, Sambre) which debouched into it, and to the land routes which crossed it, sometimes via a bridge, as in Dinant and in Maastricht, more than to international trade, which from the eighth century onwards at best extended only to Maastricht and perhaps Huy from centres like Domburg and Dorestat. Places at those confluences and intersections which had sometimes existed for a long time took on a more distinct urban character and gradually a more than regional commercial character, since the seventh–eighth centuries in the case of Maastricht, and in the second half of the ninth century in the case of Huy, Namur and Dinant. This development was partly explained by Despy when he referred to the agrarian expansion of the hinterland of the Meuse in the ninth century, whereby Huy, Namur and Dinant

[16] Despy, 'Villes et campagnes'.
[17] See chapter 2, note 1.   [18] Lebecq, *Marchands et navigateurs frisons*, I, p. 223.

became regional markets for arable farming and cattle breeding products
and for raw materials from that hinterland.[19] In the course of the tenth
century, however, they became involved in international trade, which
consisted more of industrial products from the Meuse region: especially
products of metal working (bronze, copper, tin, lead) which could boast a
long tradition and which were based largely in the countryside until into
the ninth century, as in Dinant, or pottery and bone products, sometimes
going back to older, Merovingian and even Roman traditions such as
in Huy, or products of recent origin, such as the Andenne ceramics
(tenth–eleventh centuries, midway between Huy and Namur).[20]

This was a new development and one which put the spotlight on Huy
and Dinant in the tenth–eleventh centuries at the expense of Maastricht
which they then overshadowed in economic terms. Indeed, as a result of
Liège's growing political and ecclesiastical importance in the tenth century, Maastricht lost its former prominent position on the Meuse during
the course of that century.

The destruction of Liège, Maastricht and Tongeren by the Vikings in
881, called *civitas*, *castrum* and *urbs* respectively when described by the
historian Regino of Prüm in 908, had no effect on the changes taking
place in the urban landscape along the Meuse from the ninth to the tenth
centuries, as outlined above.[21] Indeed, apart from this one raid from their
winter camp in Asselt (downriver from Maastricht near Roermond) in
881, the Vikings undertook no other destructive campaigns in the Meuse
Valley. This is in strong contrast to the western part of the area between
Somme and Meuse, where the development of urban life during the
eighth–ninth centuries is outlined below.

Between North Sea and Scheldt

Almost no written sources relating to urban life in the region between
Somme, Scheldt and North Sea in the eighth century have come down to
us, and for the ninth century the written sources are few and far between.
Archaeological data relating to this area during those two centuries exist
only for the trading place called *Walichrum* (Domburg) at the mouth of
the Scheldt on the north-west coast of Walcheren, but then we have no
real written sources. At the beginning of this chapter we provided information that may be relevant here. This information is not very plentiful
because the history of this trading place on the coast seems to have
unfurled quite separately from urban development along the rivers in-

[19] Despy, 'Villes et campagnes'.
[20] See chapter 5.
[21] A. D'Haenens, *Les invasions normandes en Belgique au IXe siècle*, Leuven, 1967, pp. 49–50.

land, except perhaps in the second half of the ninth century, by which time Domburg's heyday was over and its influence limited to just a few urban settlements along the middle reaches of the Scheldt.

With a few exceptions, most written sources concerning the region between the River Scheldt and the North Sea date from the ninth century and then, as far as the urban character and possible trade activity of these settlements are concerned, from the second half of that century. This is probably no coincidence, and in our opinion has to do with the growing importance of their commercial activity in that period.

Apart from a few indirect clues and just one mention in a literary source, this commercial activity can only really be deduced from the term *portus,* used, as in the Meuse area, shortly after the middle of the ninth century to indicate a number of places along the Scheldt, namely – downstream – Valenciennes, Tournai and Ghent. Their location along this river is interesting because the only other mention of *portus* in the ninth century in relation to the area between Scheldt, Somme and North Sea – apart from Quentovic which we can ignore here for reasons explained at the beginning of this chapter – refers to a mysterious place, which cannot be located, at one of the spots where at that time the Yser debouched into the North Sea, the so-called *Iserae portus*, where a body of Vikings disembarked in 860.[22] Downstream from Ghent along the Scheldt is the *civitas* of Antwerp, denoting a fortification with church dating from the Merovingian period 1,000 metres to the south of the later medieval city centre. It was set on fire during a raid by a Viking fleet as early as 836 and probably completely destroyed. When Antwerp again appears in a written source at the end of the ninth century, it is the only place, along with Bruges, to be called *vicus* in the middle of a summary of places all – with one exception – called *villa* in the sense of 'village' or 'manor'. As explained above in connection with Maastricht, Huy, Namur and Dinant, which were all called *vicus* at least once in the course of the ninth century, this term refers to a degree of urbanization which may have gone hand in hand with trade activity. As we have already mentioned, it is highly likely that the *vicus* in Antwerp was no longer located on the same site as the *civitas* destroyed in 836.[23] Apart from Antwerp and Bruges, called *vicus* at the end of the ninth century, Einhard attributed this qualification to Valenciennes, and also to Maastricht in the same source, around 830.[24]

[22] A. C. F. Koch, 'Phasen in der Entstehung von Kaufmannsniederlassungen zwischen Maas und Nordsee in der Karolingerzeit', in G. Droege (ed.), *Landschaft und Geschichte: Festschrift für Franz Petri*, Bonn, 1970, pp. 319–20.

[23] Verhulst, 'Origins of Antwerp', pp. 10–15.

[24] Einhard, *Translatio*, p. 258; Deisser-Nagels, 'Valenciennes', p. 75 note 84 and p. 83.

It seems that a distinction has to be drawn between a straightforward *vicus* and the frequent phenomenon of a *vicus monasterii*, which refers to a settlement near an abbey and revealing certain urban traits, such as streets where specialized craftsmen, grouped according to their specialization, and others, including merchants, in the service of the abbey, lived.[25] A particularly interesting example of this distinction is found in one of the places in the area under consideration here, namely **Arras**, in the ninth century. Both terms appear in one and the same text, a charter of 30 October 867 in which Charles the Bald set up a *mensa conventualis* in the Abbey of St Vaast, whereby specific revenue and goods from the abbey were reserved for the monks.[26] For their general maintenance, he reserved an income of half of the *vicus qui vocatur Nova Villa juxta monasterium ipsum situm*, with a *taberna* (tavern); for the *camera* of the abbey also a tavern, but located in *vico monasterii*. The separate place of the two *vici* in the description of the properties, but in particular the different names given to them (the first one even has a proper name – *Nova Villa* – whose meaning moreover suggests a recent origin), allow us to conclude that they were two different *vici*, though both were located next to the abbey.[27] This distinction takes on its full significance when we interpret it as meaning that the *vicus monasterii* is older and indicates a settlement whose inhabitants were all in the service of the abbey and employed in various métiers ranging from bakers, brewers, smiths, etc. even to merchants,[28] while this was not necessarily the case or did not apply to the whole population in the other, newer *vicus* which consequently was called *Nova Villa*. In other words, we should be able to see the nucleus of the later city in the *Nova Villa*, while the *vicus monasterii* represents an older type of settlement with urban traits, which more often than not stood next to a large abbey and did not develop into a medieval city, or perhaps not until considerably later. We should perhaps look in one of the two *vici* or in both for the workers who had to process the large quantities of flax and wool which, according to Charles the Bald's same charter of 30 October 867 in which the two *vici* are mentioned, had to be supplied to the abbey's *camera* by the abbey's seven manors, of which

---

[25] J. F. Niermeyer, *Mediae latinitatis lexicon minus*, Leiden, 1976, p. 1,098; J. P. Devroey, 'Courants et réseaux d'échange dans l'économie franque entre Loire et Rhin', in *Mercati e mercanti nell'alto medioevo*, Spoleto, 1993 (Settimane 40), pp. 383–4.

[26] G. Tessier, *Recueil des actes de Charles II le Chauve, roi de France*, II, Paris, 1955, no. 304, pp. 170–6.

[27] Kéry, *Errichtung des Bistums Arras*, p. 265 and note 76.

[28] F. Lot (ed.), *Hariulf: Chronique de l'abbaye de Saint-Riquier*, Paris, 1894, p. 306; P. Johanek, 'Der fränkische Handel der Karolingerzeit im Spiegel der Schriftquellen', in Düwel *et al.* (eds.), *Untersuchungen zu Handel und Verkehr der vor- und frühgeschichtlichen Zeit in Mittel- und Nordeuropa*, IV, *Der Handel der Karolinger und Wikingerzeit*, Göttingen, 1987, p. 54.

three were in the immediate vicinity of Arras and the others within a 25 to 60 kilometre radius. This location confirms what may *a priori* be supposed, namely that these quantities of flax and wool were delivered to the seat of the abbey. The *camera* then probably entrusted their processing to workers who either were obliged to provide the services or who were paid for it and who, as mentioned above, lived either in the *vicus monasterii*, as in the case of the first group, or, in the case of the second group, in the *vicus* called *Nova Villa*. Perhaps the *Nova Villa vicus* originated as a new settlement next to the abbey precisely because there were too few textile workers in the *vicus monasterii* to cope with the work generated by such large quantities of flax and wool.

Unfortunately the two *vici* in the immediate vicinity of the abbey cannot be located exactly, not even with the help of later data. We can assume, however, that the *vicus monasterii* was located nearest to the abbey, and that it was destroyed together with the abbey by the Vikings on 28 December 880. It may then have been incorporated into the fortification which was built around the abbey between 883 and 887, or at any rate before 891.

In the eleventh century there was an old residential area (*vetus burgus*) in the vicinity of the abbey and a more recent one (*novus burgus*), which are in their turn difficult to locate, so that it is impossible to link one of the two *burgi* to one of the two ninth-century *vici*.

According to the charter of 30 October 867, the provost of the abbey could dispose as he thought fit of the wool that was in excess of the quantity of 400 pounds which had to be supplied. It is therefore conceivable that he sold a part of it at the market where, according to the already much quoted charter of Charles the Bald, the market toll was allocated to the abbey infirmary. This market was probably also in the immediate vicinity of the abbey. The provost of St Vaast may have sold a part of the wool to free, independent workers, who we would expect to find in the *Nova Villa*.

Without at this stage examining the possible topographical aspects of this hypothesis, we have expounded it here because it may also hold true for other cities. In that case it would have greater universality which, in our opinion, could be linked to and offer an explanation for an important change in the phenomenon of the 'city' in the course of the ninth century.

Urban development in **Ghent** in the ninth century suggests a similar hypothesis to the one proposed above for Arras. Indeed, modern historical research locates the *portus Ganda*, referred to in the Martyrology of Usuard *c.* 865 (which also mentions the *portus* of Valenciennes), in the immediate vicinity of St Bavo's Abbey which is called *Ganda*.[29] This was the place at the confluence of the Scheldt and Leie where the abbey was located, and only that place was called *Ganda* well into the ninth century when the name began to peter out (Map 5). In the course of that century a new name – *Gandavum* – also began to appear and was used increasingly. This name, however, was given not to the place where the Scheldt and Leie met, but to the area *between* the Scheldt and Leie where the medieval city was to grow up. It is generally agreed that the commercial settlement relocated, probably as a result of the destruction of St Bavo's Abbey in 879 by the Vikings who had pitched their camp there for a year. A new settlement probably grew up on the left bank of the Scheldt, some 500 m upstream from the abbey, near the oldest city church (St Jans, now St Bavo's Cathedral) even before the end of the ninth century. A semicircular, D-shaped moat, whose two extremities terminated in the Scheldt, was constructed around the settlement. It is here that the basis of the medieval city, which gradually extended beyond the earlier moat to incorporate the whole area between Leie and Scheldt by the middle of the tenth century, is now sought.[30] If we were to compare this largely new settlement with the *Nova Villa* in Arras on the one hand, and the *portus Ganda*, which must have been destroyed in 879 along with the abbey, with the *vicus monasterii* in Arras on the other, then – apart from the possible similarity – we would find one distinct difference: the *vicus monasterii* near St Bavo's Abbey is called *portus* and so trading was engaged in there. In the light of the new views about the character of trade in the ninth century as recently expounded by Toubert and Devroey,[31] the trading conducted in the *portus Ganda* up to the year 879 would not have been an ordinary free trade engaged in for profit motives by independent merchants, but trade in the service of the abbey. This is to say that it was directed at the sale by the abbey of the remainder of its manorial revenue in kind and at the purchase of products needed by the abbey which it could not otherwise obtain. As a rule this trade would have been conducted by merchants in the service of the abbey who may also have carried out commercial transactions on their own behalf. At the same time, it may have attracted free and independent merchants as well. It is, we believe, even possible that the latter had settled in Ghent before the *portus Ganda* of St Bavo's Abbey was destroyed in 879, living in the newer settlement 500 m upstream on the River Scheldt, near the oldest – possibly ninth-century – city church and within the semicircular, D-shaped moat which they may have constructed themselves. Indeed, it appeared

[29] Verhulst and Declercq, 'Early Medieval Ghent', pp. 49–52, reprinted in Verhulst, *Rural and Urban Aspects*, XII, pp. 24–32.   [30] *Ibid.*, pp. 56–7, and pp. 42–5 of the reprint.
[31] P. Toubert, 'La part du grand domaine dans le décollage économique de l'Occident (VIIIe–Xe siècles)', in *La croissance agricole du haut moyen âge*, Auch, 1990 (Flaran 10, 1988), pp. 53–86; Devroey, 'Courants et réseaux d'échange'.

from the archaeological examination of a 75 m length of this moat that it does date from the ninth century and was no longer used in the tenth century. This information tallies with what we know about the size of *Gandavum* in 941: as mentioned above, at that time the urban settlement already comprised the *whole* area between the Leie and the Scheldt, extending far beyond the area of approximately 7 ha enclosed by the moat, i.e. up to the Leie and even as far as onto the left bank of the Leie.

This digression into urban development in Arras and Ghent on the strength of the terminological data *vicus* and *portus* has enabled us to determine what was possibly the most important stage in early medieval urban development. This consisted in the transition from a limited 'manorial' phase in trade – and perhaps, bearing in mind the hypothesis about Arras, also in industry, carried out in a small, adjoining abbey town near a large abbey and on its behalf mainly by people in the service of the abbey – to a wider and free phase conducted by independent merchants and workers who traded or practised a trade for profit. They still lived in the vicinity of the abbey, but a little further away than the monastic *vicus*. Clearly the Viking raids, and, in the case of Ghent, the destruction and eventual disappearance of the abbey over a longer period, accelerated the evolution from the one stage to the other. A result of this was the emancipation of the earlier abbey merchants who could now conduct trade on their own account.

This evolution was not restricted to the ecclesiastical sphere: the role which can be attributed to large abbeys, such as in Arras and in Ghent, can be ascribed to royal manors (*fisci*) elsewhere, with or without a royal residence (*palatium*). Within the area between the Somme, Scheldt and North Sea under consideration here, this was the case in Valenciennes and in Tournai on the Scheldt in the ninth century, and perhaps also in Douai, but there in the tenth century.

In **Valenciennes** the *fiscus,* to which a few villages in the area belonged, comprised a royal residence (*palatium*) in Valenciennes itself, which dates back to the end of the seventh century (693) at least, and from where the whole *fiscus* was administered.[32] The ninth-century *portus,* mentioned around the year 865, which is identified with the mooring place known as *le Rivage* on the right bank of the Scheldt near the oldest, but later city church (St Géry), was apparently part of it (Map 13). Toll and mooring fee (*ripaticum*) were levied there in the ninth century. Between 879 and 883, probably at the end of 880 or the beginning of 881, the Vikings destroyed the royal manor's operating centre (*mansus indominicatus*) along with the two churches, St Pharaïlde and St Saulve,

---

[32] Deisser-Nagels, 'Valenciennes', pp. 62–79; Platelle, 'Du "Domaine de Valentinus"', pp. 162–6; H. Platelle (ed.), *Histoire de Valenciennes*, Lille, 1982, p. 17–22.

which belonged to it. Thirty years later in 914 they still lay in ruin, and there is no trace whatsoever of commercial activity in Valenciennes in the tenth century. It seems then that here, unlike in Ghent and Arras, there was no continuity of any urban life or of trade activity from the ninth to the tenth centuries.

In the ninth century, a very large part but not the whole territory of **Tournai** was also part of a royal manor, whose centre (*caput fisci*) was very probably located within the walls of the late Roman *civitas*, where the Merovingian kings also had a residence until the end of the sixth century.[33] It is assumed that the *portus*, which is referred to as such on coins of Charles the Bald and Charles the Fat (875–87) and whose mooring place is probably on the left bank of the Scheldt near the Church of St Pierre which is described as *de media urbe* – 'in the middle of the (fortified) city' – was also located within these walls, between the cathedral and the bank of the River Scheldt to where the walls very probably reached. Within that same fortified area (*in eadem urbe*), Louis the Pious had relinquished several plots belonging to the *fiscus* to the bishop of Noyon-Tournai in 817 for the construction of the communal buildings for the canons (*claustra canonicorum*). The rest of the *fiscus* remained royal property until the end of the ninth century. Then in 898 Charles the Simple handed it over to the bishop as part of an exchange operation, together with the comital rights, including the mintage, the mooring fee (*rivaticum*), the right to hold a market (*mercato*) and the toll. These elements are sufficient indication of trade activity in Tournai within the framework of a royal manor. A literary work in verse by Milo of Saint-Amand (845–55: *Carmen de S. Amando*) sang the praises of trade in relation to Tournai (*quod aquis et merce redundat*) even around the middle of the ninth century.[34] It seems that the Viking raids on Tournai in 880 scarcely interrupted this activity.

What we should intend by trade activity as part of a royal manor can be deduced from an analogy with trade activity within the framework of an ecclesiastical manor, and in particular at the seat of a large abbey.[35] It is, however, also partly apparent from Louis the Pious' well-known *Preceptum negotiatorum* dating from 828,[36] in which the emperor guarantees those merchants who provide the imperial palace with goods supplied on the orders of the king or on their own account (*ex suo negotio ac*

---

[33] Chapter 1, note 18; chapter 2, notes 29–34.

[34] Vercauteren, *Civitates*, p. 246 note 4.

[35] A. Verhulst and J. Semmler, 'Les statuts d'Adalhard de Corbie de l'an 822', *Le Moyen Age* 68 (1962), pp. 247–51; Devroey, 'Courants et réseaux d'échange', pp. 330–8, 340–56, 367–84.

[36] F. L. Ganshof, 'Note sur le "Praeceptum Negotiatorum" de Louis le Pieux', in *Studi in onore di Armando Sapori*, I, Milan, 1956, pp. 92–112; text and commentary in Lebecq, *Marchands et navigateurs frisons*, II, pp. 435–7.

nostro) protection against all officeholders and others with power in the kingdom. To that end they had their own ships and other means of transport which they could add to for the purpose of their own trade and for that of the emperor without having to pay tolls anywhere, apart from 10 percent to the king in Quentovic, Dorestat and on the Alpine passes (*ad Clusas*).

According to a view defended in the last chapter,[37] the well-known but disputed text regarding **Cambrai** (contained in a manuscript originating from between 822 and 986 and preceded by the famous 822 Statutes of Abbot Adalhard for the Abbey of Corbie) may be applied to the period in which it was written, the ninth–tenth centuries. That text takes the form of a list of mainly exotic products, including many spices, and their quantities, that had to be purchased in Cambrai if there was money available – apparently on behalf of and for use by the Abbey of Corbie. Apart from pepper and some other items (incense, myrrh, sulphur, minium, gold dust and wax), these products are so unusual that they can scarcely be regarded as representative of what was normally on sale at a weekly market. They are so diverse, the grades of some of the products are so various (*si inveneris bonum, bonum compara*) and the quantities are so great that Cambrai must certainly have had a very special market in the ninth and tenth centuries, with products deriving from distant regions, and so visited by merchants with international contacts. So no ordinary weekly market, as information relating to the ninth century may well bear out: according to a narrative source of *c.* 900,[38] a fair (*nundinae*) was held twice a year (11 August and 18 November) on the feast of St Géry and on the day of the elevation of his relics. Otherwise particulars about trade activity in Cambrai date from the tenth and eleventh centuries. Though quite plentiful, the ninth-century information about mintage in Cambrai may not automatically be included in this. In Cambrai most of the coins were struck under Charles the Bald in the Abbey of St Géry where the fair was held, and in the *civitas* where the bishop had his seat [39] (Map 8). The old Roman *civitas* next to the Abbey of St Géry had remained of significance, whereas in Arras, in the absence of a bishop who had his seat in Cambrai until 1093, the Abbey of St Vaast was in several respects the one and only central point in the urbanizing settlement, while the early medieval *civitas* of Roman origin, with its Church of Notre Dame and dilapidated walls, lay abandoned in the ninth century. In Cambrai the bishop had his seat in the *civitas*, along with his residence, his cathedral, the communal buildings of the cathedral chapter and the houses of the

---

[37] Chapter 2, p. 34.
[38] Vercauteren, *Civitates*, p. 217 and note 2.
[39] Lafaurie, 'Monnaies émises à Cambrai', pp. 402–3.

canons. The Abbey of St Géry stood on the hill of Mont-des-Bœufs, a few hundred metres to the south-east of the *civitas*.[40]

The Viking raids

Both the *civitas* of Cambrai, whose Roman walls had apparently fallen into disrepair, and the Abbey of St Géry were destroyed by fire by Vikings from their camp in Kortrijk on the very day – 28 December 880 – that the same lot befell the *civitas* and the Abbey of St Vaast in Arras. Earlier that same year the Vikings had set fire to and destroyed the *civitas* of Tournai from the camp which, with winter approaching, they had set up in St Bavo's Abbey in Ghent in November 879. They thoroughly destroyed that as well.[41] There were reactions to these more or less contemporaneous events in the three old *civitates* of Cambrai, Tournai and Arras. In Valenciennes, which, as we have seen, was also affected in the winter of 880/1, nothing happened after that for about thirty years. We are unsure about the situation in Ghent but, as in Bruges and Saint-Omer, it produced a different kind of reaction to the Vikings.

Cambrai, Tournai and Arras still had the remains of the walls which had protected the *civitas* in each of these places since the late third–fourth centuries. These walls were rebuilt in Cambrai and in Tournai, but not in Arras. The reason for this was that in both Cambrai and Tournai the initiative came from the bishop, whereas in Arras the lay abbot of St Vaast had the abbey rather than the *civitas* fortified with walls. As well as having the walls of the *civitas* in Cambrai rebuilt between 880 and 901, Bishop Dodilo also extended them so as to incorporate the Abbey of St Aubert. The Abbey of St Géry remained outside the walls, within its own, possibly older and unfortified enclosure.[42] In Tournai King Charles the Simple gave permission in 898 to the bishop residing in Noyon to rebuild the old fortification (*firmitas*), at the same time granting him the comital rights. It is believed that *firmitas* referred to the walls of the old *civitas* whose towers had collapsed in the middle of the ninth century according to the well-known passage in Milo of Saint-Amand's *Carmen de S. Amando*.[43] It is assumed, though this is not entirely certain, that the *portus* on the Scheldt in Tournai, which had existed before the Viking raid, was incorporated inside the restored walls between the river and the cathedral.

In **Arras** lay abbot Raoul, who was also lay abbot of St Bertin in Saint-Omer and organized the defence against the Vikings there as well,

[40] Vercauteren, *Civitates*, pp. 214–17.
[41] D'Haenens, *Invasions normandes*, pp. 47–9.
[42] *Ibid.*, p. 113, note 102.
[43] *Ibid.*, pp. 113 and 201; Pycke, 'Urbs fuerat quondam', pp. 227–30.

did not fortify the old *civitas* but built a fortification around the Abbey of St Vaast.[44] This was done after the Vikings had set fire to the *civitas*, the abbey and the abbey town (*vicus monasterii*), with the exception of the churches, on 28 December 880, from the camp they had established in Kortrijk in November of that year, and after they had set fire to the Church of Our Lady of the *civitas* in Arras. Between 883 and 887 Charles the Fat had given permission for the abbey to be fortified, and it was called *castrum* and *castrum sive monasterium* for the first time in 890. The fortification formed a rectangle measuring approximately 330×150 m, which can be projected fairly well onto the modern-day street plan of Arras between the present-day cathedral in the north and rue St Aubert in the south, rue Albert Ier (formerly rue des Murs St Vaast) in the east and rue des Teinturiers (along the earlier course of the Crinchon, now underground) in the west (Map 6). The whole fortification covered an area of some 5.25 ha and, apart from the abbey church of St Vaast and the abbey buildings, comprised the parish church of S Pierre-du-Castel (replaced in the thirteenth century by the Church of La Madeleine-du-Castel near the present-day place de la Madeleine)[45] and the palace of the king next to the southern wall (on the place de la Madeleine) which, as *Cour-le-Comte*, was the residence (*domus mea*) of the count of Flanders at the beginning of the twelfth century at the latest.[46] The abbey town (*vicus monasterii*) was probably also located within the fortification, but in our view this is unlikely to have been the case for the *vicus* called *Nova Villa* in 867. Perhaps we should look for this *vicus* to the east of the abbey, in the area immediately adjacent to rue Albert Ier, which was incorporated into the fortified abbey area when the fortification was extended in that direction in the eleventh century. The fortified character of the abbey was so striking that in 890 King Odo (Eudes) found it necessary to emphasize that it was still an abbey whose monastic character should not be marred. Yet it was very probably a wooden fortification rather than one with stone walls, which explains why it was totally devastated by an accidental fire in 892, along with the churches of St Vaast and St Pierre which were located inside it. Though a fortified abbey was a frequent phenomenon in the ninth century,[47] the one in Arras was rather unusual because its location next to the old and unfortified *civitas* was something new, whereas the *civitates* in the nearby cities of Cambrai and Tournai were fortified at about the same time.

[44] D'Haenens, *Invasions normandes*, pp. 117–19; Kéry, *Errichtung des Bistums Arras*, pp. 265–7; Brühl, *Palatium*, pp. 92–5.

[45] Delmaire, *Diocèse d'Arras*, II, pp. 426–7.   [46] Brühl, *Palatium*, p. 99.

[47] See list of fortified abbeys in A. Verhulst, 'Over de stichting en vroegste geschiedenis van de Sint-Pieters- en Sint-Baafs-abdijen te Gent', *Handelingen van de Maatschappij voor Geschiedenis en Oudheidkunde te Gent*, new series, 7 (1953), p. 22, note 100.

Partly because the new defence against the Vikings in Arras was probably created on the initiative of a lay abbot who was charged with
defending a larger area and had (among other things) a new fortification
built in Saint-Omer, it can be compared not only to the latter place but
also to what was undertaken as part of the defence against the Vikings in
the ninth century more to the north, along the Flemish coast and along
the Scheldt, as well as in Bruges and in Ghent. As in Arras, no Roman
ruins were used and/or rebuilt as defence against the Vikings in these
more northerly areas either, even if they were already there. Oudenburg,
on the Flemish coast, is a case in point. There the ruins of the late Roman
fortified camp were used as a stone quarry in the tenth–eleventh centuries.[48] Though as an earlier Roman fortification, situated on what was
then an inlet of the sea to the north-east of Bruges (the later Zwin),
Aardenburg was reinhabited in the tenth century and perhaps even earlier; it was very probably not fortified against the Vikings at the end of the
ninth century either. This function was taken over by Oostburg (6.5 km
to the north-east of Aardenburg), where a round stronghold, which will
be discussed below, was erected at the end of the ninth century.[49]

The situation in **Ghent** is rather more complicated, partly because St
Bavo's Abbey was allocated a role in the general coastal defence of the
north-west of the Carolingian kingdom at the beginning of the ninth
century.[50] Several of its vassals in the Flemish coastal region and on the
Zealand islands were charged with guard duties during the first half of the
ninth century. In Ghent itself, probably in the immediate vicinity of St
Bavo's Abbey, Charlemagne had ships built for deployment against the
Vikings, and in 811 he came in person to inspect them. Perhaps St Bavo's
Abbey was itself fortified, which would explain why it was called *castrum
Gandavum*[51] by a contemporary source, the *Vita Bavonis*, dating from the
second quarter of the ninth century, though its textual tradition does not
date back further than the tenth–eleventh centuries and so it may have
been manipulated on that point. Despite this possible fortification, the
abbey was set on fire by the Vikings in 851 and totally destroyed in 879
when they pitched their winter camp there. A new, late ninth-century
commercial settlement 500 m upstream on the River Scheldt was left
open and unprotected on its waterfront, although it was enclosed by a
D-shaped moat on the landward side (Map 5). A donjon, recognizable in
a tower in the largely rebuilt and restored Gerard de Duivelsteen, may
have been built on the river bank at that time, but in our opinion it can

[48] Verhulst, 'An Aspect of the Question of Continuity', pp. 190–1.
[49] *Ibid.*, pp. 194–5; Van Heeringen *et al.*, *Ringwalburgen*, p. 96.
[50] Verhulst and Declercq, 'Early Medieval Ghent', p. 49 (p. 24 of the reprint in Verhulst,
Rural and Urban Aspects, XII).   [51] *Ibid.*, pp. 46–9 (pp. 20–4 of the reprint).

hardly be regarded as a defence against the Vikings.[52] Neither can the predecessor of the twelfth-century Count's Castle in Ghent, consisting largely of a donjon, and dating back only to the middle of the tenth century, when it was built of wood.[53] So, contrary to an earlier, generally accepted view, it had nothing to do with defence against the Vikings. The island, surrounded partly by excavated water courses, on which the donjon of the Count's Castle was built in the south-west corner as *novum castellum* in the middle of the tenth century, and which in its totality was called Oudburg (*Vetus Burgus, Vetus Castellum*) as of the twelfth century, can at best be regarded as a defensive element which was older than the *novum castellum* and so was perhaps constructed against the Vikings before the tenth century. We do not know who took the initiative for this. It was not necessarily the count of Flanders, whom we only encounter with certainty as a ruler in Ghent in the tenth century. It could have been someone like the lay abbot of St Bavo's Abbey on whose manor the fortification may after all have been built. Around the middle of the ninth century this was the count of Laon, Adalelm, who as lay abbot was charged with defending the entire area to the north of Ghent against the Vikings. It is possible that his son Walcher continued to be lay abbot of St Bavo's Abbey until 892 and that, while St Bavo's Abbey itself lay in ruins and abandoned, he made the Oudburg into a fortified island, where he may have had residency.

We first hear something about **Bruges** around the middle of the ninth century.[54] Fearing the Viking raids of 851, when the abbey was probably set on fire for the first time, the canons of St Bavo's Abbey in Ghent took some valuables to Bruges for safekeeping, including a gold cross which was never returned to the abbey. This implies the existence of a fortification in Bruges around the middle of the ninth century. A few traces of this may perhaps be discerned in parts of a curved ditch which were discovered there during excavation work in 1987–9 in the northern half of the later castle, the modern-day square known as Burg (Map 9). This ditch is older than the Church of St Donatian which was built there around the middle of the tenth century, and so could have been part of a fortification which we know beyond doubt from a written source existed

[52] *Ibid.*, pp. 49–53 (pp. 25–32 of the reprint).
[53] *Ibid.*, pp. 55–6 (pp. 39–42 of the reprint).
[54] H. De Witte (ed.), *De Brugse Burg*, Bruges, 1991, esp. G. De Clercq, 'Oorsprong en vroegste ontwikkeling van de burcht van Brugge (9de–12de eeuw)' (with a summary in English), pp. 15–45; M. Ryckaert, 'Les origines et l'histoire ancienne de Bruges: l'état de la question et quelques données nouvelles', in Duvosquel and Thoen (eds.), *Peasants and Townsmen*, pp. 117–34; H. De Witte, 'La fortification de Bruges. Les fouilles de 1987–1989 au "Burg" de Bruges', in P. Demolon, H. Galinié and F. Verhaeghe (eds.) *Archéologie des villes dans le Nord de l'Europe (VIIe–XIIIe siècle)*, Douai, 1994, pp. 83–91.

in 892 and was then in the hands of the count of Flanders. This fortification very probably had its origins in one of the fortified sentry posts
(*presidia, seditiones*) which were set up as of the early ninth century along
the coasts of Flanders and Zealand, preferably in places accessible by ship
from the sea,[55] against the Viking raids which were beginning to threaten.
This was the case, for example, in Bruges, and also in many other places
along the coast where, later in the ninth century and particularly in the
years before 891, circular fortifications (*castella recens facta*) were built,
which, with an average diameter of 200 m, could also serve as refuges.
These round boroughs were constructed in Bourbourg, Sint-Winoksbergen and Veurne on the western part of the Flemish coast, in Oostburg in
Zealand Flanders and on the Zealand islands (Domburg, Middelburg
and Souburg on the island of Walcheren and Burgh on Schouwen).[56]
Later, in the tenth–eleventh centuries, some of these round boroughs
were permanently inhabited and became small towns whose circular
shape is still preserved in their street plan. **Veurne,** situated on one of the
then estuaries of the River Yser, is an early example of this. The development in Veurne may even have been under way at the end of the ninth
century as the continuation or successor of a mysterious *Iserae portus*. In
the list of *villae* from the late ninth century in which Bruges and Antwerp
are called *vicus*, Veurne is the only place without the qualification of
villa.[57] In 860 the Vikings journeyed from this *Iserae portus* to the Abbey of
St Bertin in **Saint-Omer,** which they did not attack and set on fire until
the summer of 879, apparently without serious consequences. Shortly
before that, Abbot Fulco (872–82) had tried in vain to fortify the cloister
with an enclosure. He had abandoned the work because its periphery was
much too large.[58] In response to the raid of 879, the hill of Saint-Omer,
which rose up about 1000 m to the south-west of St Bertin from a
low-lying, swampy area and on which the Church of Notre Dame stood,
was fortified a few years later, or at any rate before 891, perhaps on the
initiative of lay abbot Raoul who had also fortified St Vaast Abbey in
Arras.[59] The top of the hill was not large (approximately 2 ha) and,
according to a contemporary description, wide, deep ditches and an earth
wall with a wooden palisade on top made access to it more difficult (Map
10). This pattern can still be seen in today's street plan of Saint-Omer as a
half-circle around the hill. It may once have been a completely circular
fortification like those in Bourbourg, Sint-Winoksbergen and Veurne in
the vicinity of Saint-Omer, which were also built at the end of the ninth

[55] Van Heeringen *et al.*, *Ringwalburgen*, p. 82; D'Haenens, *Invasions normandes*, p. 107–8.
[56] Van Heeringen *et al.*, *Ringwalburgen*; D'Haenens, *Invasions normandes*, p. 118.
[57] Koch, 'Kaufmannsniederlassungen', p. 320.
[58] D'Haenens, *Invasions normandes*, pp. 46, 117.   [59] *Ibid.*, pp. 117–22.

century. The fortification served as a safe borough for the local population, who took shelter there in 891 when the Vikings came to steal the cattle from the area, yet were kept at a distance from the fortification with arrows and other weapons and eventually dispelled. In this respect Saint-Omer is one of the series of fortifications (*castella recens facta*) built along the coast shortly before 891 which, with their usually round shape, served as refuges and within which a city did not develop until later. In Saint-Omer this development took place in the course of the tenth century, though outside the fortification. The old market square (Vieux Marché) and the big market square were created at the foot of the fortified hill in the tenth and eleventh centuries respectively.[60]

Apart from the case of Saint-Omer, it strikes us that in two places where a fortification was built against the Vikings in the ninth century, but not in the form of a round borough, there are signs of urban development even earlier than in the case of these round boroughs. This is undoubtedly the case in **Bruges** before the end of the ninth century; together with Antwerp it was called *vicus* in a summary of places which were all rural and qualified as such (*villa*). This poses not only the question of where in Bruges this settlement with early urban characteristics and distinguishable from a possible fortification was located, but above all what the relationship was of the *vicus* to a possible fortification in the area. Some believe that in Bruges the oldest urban settlement was in the area later known as Oudeburg, to the west of the castle, yet separated from it by the Reie.[61] If, as some believe, the Oudeburg had its own bulwark in the eleventh century, then the Bruges Oudeburg was probably a sort of small borough town (*bourg castral*) comparable with the small abbey towns (*vicus monasterii*) near the abbeys in Ghent and Arras. If, moreover, the Oudeburg in Bruges can be identified with the above-mentioned *vicus* dating from the end of the ninth century, then the Oudeburg would not be much later than the count's fortification in Bruges and would also date from the ninth century. The qualification 'oud' meaning 'old' in Oudeburg does at any rate denote the contrast with a younger urban settlement which together with the market square, developed in the tenth–eleventh century just to the north of Oudeburg and Steenstraat.

Originally, i.e. before the eleventh century, there may have been not only a difference in age between the Oudeburg and the area around the market square, but also a juridical difference. This can be assumed by analogy with the Oudburg in **Ghent**.[62] Around the middle of the tenth century the long, fortified, 5.5–ha island in Ghent not only comprised a

[60] A. Derville, *Saint-Omer des origines au début du XIVe siècle*, Lille, 1995, pp. 30–1, 41–3.
[61] Ryckaert, 'Origines de Bruges', pp. 132–3.
[62] Verhulst and Declercq, 'Early Medieval Ghent', pp. 55–6 (pp. 39–42 of the reprint).

wooden donjon in the south-west of the island; leather workers (*coriarii*) lived next to this then-fortified nucleus (*novum castellum*) on the island which, as a whole, was called *castrum* at the time (Map 5). We may assume they were in the manorial service of the count of Flanders, lord of the donjon, as we were also able to assume for the inhabitants of the *vicus monasterii* near the Abbey of St Vaast in Arras. So the Oudburg in Ghent can perhaps be compared to the manorial settlement within the fortification of the Abbey of Arras and to the walled Oudeburg near the castle in Bruges. Indeed the Oudburg in Ghent was not juridically part of the actual medieval city until the thirteenth century. During the first half of the tenth century a new *portus* grew up across the River Leie opposite the Oudburg and on both banks of the Leie to the south of it. That *portus* was to become the second nucleus of the medieval city, alongside the ninth-century settlement on the River Scheldt near the oldest city church.[63] As in Bruges, the 'oud' ('old') element in the name Oudburg indicates the chronological contrast with this more recent urban area on the Leie and perhaps at the same time the contrast with the new donjon (*novum castellum*) dating from the mid-tenth century in the south-west of the Oudburg island. In Ghent, as in Bruges, the 'burg' element in the name has its double, respectively Romance and Germanic meaning of 'settlement' (Fr. *bourg*) and 'fortification' (Ger. *burg*).[64]

Things are less clear when we look at **Antwerp**, which is called *vicus* in the same late ninth-century list in which Bruges is given that designation. When shortly before 980 the German Emperor Otto II built a semicircular fortification on the right bank of the Scheldt in Antwerp, of which the famous 'Steen', a piece of wall and the street plan are the still visible vestiges, a settlement with urban characteristics (streets, plots of land for houses) was located within this fortification (Map 12). In the terminology of the ninth–tenth centuries, such a settlement could be labelled *vicus*.[65] The question is simply whether the tenth-century fortification dates back to a more primitive, semicircular, late ninth-century fortification, and consequently perhaps the settlement too, as the late ninth-century attestation of *vicus* in Antwerp suggests. If so it would probably have had a manorial character, like other *vici* elsewhere (Arras, Ghent, Bruges). Unfortunately the archaeological research carried out in the Antwerp castle area provided no clear findings about the late ninth century. But in Antwerp, too, the real medieval city, with marketplace, city church, etc.,

---

[63] *Ibid.*, pp. 56–7 (pp. 42–5 of the reprint).
[64] H. Van Werveke, *'Burgus': versterking of nederzetting?*, Brussels, 1965 (with a summary in French) (Verhandelingen van de Koninklijke Vlaamse Academie voor Wetenschappen van België, Klasse der Letteren, XXVII, no. 59).
[65] Verhulst, 'Origins of Antwerp', pp. 13–16.

did begin to develop outside the castle and at the foot of it in the eleventh century.

Conclusion

Compared to the Meuse Valley, the western part of the area under consideration here, primarily the Scheldt Valley, gives the impression of greater dynamic force with regard to urban development in the ninth century. That was perhaps the beginning of the superiority in terms of urbanization of the areas located nearer the sea over those more inland, which characterized the mid and late Middle Ages. Since the Vikings operated mainly from the sea and in the coastal areas, whereas in the Meuse region they ravaged just Maastricht and Liège, there is the obvious question of whether there was a link between the two phenomena, such as the Viking threat giving rise to greater activity in terms of building fleets, fortification work, etc. While one certainly cannot argue that the Viking raids stimulated urban life, they did not cause a long interruption in the evolution of the settlements to cities either, unless exceptionally as in Valenciennes.[66] Indeed, in many places there are signs of continuity which lead us to believe that the destruction wreaked by the Vikings, as for example by fire, was often quickly repaired. When that destruction was severe, as in Ghent, continuity was nevertheless provided by relocation to a new settlement in the area. Finally – and this seems to us the most important result of recent historical research – it is untrue to say that in every case the fortifications or castles erected against the Vikings formed the pre-urban core, giving rise to a trade settlement in the tenth–eleventh centuries, once the raids were over. This was long the normative and well-known theory of Henri Pirenne.[67] The influence exerted by fortifications as centres of power and wealth in their area rather than as protective elements, as Pirenne thought, certainly cannot be denied. In particular the new, tenth-century feudal castles saw the emergence of new trade settlements (e.g. Douai) or new extensions of existing trade settlements (e.g. Ghent on the Leie) in their vicinity.[68] But even before the Viking raids in the ninth century, centres of power and wealth – such as abbeys and royal residences or palaces, even if they were not yet fortified – or early fortifications, such as Bruges around the middle of the ninth century, gave rise to settlements in their immediate vicinity whose inhabitants were engaged in artisanal and even commercial activities. These then were usually practised in a manorial connection of dependence and subordination relating to the maintenance and care of the abbey or of the

---

[66] D'Haenens, *Invasions normandes*, pp. 158–9.
[67] Verhulst, 'Origins of Towns', pp. 3–5.   [68] See chapter 4.

king.. These small abbey towns and castral or small borough towns, frequently part of the fortification of an abbey, as in Arras, continued to exist as such and preserve their manorial character after the ninth century, if they were not destroyed by the Vikings as in the case of St Bavo's Abbey in Ghent. In the tenth century new castral settlements would even emerge at the foot of the new feudal castles, as in the Oudburg in Ghent and the Oudeburg in Bruges. Even in the ninth century, however, new settlements with an urban character and urban functions emerged outside the fortifications. The inhabitants of those new settlements were not in the service of a lord but worked on their own account and for profit. We have seen examples of such settlements even in the ninth century in Arras and in Ghent, where they became the core and the starting point of the medieval city. They developed and expanded in the tenth century in particular, first still under the effect of the stimulus deriving from the abbey or feudal castle, but before long against the background of the burgeoning international trade in which they participated.

We have no information about the commercial and/or artisanal activities practised there in the ninth century. The example of Arras indicates that textiles were already an important part of that activity. The same may be assumed of Ghent where, even at the beginning of the ninth century, the two large Benedictine abbeys of St Bavo and St Peter had large flocks of sheep in the coastal region near Bruges and in Zealand. Their wool production may have been too large to be worked locally and the geographical conditions unsuitable, so that even at that stage the wool may have been taken to Ghent for processing. This was certainly the case at the end of the tenth century.

4 The urbanization of the high Middle Ages (tenth–eleventh centuries)

The urbanization which had begun in the ninth century continued during the tenth century, despite the Viking raids in the late ninth century, and reached its first peak in the eleventh century. That process can be divided into four phases and is visible in as many groups of cities, at least within what were then the most urbanized regions in the area between the Somme and the Meuse, namely the Meuse and the Scheldt valleys and the North Sea and Channel coast.

First, there was the expansion of the urbanized area from several nuclei which had begun to display signs of an urban character back in the ninth century: this was primarily the case in Ghent, even in the first half of the tenth century, in the Meuse Valley – particularly in Liège – in the second half of the tenth century, and in the old ecclesiastical centres of Arras, Tournai and Cambrai.

Second, in the course of the tenth century new urban settlements emerged in the county of Flanders, namely in Saint-Omer and in Douai. Though older, Bruges was in a sense part of this group.

Third, around the year 1000, new trade settlements grew up along the River Scheldt in Antwerp, Ename and Valenciennes, near castles erected on the right bank by the German emperor at the end of the tenth century to protect the border with the county of Flanders which had been provided by the River Scheldt since 925. At the beginning of the eleventh century a castle was built in Oudenaarde, immediately opposite Ename on the left bank, then part of the county of Flanders, and subsequently a trade settlement emerged at its feet.

Eventually Ypres and Lille, also in the county of Flanders, began to emerge in the middle of the eleventh century and developed during the second half of that century. It was not long before they, together with Ghent and Bruges, were among the most important cities in the county.

In Brabant, which scarcely merits a mention before the tenth century since it had no urban settlements at that stage, a fifth group of cities can be distinguished as from the late tenth and in the eleventh centuries as part of a very specific urban development within this future duchy. These cities did not stem from older predecessors; they were new. Apart from Antwerp, a Brabantine city which economically speaking can be regarded as an older Flemish Scheldt city up to and including the eleventh century, these were primarily Nivelles and Gembloux, Brussels, Mechelen and Leuven.

In the ninth century it had been abbeys (sometimes fortified) and royal residences with a manor attached (*fiscus*) that influenced the emergence of urban settlements. In the tenth century the establishment of a feudal castle in the various places mentioned above was the most important factor to influence urbanization, apart from in the ecclesiastical centres of Liège, Arras, Tournai and Cambrai and the small abbey towns of Nivelles and Gembloux. Moreover, these new feudal castles were often built on the sites of those residences and manors of which they were in a sense the successors, though now under the dominion no longer of the king, but of a territorial prince.[1] International trade played no visible role in this development during the tenth century. In fact, it did not begin to do so until the end of the tenth century, and in the eleventh century in particular, when industrial activity, which had until then been restricted almost exclusively to the countryside as an aspect of the manorial economy, shifted to the cities. As a result of the weakening manorial system and the feudalization of rural society, which in some regions began in the late ninth century but became more widespread in the tenth–eleventh centuries, industry – and wool and metal processing in particular – began to secure a foothold in the urbanizing centres, thereby paving the way for division of labour and industrial serial production. From then on products were manufactured on a large scale in the cities and exported, so that, along with industrialization, international trade became the most important factor in urbanization and reached a high point in the eleventh century for the first time in the Middle Ages.[2] Signs of this expansion were to be seen in the cities which had existed before the tenth century, and after that also in the younger cities where new residential areas emerged, new parishes were founded, markets were established and a city wall was constructed.

[1] F. L. Ganshof, *Etudes sur le développement des villes entre Loire et Rhin au moyen âge*, Paris, 1943, pp. 18–3; Van Werveke, '*Burgus*'; H. Patze (ed.), *Die Burgen im deutschen Sprachraum: ihre rechts- und verfassungsgeschichtliche Bedeutung*, 2 vols., Sigmaringen, 1976 (Vorträge und Forschungen 19); A. Verhulst, 'Die gräfliche Burgenverfassung in Flandern im Hochmittelalter', in Patze (ed.), *Die Burgen*, pp. 267–82; G. Streich, *Burg und Kirche während des deutschen Mittelalters: Untersuchungen zur Sakraltopographie von Pfalzen, Burgen und Herrensitzen*, 2 vols., Sigmaringen, 1984 (Vorträge und Forschungen 29); A. Verhulst, 'Grundherrschaftliche Aspekte bei der Entstehung der Städte Flanderns', in A. Verhulst and Y. Morimoto (eds.), *Economie rurale et économie urbaine au moyen âge*, Ghent and Fukuoka, 1994, pp. 157–64 (Centre belge d'histoire rurale, publication no. 108).
[2] See chapter 5.

We will now examine the topographical aspects of the expansion of the older urban centres in the tenth–eleventh centuries and the emergence of new cities. It is difficult to do this other than city by city, but we will take a global look at trade and industry in these cities and at the social aspects of the urban population and institutional development in the tenth, eleventh and twelfth centuries in chapter 5.

The Meuse Valley

Of the urban centres along the Meuse it was **Liège** that underwent the most significant development in the tenth century, especially under the bishopric of Notger (972–1008), put on the throne by Otto II as a pillar of the imperial church in Liège.[3] Even before his appointment, various churches had been built in Liège during the period of redevelopment that followed the Viking raid of 881. However, as of 987 Notger implemented an impressive building programme (Map 4): the Abbey of St John the Evangelist (before 997), the Church of St Croix on the Publémont (before 1005), the Chapter of St Denis (1008) and the – since vanished – Cathedral of St Lambert in the centre of the old *vicus*, next to the prince-bishop's palace. In constructing a wall, around the year 1000, Notger incorporated not only the buildings in the lower town (cathedral and palace) into a single defence zone designed to protect the 'holy city' (*urbs sancta*), but also the market square and the new commercial district to the south of that, between the market and the Meuse, the *novus vicus* (1194: *Noviz*; now rue Neuvice), and the churches on the Publémont, the hill above the lower town. Furthermore, Notger may have urbanized the island, formed by a branch of the Meuse to the south-west of the walled city, by laying out the streets according to a planned and regular network and by building two chapters there (including St Paul's, the modern-day cathedral).

In the first quarter of the eleventh century two more abbeys and a chapter were built on this island, which was linked to the left bank of the Meuse by two bridges (*Pont d'Ile*, Pont d'Avroy) around the same period, while the Pont des Arches, which linked the city with the right bank (quartier d'Outremeuse), was built between 1025 and 1037. A direct road led from the Pont des Arches to Aachen. Though all this building work underlined first and foremost the role of Liège as an ecclesiastical centre and as capital of the prince-bishopric, which was certainly the

[3] J. L. Kupper, *Liège et l'église impériale, XIe–XIIe siècles*, Paris, 1981; Kupper, 'Archéologie et histoire: Aux origines de la cité de Liège (VIIIe–XIe siècle)' in *La genèse et les premiers siècles*, pp. 377–89; Kupper, 'Notger de Liège revisité', *Cahiers de Clio* 124 (1995), pp. 5–16.

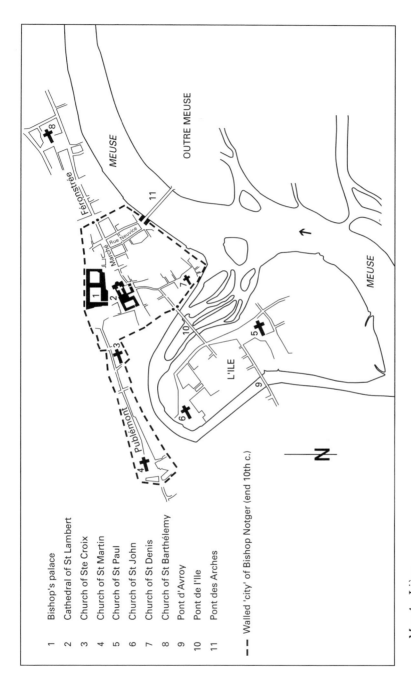

1   Bishop's palace
2   Cathedral of St Lambert
3   Church of Ste Croix
4   Church of St Martin
5   Church of St Paul
6   Church of St John
7   Church of St Denis
8   Church of St Barthélemy
9   Pont d'Avroy
10 Pont de l'Ile
11 Pont des Arches

-- - Walled 'city' of Bishop Notger (end 10th c.)

Map 4 Liège

intention, it must also have served as an economic boost for the city towards the end of the tenth century. This is apparent from the existence of the *novus vicus*, the new, tenth-century part of the city where the merchants lived who were mentioned between 991 and 1002 in the famous toll tariff of London and who later frequented the markets in Cologne and appeared in the well-known toll tariff of Koblenz in the eleventh century. Though the merchants are referred to as *cives* in a 1052–6 source, unlike the knights (*viris militaribus*) who also lived in Liège, they did not yet have a freedom charter. It was not until 1107, forty years later than in Huy, that as merchants they were granted a special market prerogative (*judicium forense*).[4]

The prosperity of Liège in the tenth–eleventh centuries was probably at the expense of **Maastricht**, about which we hear almost nothing in that period, except that Louis the Child gave the toll and the mintage of Maastricht to the bishop of Liège in 908. According to a later source, Duke Giselbert of Lotharingia (915–39), who regarded Maastricht as his seat, had a wall built around the cloister of St Servaas and the ducal residence there. With the laying out of the Vrijthof as a large square, which dates from around 1000 archaeologically, the then built-up part of Maastricht was bordered to the west, creating a sort of link between it and the St Servaas complex (Map 2). Merchants from Maastricht were not seen in distant parts, such as Austria and Hungary, until the end of the twelfth century.[5]

The first written data relating to the topography of **Huy** and its urban development date from the eleventh century, though frequently they derive from later sources.[6] In the eleventh century, the term *castrum*, which was often used for Huy in the eighth–ninth centuries, refers not only to the rock near the confluence of Meuse and Hoyoux, on which a donjon probably stood at that time (the so-called *Tour Basin*), but also to the area at the foot of the rock, between the two rivers (Map 3). There, in the triangle at the confluence, stood the monastic immunity of Notre Dame, on an area of land measuring 1 ha, and to the south-east of it, between the rock and the Hoyoux, lay the parish of St Etienne, likewise no bigger than 1 ha. The palace of the bishop of Liège was located in this parish. The bishops had often resided in Huy since the early Middle Ages, and in the tenth century, before Notger's large-scale building programme

---

[4] F. Vercauteren, 'De wordingsgeschiedenis der Maassteden in de hoge Middeleeuwen', *Bijdragen en Mededelingen van het Historisch Genootschap te Utrecht* 71 (1957), pp. 12–28; Vercauteren, 'Marchands et bourgeois dans le pays mosan aux XIe et XIIe siècles', in *Mélanges Felix Rousseau*, Brussels, 1958, pp. 655–72, esp. pp. 664–71.

[5] Panhuysen and Leupen, 'Maastricht', pp. 447–9; Van Ommeren, 'Bronnen voor de geschiedenis van Maastricht', pp. 42–6; Devroey and Zoller, 'Villes, campagnes', pp. 250–1.   [6] Joris, *Huy*, pp. 135–52.

in Liège, one of them had thought of making Huy his residence. The area covered by the parish of St Etienne, where the main street is rue Sous-le-Château, is called *bourc desoubz* in a fifteenth-century Romance translation of a Latin text dating from 1149. So, as part of the *castrum*, this *burgus* was a sort of appendage of the donjon on the rock and probably fortified. In this respect it can be compared to the *vetus burgus* in Arras and the Oud(e)burg in Ghent and in Bruges, which also date from the tenth–eleventh centuries.[7] Its population consisted largely of *clerici* and of vassals of the bishop of Liège rather than of merchants, even though the name of *Apleit* – meaning mooring place – on the right bank of the Meuse, the Church of St Nicolas at the confluence with the Hoyoux and the name *burgenses* in the famous charter for Huy of 1066 all recall the earlier presence of traders. However, in the eleventh–twelfth centuries the merchants, like the craftsmen, lived on the right bank of the Hoyoux, near the market where the Church of *St Martin-in-Foro* stood. As had been the case in the first centuries of the Middle Ages and even before that, craftsmen also lived on the left bank of the Meuse, which was joined to the right bank by a bridge in 1066.[8] As we show in another connection, merchants from Huy were present in London around the year 1000 and a little later in Cologne, where they sold the copper and tin basins and kettles which accounted for the fame of Huy's metal industry in the eleventh and twelfth centuries. As we will see, these merchants, called *burgenses* in 1066 though the place where they lived at that time was not called *burgus*, purchased from the bishop of Liège, lord of the city, a certain limitation of his seignorial rights in that same year.[9]

The topography of **Namur** in the tenth–eleventh centuries was in many ways similar to that of Huy. Here, too, its development into a city started in the area at the confluence of the Sambre and the Meuse.[10] This was the site of the rock on which the count of Namur's residence (*domus*) stood, probably fortified as a donjon. At the foot of the rock, on the triangular peninsula between the two rivers – the so-called *pointe du Grognon* – there were two churches in the tenth century, the chapter of Notre Dame and that of St Hilaire. This area was fortified in 960 together with the donjon, and in 1188, like Huy, it was called *burgus*.[11] It may have been inhabited by the count's servants because, according to eleventh- and twelfth-century data, the merchants and craftsmen lived in a *vicus* on the left bank of the Sambre. This topographical configuration also resem-

[7] A. Joris, 'A propos de "burgus" à Huy et à Namur', in *Die Stadt in der europäischen geschichte: Festschrift Edith Ennen*, Bonn, 1972, pp. 192–9. [8] Joris, *Huy*, pp. 144–9.
[9] See chapter 5.
[10] Despy, 'L'agglomeration urbaine', pp. 66–78; Devroey and Zoller, 'Villes, campagnes', p. 255. [11] Joris, 'Burgus', pp. 196–9.

bles that of Huy. Moreover, as in Huy, we may well wonder if perhaps the first merchants lived in the *burgus* beneath the rock. According to a late tenth-century source that deals with events of 954, the *portus* of Namur – where in the 960s the Abbey of Lobbes had parcels of land divided up into many lots (*in Namuco portu sessi*) – was located around the Church of St Hilaire at the foot of the rock, where – again as in Huy – the toponym *Apleit*, meaning mooring place, occurs. However, as we have said, the further expansion of the city took place on the left bank of the Sambre, around the Church of St Aubain. At the end of the twelfth century the left bank was linked by a bridge to the *burgus* between Sambre and Meuse.

Indications of a topographical nature with regard to **Dinant** are more numerous for the ninth century than for the tenth. Conversely the data about the economic significance of Dinant are more plentiful for the tenth century than for the ninth. So, according to the proposition of G. Despy,[12] continuous expansion must have taken place between the two centuries. More recently, however, it has been shown that we must be wary of associating the Church of St Pierre, which was located near the market to the north of Notre Dame Church, both on the right bank of the Meuse, with small parcels of land (*sessi*) which the Abbey of Lobbes probably owned there at the end of the ninth century (889). Though in Dinant such parcels (*sedilia*) had been in the possession of the Abbey of Stavelot a few years earlier, it is no longer certain that those of Lobbes were located in Dinant.[13] Consequently, the interpretation of the Church of St Pierre as a sign of ninth-century urban expansion to the north of Notre Dame cannot be upheld. This then must mean that the foundation of new churches and parishes in Dinant must have been deferred to the tenth century, which is more consistent with the information about the city's economic significance in the tenth century. This information is as follows: its listing as *portus* and as *emporium*, the existence of a mooring place (*statio navium*) and above all the fact that it had an annual fair (*nundinae*), though this seems to have been of no more than regional significance. In fact we have to wait for the middle of the eleventh century to find indications in Dinant of the metal working for which the city became famous in the twelfth century.[14]

Apart from Liège, which evolved in the ninth century from a rural manor to an episcopal residence with urban traits to which it also owed its

---

[12] G. Despy, 'Note sur le "portus" de Dinant aux IXe et Xe siècles', in *Miscellanea mediaevalia in memoriam J. F. Niermeyer*, Groningen, 1967, pp. 61–9; Devroey and Zoller, 'Villes, campagnes', pp. 255–6.

[13] J. P. Devroey, *Le polyptyque et les listes de biens de l'abbaye Saint-Pierre de Lobbes (IXe–XIe siècles)*, Brussels, 1986, p. 22, note 50.

[14] Despy, 'Note sur le "portus" de Dinant', pp. 67–9; Gaier-Lhoest, *Evolution topographique de Dinant*, pp. 26–7 and 33–4.

urban expansion in the tenth century, all the settlements in the Meuse Valley which can be characterized as urban in the tenth–eleventh centuries go back to antecedents from Roman times or from the first centuries of the Middle Ages. In other words, apart from Liège whose origins were purely ecclesiastical, for economic reasons not a single new settlement along the Meuse evolved into a city in the course of the ninth, tenth or eleventh century. Even the geographic expansion of the Meuse cities was modest, again with the exception of Liège. It has, however, been established that the merchants in Huy and in Namur who were perhaps originally based in the small fortified appendage of the castle, which was called *burgus*, may later have settled *outside* the area of the castle, but then right opposite and linked to it by a bridge. We encounter the same topographical situation in a number of Flemish cities where there was a feudal castle in the tenth–eleventh centuries which influenced urban development there.

From the North Sea to the Scheldt Valley

The western part of the area between Somme and Meuse, more specifically the area from the North Sea coast up to and including the valley of the Scheldt and its tributaries, gives a much more dynamic picture with regard to urban development in the tenth–eleventh centuries than the Meuse Valley. This applies both to topographical growth within the cities themselves and to the number of new cities.

Ghent

The most spectacular and also the earliest growth took place in **Ghent**. As indicated briefly in chapter 3, following the destruction by the Vikings of the *portus* next to St Bavo's Abbey in 879, a settlement had grown up or become important 500 m upstream from there on the left bank of the Scheldt, in the vicinity of the oldest city church (St John's, now St Bavo's Cathedral), and expanded in a westerly direction towards the Leie and beyond this river even before 941 (Map 5). As a result, the ninth-century semicircular moat which surrounded the settlement on the landward side lost its significance and was gradually filled in. This expansion in a westerly direction led to the urbanization of the whole area between the Scheldt and the Leie and even of a strip on the left bank of the Leie. This was done partly by dividing the land into small plots and building houses on them, called in contemporary sources *mansioniles* or *mansiones*, and around the year 1200 *mansurae*. Topographically and perhaps also economically this expansion and more specifically the direction it took, as

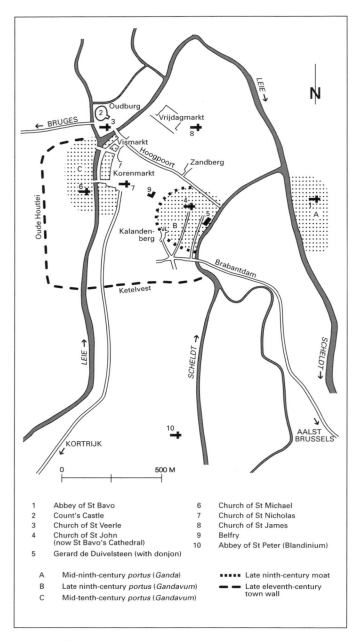

Map 5   Ghent

indicated by the main street of the later town – which still has the meaningful name of Hoogpoort ('Hoge stad', 'uptown') – are explained by the draw exercised by the manor and residence on the left bank of the Leie, of which the existing Count's Castle is a vestige, and by the growing importance of the River Leie.[15] The manor around the Count's Castle was perhaps an autonomous element of a vast, early medieval royal estate (*fiscus*) in the ninth century which encompassed the west side of Ghent as far as the left bank of the Leie. Up until the tenth century this element must have been a rural entity, corresponding more or less to the elongated, approximately 5 ha island to the west of the Leie between two branches of this river and two ditches. This area was termed *castrum* in the tenth century, and in the twelfth century *vetus castellum* or Oudburg.[16] So in the tenth century, and perhaps even in the late ninth century, it was a fortified island whose larger north-east half comprised a settlement where leather workers were based. More specifically this settlement was referred to by the name of Oudburg, which is still the name of the main road running through this part of the original island. It is believed that the name originated because, opposite the old *burgus* – used in the sense of a fortified settlement as an appendage to a castle, as in Arras, Bruges, Huy and Namur – a new *burgus* had developed from the Scheldt in the east in a westerly direction along the Hoogpoort, up to the right bank of the Leie, right opposite the Oudburg. A wooden donjon, enclosed at its base by an earthen motte, was built around the middle of the tenth century in the smaller south-west half of the island, in the corner between the two branches of the Leie. It is probably this new fortified element which was called *novum castellum* in a more or less contemporary text. This may also explain why the rest of the originally fortified island was named Oudburg. After all, in the Flemish region 'burg' could be used in two senses: the Germanic one, as in the latter case, usually meaning 'fortification', or the Romance one, as in the origin of the name outlined above, usually meaning 'settlement'. Both are combined in the sense of 'fortified settlement as an appendage of a castle' as was normally the case within the area between Somme and Meuse, close to the Germanic–Romance linguistic border.[17]

By analogy with the excavated donjon in Douai, the wooden donjon in the Oudburg in Ghent dating from the middle of the tenth century may have been built on the site of an earlier, fortified farmstead which served as the operating centre of the manor which had comprised the area of the Oudburg and its surroundings. Even after this rebuilding, and especially once the count of Flanders had reorganized the county administratively

[15] Verhulst and Declercq, 'Early Medieval Ghent', pp. 50–9. [16] *Ibid.*, pp. 55–6.
[17] Van Werveke, '*Burgus*'.

into so-called 'kasselrijen' ('castellanies') around the year 1000 – the centre of these 'castellanies' being a castle to which the produce and supplies from the rural manors were brought – this castle took on great economic importance with its storehouses and cellars (*spicaria*)[18] and was rebuilt in stone around the middle of the eleventh century.[19] Pirenne did not consider the active economic role of the castle, seeing it as an economically passive and purely consumptive organism, which had no contact with the nearby city from which it was to remain juridically and militarily separate. In particular, he failed to realize the consequences of the fact that this and other manorial centres inside castles stored agricultural products, many of which were sold at the town market.[20] That is why in Ghent, as in Bruges and in most other Flemish cities, the oldest market was located right opposite the count's castle, separated from it by a river or moat. From both a topographical and even an economic viewpoint, Ghent is a good and early example both of urban development in the tenth–eleventh centuries and of the part played by the feudal castle, partly because it has been studied so thoroughly. This does not of course exclude other factors of, for example, a more general economic nature as an explanation. These factors will be treated globally for various cities together in the next chapter. Perhaps that will explain the earliness in the example of Ghent, albeit within the urban development of the tenth–eleventh centuries.

The topographical expansion of the urban area of Ghent, from the oldest city church on the Scheldt to the Count's Castle on the other side of the Leie, must have been a gradual process. Two new parishes, St Nicholas and St James, were separated only in the late eleventh century from the oldest urban parish, which comprised the whole area between Scheldt and Leie.[21] Then a new parish, St Michael, was formed in the west as well, on the left bank of the Leie. It had split away from the ecclesiastical district that comprised the whole of the vast, early medieval crown estate to the west of Ghent, at the centre of which was the rural Church of St Martin of Akkergem manor. St Nicholas and St Michael were situated very close together, but on different sides of the Leie. This river had formed the border in Ghent between the patronage areas of the two large, vying Benedictine abbeys, St Peter's (with ecclesiastical authority over the area between Scheldt and Leie) and St Bavo's (which had

[18] A. Verhulst, 'Die gräfliche Burgenverfassung', pp. 267–82.
[19] D. Callebaut, 'Résidences fortifiées et centres administratifs dans la vallée de l'Escaut', in Demolon *et al.* (eds.), *Archéologie des villes*, pp. 102–9.
[20] A. Verhulst, 'The Alleged Poverty of the Flemish Rural Economy as reflected in the Oldest Account of the Comital Domain, known as "Gros Brief" (A.D. 1187)', in E. Aerts *et al.* in *Studia historica oeconomica: liber amicorum Herman Van der Wee*, Leuven, 1993, pp. 369–82.   [21] Verhulst and Declercq, 'Early Medieval Ghent', p. 59.

ecclesiastical control over the areas on the left bank of the Leie). The close proximity of St Nicholas and St Michael may then have been a result of this rivalry, though each parochial area was sufficiently extensive and also densely populated to support a church. We can nevertheless deduce from the location of two markets on the right bank of the Leie – the oldest, called *Vismarkt* (actual Groentenmarkt), opposite the Count's Castle, the other, called Korenmarkt, opposite the densely populated *Overleie* neighbourhood, with the Church of St Nicholas on the edge of the market – that the western part of the city was at first still able to accommodate these markets, i.e. in the tenth century. The oldest core of the city, later called *Kuip van Gent*, with the belfry and the town hall in the late Middle Ages, lay more to the east, near the oldest city church of St John (now St Bavo's Cathedral), from where expansion in a westerly direction had begun early in the tenth century. The building of the oldest city wall in Ghent is usually believed to have taken place around 1100, though we have no direct information about this.[22] The Leie, which forms a large northerly curve around the Ghent city area, constituted the basis of this line of defence in the north and the Scheldt in the east. A canal – the still existing Ketelvest – was dug in the south, between the Scheldt and the Leie. The Houtlei - now filled in - was excavated in the west around the *Overleie* area on the left bank of the Leie. The Oudburg area belonging to the count, together with the Count's Castle, remained outside this wall, whose construction was probably undertaken on the initiative of an autonomous city council. We will look at its formation in a wider context in the next chapter.

The group of ecclesiastical towns: Arras, Tournai, Cambrai

Without showing the many topographical similarities of cities like Ghent, Bruges and Douai, where a feudal castle of the count of Flanders played an important role, older cities like Arras, Tournai and Cambrai, where bishops, abbots and canons held sway, can nevertheless be treated as one group as regards their topographical development in the tenth–eleventh centuries.

Arras became the most important of these three cities in the twelfth–thirteenth centuries. As we saw when we touched on the topographical development of Arras during the tenth–eleventh centuries in chapter 3, the fortification work carried out around the abbey between 883 and 887 initially comprised not only the abbey church of St Vaast and the abbey buildings, but also the parish church of St Pierre-du-Castel and the

---

[22] L. Milis, 'The Medieval City', in Decavele (ed.) *Ghent*, pp. 61–2.

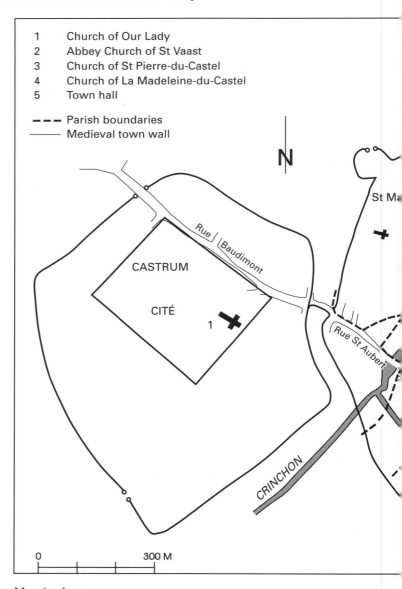

1   Church of Our Lady
2   Abbey Church of St Vaast
3   Church of St Pierre-du-Castel
4   Church of La Madeleine-du-Castel
5   Town hall

--- Parish boundaries
—— Medieval town wall

Map 6   Arras

residence of the king near the southern wall, which came into the hands of the count of Flanders in the tenth century and was called his home (*domus mea*) no later than the beginning of the twelfth century, and later *Cour-le-Comte* (Map 6). The small, ninth-century abbey town next to the abbey (*vicus monasterii*) was probably also located inside the fortification, though we hear nothing more about it after the ninth century. Neither do we hear anything more of another, later settlement next to the abbey, called *Nova Villa* in the ninth century. Perhaps it lay to the east of the abbey and was incorporated into the fortification when the area adjacent to the present-day rue Albert Ier (formerly rue des Murs St-Vaast) was absorbed by a new eastern wall built in the tenth or eleventh century, whereby the castle of St Vaast was enlarged from 5.25 ha to around 8 ha.[23] This maximum expansion was consistent with the parish of St Pierre-du-Castel, whose church was replaced in the thirteenth century by the Church of La Madeleine-du-Castel, 100 m to the south of St Pierre, though without altering the parish borders which continued to correspond to the castle walls.[24]

In several respects, both topographical and functional, this fortification can be compared to the great feudal castles of Ghent or Bruges. New population nuclei also emerged in the immediate vicinity of the fortification, their location marked by the churches of St Aubert, just outside the south-west corner of the fortification, and St Géry, just outside its eastern wall.[25] Their parochial area even enclosed the whole fortification: St Aubert on the south and west sides, St Géry along the east and north. Neither church dates from later than the early eleventh century; St Aubert is even mentioned in 1015–25. We can expect to find the *Vetus Burgus*, named along with a *Novus Burgus* in connection with a quarrel that broke out around 1113 between the Abbey of St Vaast and the episcopal Notre Dame chapter in the old Roman cité (*civitas*), on the territory of one or both of the parishes.[26] After a bishop was appointed to Arras in 1093 (who was independent of the bishop of Cambrai who had exercised ecclesiastical control over the bishopric of Arras since the early Middle Ages), the chapter of Notre Dame claimed its rights over the parishes of Arras, all of which (with the exception of St Pierre inside the castle) depended on the chapter and not on the abbey. To the north of the fortified abbey complex and of the parish of St Géry, a third and new population nucleus developed no later than around the middle of the eleventh century, for which St

---

[23] Vercauteren, *Civitates*, pp. 197–204; Brühl, *Palatium*, pp. 95–9; Kéry, *Errichtung des Bistum Arras*, pp. 277–85; Delmaire, *Diocèse d'Arras*, I, pp. 79–86, II, pp. 425–31.
[24] Delmaire, *Diocèse d'Arras*, II, pp. 426–7.
[25] *Ibid.*, p. 427.
[26] *Ibid.*, pp. 428–9; Vercauteren, *Civitates*, pp. 197–8.

Vaast Abbey built a small chapel close to the market (*Petit Marché*) before 1060. By 1113 this chapel had already become the parish church of Ste Croix. Within its jurisdiction we would expect to find the *Novus Burgus* over which St Vaast Abbey and the cathedral chapter had started to quarrel that same year, unless perhaps *Novus Burgus* also referred to a part of the parish of St Maurice, which like Ste Croix was built as a chapel in the gardens (*pomerium, hortus*) of St Vaast Abbey, to the north-west of the abbey wall, shortly before 1060. The later street names show that mainly textile workers settled here along the little River Crinchon on the site of the earlier garden which had been divided very systematically into parcels of land around 1150 or perhaps even earlier. The famous 'Cartulary of Guiman' which was drawn up in St Vaast Abbey around 1170 to defend the rights of the abbey against the cathedral chapter, lists the names of more than 200 tax payers for these new plots, together with the amounts payable. Many names refer to migrants from up to about 30 km around Arras. The new parish of *La Chapelette au Jardin*, also called *Sainte Marie* or *Notre Dame du Jardin* (*Sancta Maria in Horto, SM in Pomerio*) was established in the middle of these plots in 1152.[27]

In contrast to the cities in Germanic-speaking areas, such as Ghent, Bruges and originally also Saint-Omer where *burgus* (in the vernacular: 'Oud(e)burg', 'Bourc') is used both in the Germanic sense of 'fortification' and in the Romance sense of 'settlement', in the French-speaking Arras the *Vetus* and *Novus Burgus* are simply used in the Latin sense to mean parts of the town which had no fortification of their own. Together with the emergence of new churches and chapels and the parcels of land that Guiman mentions, they provide a picture of the rapid topographical growth of Arras from the late tenth to the end of the twelfth century. This growth was already so far advanced by around 1100 that between 1100 and 1111 Robert II, count of Flanders, had the existing above-mentioned parishes and neighbourhoods enclosed by a great wall, including some which were not yet densely populated such as the later *La Chapelette (Notre Dame) au Jardin* (1150). The *cité*, the old Roman *civitas* with Notre Dame Chapter and episcopal residence, was not made a part of this fortification, which enclosed an area of approximately 100 ha.[28]

This topographical expansion was of course driven by Arras' economic development, which, as we will see in the next chapter, peaked in the twelfth century.

The topographical development of **Tournai** between the tenth and the twelfth centuries is quite straightforward, despite a dearth of con-

[27] Vercauteren, 'Un exemple de peuplement urbain', pp. 18–27.
[28] Brühl, *Palatium*, p. 96.

temporary sources – we have to rely largely on two chronicles dating from the middle of the twelfth century and on the later topography.[29]

After the walls of the Gallo-Roman *civitas* had been rebuilt – Charles the Simple having given the bishop of Noyon-Tournai the go-ahead in 898 – their line following that of the wall dating from late antiquity, new churches were built outside the surrounding episcopal wall in the tenth and again in the eleventh century. Apart from the cathedral, there was just one church inside the wall, that of St Pierre, which was located between the cathedral and the left bank of the Scheldt (Map 7). It was first mentioned in 951 as *S. Petrus de media urbe*, yet may even have existed at the beginning of the tenth century. In this case *urbs* means 'fortified city' or 'fortification', and the Church of St Pierre was indeed located in the middle of it. Because of its location close to the Scheldt and, more precisely, near the Quai du Marché aux Poissons, it is considered to be the ninth/tenth-century church of the commercial district (*portus*) which was located there. Indeed, in many cities the location of a fish market denotes one of the oldest urban nuclei. Moreover, a number of streets in the vicinity of the former Church of St Pierre bear the names of artisanal crafts often practised near a fortified power centre (cf. Ghent, Bruges), such as leather workers or nail and spur makers. Outside the surrounding wall, immediately to the west of the cathedral, was the Grand Marché (lat. *forum*, actual Grand-Place) with the existing Church of St Quentin on the north-west side of this triangular square. Like St Pierre, it too was named in 951 and designated *S. Quintinus de foro*. This reference to a market square (*forum*) is one of the oldest in the area under consideration and is evidence of the city's early development. While the Marché aux Poissons apparently catered for the local area, the larger market (Grand Marché/Grand Place), where the clothmakers' hall (Halle aux Draps) was located, attracted regional and international trade. There is in fact written evidence of this trade, more specifically in wool, from the end of the tenth century.

To the south-east of the cathedral and also outside the surrounding wall, the foundation of the Church of St Piat around the middle of the eleventh century testifies to a new residential area, still on the left bank of the Scheldt. Here wood and in particular the well-known Tournai stone were worked and shipped (cf. the Quai de Taille-Pierres).

But economic and demographic expansion also made itself felt on the right bank of the Scheldt. In 1054 there is reference to the Church of St Brice, opposite and close to the oldest and long the only bridge over the Scheldt, the Pont à pont, which some believe had been there since Roman times, though these days it is generally not thought to have been built

[29] Vercauteren, *Civitates*, pp. 251–3; Vercauteren, 'Tournai', in *Villes belges en reliëf*, Brussels, 1965, pp. 185–93.

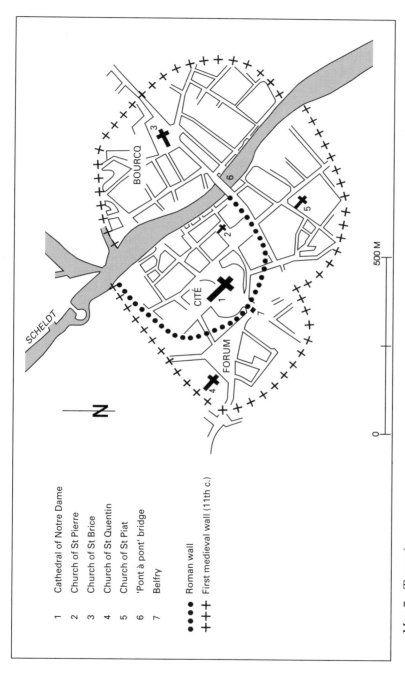

N

SCHELDT

BOURCQ

CITÉ

FORUM

1 Cathedral of Notre Dame
2 Church of St Pierre
3 Church of St Brice
4 Church of St Quentin
5 Church of St Piat
6 'Pont à pont' bridge
7 Belfry

● ● ● Roman wall

+ + + First medieval wall (11th c.)

0   500 M

Map 7 Tournai

before the second half of the eleventh century.[30] In the early Middle Ages, from the fifth to the eighth centuries, there was a cemetery here where the grave of Childeric, the father of Clovis, who died in 481, was discovered in 1653. The area was called *le Bourcq* in the late Middle Ages, in the Romance sense of 'residential district', perhaps also to convey the contrast with the *cité* (Lat. *civitas*) on the left bank; as in other cities the *burgus* was distinguished from the fortification close to which it was located. The new residential areas outside the late Roman and early medieval wall, around the churches of St Quentin, St Piat and St Brice, so now extending also to the right bank of the Scheldt, were protected by a new enclosure between 1054 and 1090. Parts of it were still visible on sixteenth-century and later city plans and can still be seen today. In the thirteenth century, between 1202 and 1304, a new surrounding wall was built on the initiative of the French king who had been the master in Tournai since 1188. Its purpose was to enclose the new neighbourhoods which had grown up outside the eleventh-century wall. That surrounding wall survived until 1864–8.

Meanwhile, in the course of the twelfth century many churches were demolished and rebuilt in Romanesque style, including the cathedral, whose Romanesque choir, which was replaced by the extant Gothic choir in the thirteenth century, was completed by around 1149. At the end of the twelfth century the belfry was built to the south-west of the cathedral at the south-eastern point of the Grand Marché. It is one of the oldest belfries in the area under consideration and it was rebuilt in its present form and fortified in 1294.[31]

The topographical development of **Cambrai** in the tenth–eleventh centuries was determined, on the one hand, by the presence of the late Roman fortification (Lat. *civitas*, Fr. *cité*) where the bishop resided and, on the other, by the Abbey of St Géry, a few hundred metres to the south-east of the episcopal fortification, where the citadel stood after the demolition of the abbey by Emperor Charles V in the sixteenth century (Map 8)[32]. After the destruction of both complexes by the Vikings in 880, the dilapidated walls of the late Roman *civitas* were rebuilt several years later on the initiative of Bishop Dodilo (880–post 901) in such a way that thereafter the Abbey of St Aubert was also inside the fortification. For its

---

[30] C. Dury, 'Les ponts des Tournai des origines à la fin du XVIIe siècle', in F. Thomas and J. Nazet (eds.), *Tournai: une ville, un fleuve (XVIe–XVIIe siècle)*, Brussels, 1995, pp. 120–1.

[31] R. Van Uytven, 'Flämische Belfriede und südniederländische städtische Bauwerke im Mittelalter: Symbol und Mythos', in A. Haverkamp (ed.), *Information, Kommunikation und Selbstdarstellung in mittelalterlichen Gemeinden*, Munich, 1998 (Schriften des Historischen Kolleges Kolloquien, 40), pp. 125–59.

[32] Vercauteren, *Civitates*, pp. 223–32; L. Trenard (ed.), *Histoire de Cambrai*, Lille, 1982, pp. 37–8.

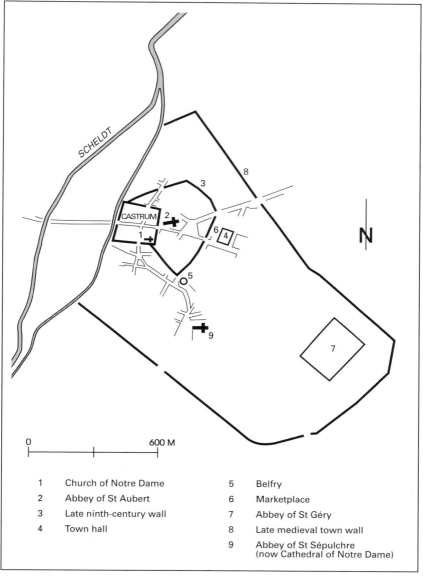

Map 8   Cambrai

part, the Abbey of St Géry on the Mont des Boeufs formed a small separate agglomeration with its own enclosure. Merchants and also craftsmen settled between the episcopal fortification and the Abbey of St Géry no later than towards the end of the tenth century. Around the middle of the eleventh century several of these merchants, who sometimes engaged in long-distance trade, are known by name. A charter drawn up by Otto III in 1001 guaranteed them market peace, which confirms the existence of a marketplace. This was probably the later Grand Marché or Grande-Place, near the east wall of the episcopal fortification, but outside it. Later on, the town hall, the butchers' hall and the clothmakers' hall were located on this market square. New churches were built in its vicinity around the middle and in the second half of the eleventh century on the initiative of the bishops who were then also master over this part of the city and over St Géry Abbey. Bishop Gerard II had the whole area between the late ninth-century wall and the Abbey of St Géry, which had been built over during this expansion, enclosed by a stone wall between 1076 and 1092. It even incorporated the restored episcopal fortification.

Bruges, Saint-Omer, Douai

Saint-Omer and Douai, and, though older, in a sense Bruges as well, form a group of cities where, as in Ghent, a fortress belonging to the count of Flanders influenced their topographical and partly also their economic development as of the tenth century.

As already explained briefly in the last chapter, in **Bruges** a fortification, built against possible Viking raids during the first half of the ninth century, was extended in a second phase during the second half of that century to form a moated wall which stood like a semicircle on two branches of the Reie (Kraanrei and Groene Rei) which divide there (Map 9).[33] This wall, of which an arched fragment several metres long was excavated in 1987–9, was taken out of use around the middle of the tenth century, allowing the construction of the first Church of St Donatian in the northern half of the fortress (third phase) at this time by Count Arnulf I of Flanders. The foundations of this church, excavated in the 1980s and following a central plan based on the model of the palatine chapel in Aachen, appeared to cut through the excavated fragment of the moat. The new fortress was much larger than its predecessor (approximately 1.5 ha), had a square rather than a (semi)circular ground plan, and was surrounded by high walls built at least partly with stones taken from the

---

[33] De Witte (ed.), *De Brugse Burg*. See chapter 3, note 54.

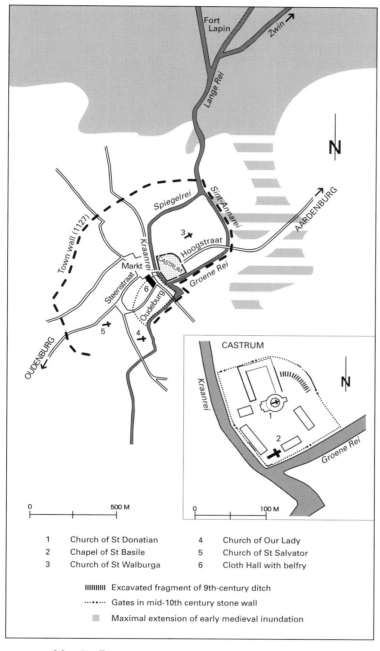

Map 9   Bruges

Key (within map):

1   Church of St Donatian
2   Chapel of St Basile
3   Church of St Walburga
4   Church of Our Lady
5   Church of St Salvator
6   Cloth Hall with belfry

|||||||| Excavated fragment of 9th-century ditch

····•···· Gates in mid-10th century stone wall

░░ Maximal extension of early medieval inundation

ruins of the Roman fort of Oudenburg, about 20 km to the west of Bruges. Inside these walls there was room for the chapter house which was attached to St Donatian Church and for buildings for the count, as well as for a large open square. While the west and south walls were protected by the water of two branches of the Reie, this was not the case for the north and east walls. These had to rely for their defence on a sort of 'Vorburg', a large square island to the north and to the east of the castle, surrounded by water on all sides, partly by the two above-mentioned branches of the Reie (the Kraanrei and Groene Rei), and partly, on the north and the east, by the Spiegelrei and the Sint-Annarei. In the south-west corner of this large island was the walled castle, and in the middle of it St Walburga Church. Though known only from texts written a few centuries later, this church is regarded by some historians either as the predecessor of the Church of St Donatian and so as the count's fortress chapel before the middle of the tenth century, or as the church of a hypothetical ninth–tenth-century trade settlement. This area is thought to be the site of a trade settlement because it was at this point that the tideway, which linked Bruges to the sea in Roman times and again during the first centuries of the Middle Ages, reached the later city area. As in many other places, the trade settlement would thus have been situated in or near an important power centre. In later centuries several street names appear on the 'large island' to the north of the castle which refer to the presence of leather workers and weapon makers. These street names may recall an early situation when perhaps such craftsmen, whose military significance is clear, worked as dependants of the count and were based in the 'Vorburg', like the leather workers in the tenth-century Oudburg in Ghent, to which the 'Vorburg' in Bruges can be compared.

The link between Bruges and the sea played an important role in the emergence and the topography of the city right up until the late twelfth century.[34] It seems to have been no coincidence that at its various stages the castle of Bruges was located at the intersection of the Reie, which flowed into a tideway to the north of the city, and the road of Roman origin which linked the Roman forts of Oudenburg and Aardenburg. This road ran from west to east through Bruges, along the Steenstraat and the Hoogstraat, straight through the castle. It was situated on the sand ridge which bordered the Pleistocene sands 5 m above the flood area to the north of it. Bruges' link with the sea was, however, in a state of flux throughout the whole of the Middle Ages. This was the result of flooding and/or recessions of the sea associated with phases of transgression and regression until into the twelfth century. Without flooding in the area to

[34] A. Verhulst, 'Les origines et l'histoire ancienne de la ville de Bruges (IXe–XIIe siècle)', *Le Moyen Age* 66 (1960), pp. 37–63 (reprinted in Verhulst, *Rural and Urban Aspects*, XIII).

the north of Bruges, access to the sea was difficult in the early Middle Ages, if not impossible. Access seems to have been difficult in the tenth century and again in the second half of the eleventh century, as well as in the first half of the twelfth century. A fleet of small ships carrying Queen Emma, who had fled from England, landed in Bruges in 1037, as a contemporary source tells us, at a place 'not far from the castle' (*haud longe a castello*). This is often interpreted as a place to the north of Bruges where the Reie discharged into a tideway which must still have been navigable up to that point for flat-bottomed ships, probably as a result of flooding in 1014 and 1042. In the late eleventh to early twelfth centuries, by which time Bruges had become a fully fledged city, and again in the second half of the twelfth century, a solution was found to the problem by linking Bruges by means of a man-made canal to the navigable creeks which had formed during flooding, this time from the bay to the north-east of Bruges which was called *Sincfal* until into the eleventh century and *Zwin* from the twelfth century onwards. These creeks did not in fact reach as far as Bruges. Perhaps this explains why it was that a settlement developed in the tenth–eleventh centuries to the west – and not to the north – of the castle in the district of the Oudeburg, to the south of Steenstraat and the Grote Markt and opposite the castle. Three land routes led from this settlement to Ypres, Kortrijk and Ghent.

As we explained in the last chapter, the Oudeburg in Bruges, like the Oudburg in Ghent, may perhaps originally have been a fortified appendage of the castle, housing a population of craftsmen and perhaps also of merchants who were dependent on the castle. It is usually thought to explain the siting of the city's two oldest churches, St Salvator and Our Lady, immediately to the west and to the south of the Oudeburg respectively. Initially, in the tenth century, they were chapels at the far corner of two large rural manors, whose church they were dependent on. It seems they were founded in competition with each other to serve the burgeoning settlement of the Oudeburg. Like the Oudeburg, they too became an integral part of the actual city, and fully fledged urban parish churches in the course of the eleventh century. As such, the elongated area along the Steenstraat with the two churches was incorporated into the primitive city fortification which may have been built at the end of the eleventh century and certainly existed by 1127. That area occupied most of the western half of the urban area inside the walls. The eastern half consisted mainly of the count's castle area and of the large square 'Vorburg' island around St Walburga. While leather workers and weapon makers, possibly in the service of the count, must have lived in the southern half of this 'island', close to the actual walled castle, the northern half was urbanized in the twelfth century, as can still be seen in the fairly regular street plan, following the possible disappearance of the hypothetical late ninth-century trade settlement near St Walburga.

So we can conclude from all this that the castle in Bruges played an even greater role in the topographical development of the city than did the castle in Ghent. With its first two ninth-century phases, it was older than the Ghent castle. Moreover, it was surrounded by ramparts even in the middle of the tenth century, while the castle in Ghent consisted only of a donjon at that time. Furthermore, there was a 'Vorburg' in Bruges next to the actual walled castle, and in terms of size and function that 'Vorburg' can perhaps be likened to the Ghent Oudburg as an appendage of the actual castle. Though outside the large castle area on the right bank of the Reie, in Bruges there was a neighbourhood called Oudeburg on the left bank of this river, which can also, if only because of the name, be compared to the Ghent Oudburg as a sort of appendage of the castle, with a settlement and its own fortification. Unlike Ghent, however, the Oudeburg in Bruges, with the two oldest city churches which belonged there functionally, was the nucleus from which the city developed in the tenth–eleventh centuries. In Ghent, on the other hand, the Oudburg remained a dependency of the castle and was only incorporated into the urban area in 1274, placing it under the authority of the city aldermen. The explanation for this difference may perhaps lie in the fact that in Ghent the urbanized area expanded from a nucleus which was much further from the castle and older than the castle itself, so that the Oudburg was not considered as a possible nucleus of the city. In Bruges the Oudeburg was situated on the Steenstraat, a road of Roman origin where Roman remains have been found. So the settlement inside the Oudeburg in Bruges may well be very old. With the decline of a hypothetical ninth-century trade settlement around St Walburga near the count's castle complex and close to a navigable link with the sea, it is possible that as soon as the latter lost its significance as a result of silting, the inland-looking settlement in the Oudeburg developed to such an extent during the tenth–eleventh centuries that it freed itself of any original dependence on the castle.

In the last chapter we saw how at the end of the ninth century the hill of **Saint-Omer**, in the south-west of the medieval city, was fortified with a wall and a moat to form a stronghold for the local population in the face of the Viking threat (Map 10). Like other Flemish coastal strongholds from the same period and in the same area (Bourbourg, Sint-Winoksbergen, Veurne), it was probably round in form. This form is still partly recognizable in the street plan, though the south-west half was destroyed by the later city wall. In the tenth century, when the fortification was in the hands of the count of Flanders and it had lost its function as a stronghold,

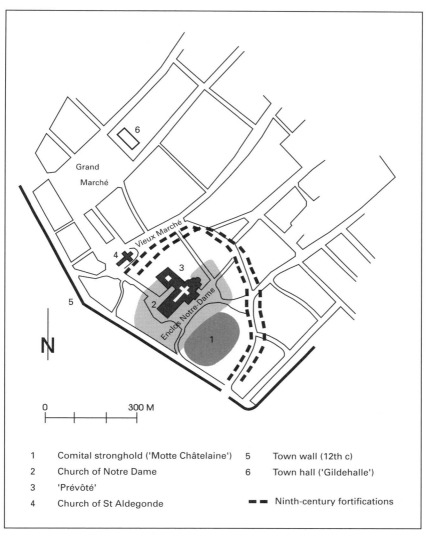

Map 10 Saint-Omer

it contained:[35] the collegiate church of Notre Dame and its annexes (deanery, buildings for the canons, garden – later known collectively as *enclos Notre-Dame)*; a donjon (later called *'bourc'*, in the Germanic sense of 'fortification', later under the dominion of the powerful viscounts of Saint-Omer whose predecessor Folcuin referred to in 938 with the ambiguous name of *praetor urbanus*, in which *urbs* means 'fortification' and not yet 'city'); and a storehouse (granary) for supplies. In the eleventh and twelfth centuries the land inside the fortification seems to have consisted mainly of built-up plots *(mansurae)* held in fief from the count. Even before the middle of the twelfth century these were increasingly integrated into the city as the free property *(allodia)* of burghers *(cives)*. Meanwhile, a market square *(Vieux Marché*, now Place Victor Hugo) was created at the foot of the north-west side of the hill and on it the first city church, St Aldegonde, built or rebuilt in 1042 *infra ambitum castelli*. It is not clear if this expression means inside the wall of the earlier (ninth–tenth century) fortification or inside a new enclosure of the 'city' (in the sense of *castellum)*, which must have been built around the year 1000. Apart from the *Vieux Marché* and St Aldegonde, built on the very site of the old rampart, this new enclosure would also have encompassed the *Grand Marché*. So this market square would have been created fairly early on, before *c.* 1000. In view of Saint-Omer's economic development, about which more later, this seems rather unlikely. The city did expand considerably in a north-westerly direction from both market squares in the course of the eleventh century, i.e. in the direction of the Abbey of St Bertin and the River Aa, and around the year 1100 it was provided with a new enclosure. This expansion was stimulated by Saint-Omer's access to the sea, the result of flooding during the first half of the eleventh century.[36] It caused the River Aa to broaden out between Saint-Omer and the sea to form a bay which, after canalization towards the end of the eleventh century, made the city accessible for small ships. Only after the foundation of the city of Gravelines at the mouth of the Aa by the count of Flanders in 1163 would ships of between 100 and 200 tons have been able to reach the city of Saint-Omer via the canalized Aa (which belonged to the city). The similarity with the history of Bruges' links with the sea and with its economic development are striking. After a modest revival in the tenth century as an urban settlement at the foot of and under the influence of a stronghold built at the time of the Vikings, in the

[35] Derville, *Saint-Omer*, pp. 30, 36–43; F. L. Ganshof, 'Note sur une charte de Thierry d'Alsace, comte de Flandre, intéressant la propriété foncière à Saint-Omer', in H. Aubin *et al.* (eds.), *Beiträge zur Wirtschafts- und Stadtgeschichte: Festschrift für Hektor Ammann*, Wiesbaden, 1965, pp. 84–96.
[36] Derville, *Saint-Omer*, pp. 62–73.

eleventh century, and especially in the twelfth, its improved link with the sea made Saint-Omer an important seaport, particularly with regard to England.

After Ghent, Bruges and Saint-Omer, **Douai** was the youngest in a group of cities in the county of Flanders whose evolution to city began before the year 1000 and in which a count's fortification played an important role.[37]

It is interesting that at the beginning of this evolution, namely during the first quarter of the tenth century, there was a shift in the urban nucleus, as was the case in Ghent and perhaps even in Bruges at the end of the ninth and the beginning of the tenth centuries. Around the year 900 the place where Douai was to emerge was in fact only a part of an extensive royal manor (*fiscus*) with several dependencies. The centre of this manor was in Lambres, some $1\frac{1}{2}$ km upstream from Douai on the Sensée, at a place called *vicus* in sixth- and seventh-century texts. A trade settlement with mooring place (*portus*) developed there in the ninth century – as we have ascertained was the case with other large royal and ecclesiastical manors (Valenciennes, Tournai and Ghent) – and a toll was levied on behalf of the king. A canal was laid around the middle of the tenth century and the River Sensée diverted northwards to the River Scarpe. There was then sufficient water power for watermills on this river upstream from Douai (e.g. in Brebières and in Lambres) as well as in Douai itself.[38]

At the same time, the Lambres toll was transferred from the *portus* there to a fortification which was built in Douai itself, on the River Scarpe, the so-called *Viese Tour* (*Vetus Turris*), later also called *Tour du Châtelain*. It is likely that all this was the work of Arnulf I, count of Flanders (918–65). Douai was first mentioned under his rule, as *oppidum nomine Duagium* (930) and as *Duagium castellum* (941), by which a fortification that encompassed more than the aforementioned donjon was probably intended. On the basis of later data, confirmed by archaeological research, this fortification, whose walled area covered almost 5 ha, comprised not only the aforementioned oldest donjon in the *ville basse* or lower town on the bank of the River Scarpe (Map 11), but also a church located in the *ville haute* or upper town, on a spur at a height of 5 m above the marshy course of the River Scarpe. The church was originally a chapel dedicated to Our Lady but it was turned into a collegiate church dedicated to St Amé by

---

[37] M. Rouche (ed.), *Histoire de Douai*, Dunkirk, 1985; P. Demolon and E. Louis, 'Naissance d'une cité médiévale flamande. L'exemple de Douai', in P. Demolon, H. Galinié and F. Verhaeghe (eds.), *Archéologie des villes dans le Nord-Ouest de l'Europe* (VIIe–XIIIe siècles), Douai, 1994, pp. 47–58.

[38] D. Lohrmann, 'Entre Arras et Douai, les moulins de la Scarpe au XIe siècle et les détournements de la Satis', *Revue du Nord* 66 (1984), pp. 1023–50.

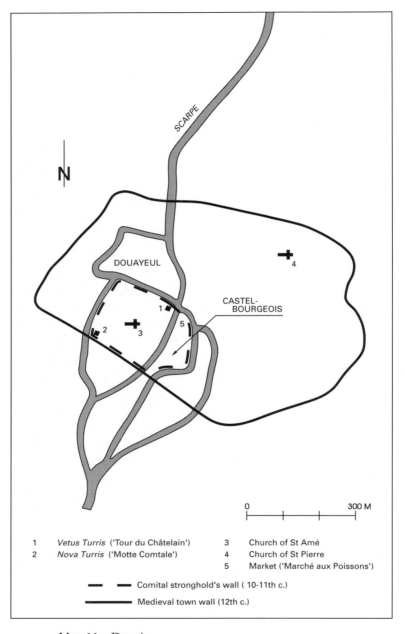

Map 11   Douai

Count Arnulf I after he had transferred relics of the saint from Soissons to Douai. There was also a second donjon at this height, to the south of St Amé, in the south-west corner of the enclosure. This second donjon was first called *Nova Turris* in the count's account dated 1187 (which also mentions a *Vetus Turris*) and was later known as *Motte Comtale*. In 1187 this was probably the more important of the two donjons and it is this *Nova Turris* whose foundations were laid bare during the spectacular excavations of 1976–81.[39] It would nevertheless be wrong to regard this later donjon as the heart of Douai castle from its beginning in the tenth century. Neither can the archaeologically established building phases of this later donjon be linked to and dated from the scanty tenth-century texts which mention a castle in Douai, but always without details of its location. These texts probably relate to the oldest donjon, the *Vetus Turris*. The *Nova Turris* was originally a wooden tower, perhaps belonging to the viscount of Douai or his predecessor. It may not have been erected in stone until the twelfth century and so then called *Nova Turris*. The later name *Motte Comtale* suggests that the count took possession of it, leaving the old donjon to the viscount. Up until then the older and probably strategically very favourably located donjon had been the centre of the castle of Douai. It is a pity that the excavations could not have been extended as far as here. In the *ville basse* the castle enclosure encompassed not only the oldest donjon, but also a settlement measuring some 2 ha which was later given the significant name of *Castel-Bourgeois*. It was here, directly opposite the older donjon as in many Flemish cities, that the oldest market – again called *Marché aux poissons* – was located, the first mention of which dates from 986. As the name of this part of the stronghold suggests, the *Castel-Bourgeois* settlement was fortified through its incorporation into the enclosure of the whole castle area which, according to the archaeologists, was built in stone shortly before the year 1000. So, as a fortified appendage of the castle where craftsmen and perhaps initially even merchants may have lived, the *Castel-Bourgeois* can be compared to the Oud(e)burg in Ghent and in Bruges. The actual city, on the other hand, with a second market square and covered hall (*Marché au Blé*) and Church of St Pierre (second quarter of the eleventh century), developed to the east of *Castel-Bourgeois* in the eleventh–twelfth centuries and was incorporated into the second, actual city enclosure, which was built in the late eleventh or early twelfth century.

[39] Demolon and Louis, 'Naissance d'une cité médiévale', p. 55.

The tenth-century fortresses on the River Scheldt: Antwerp, Ename, Valenciennes

In 925 the River Scheldt became the border between the West Frankish kingdom, the later France, and the German Empire. To protect this border against the increasing power of the counts of Flanders and their drive to expand in an easterly direction over the Scheldt, during the second half of the tenth century the German emperors Otto I (936–73) and Otto II (973–83) established three military districts on the right bank of the Scheldt, under the control of a margrave and known as 'margraveships'. The centre of each of these was a fortress on the Scheldt, upstream from north to south: Antwerp (before 980), Ename (974) and Valenciennes (before 973).[40] Soon after each of these fortresses had been erected, a trade settlement began to flourish. Only in Ename can no antecedent be shown for this settlement and the one in Ename disappeared for good some fifty years after it had appeared. So there ends the similarity between Ename and the two other places.

Antwerp was called *vicus c.* 900, almost a century before the imperial fortress was built there. In the last chapter the conjecture was formed that the *vicus* was located in or near the later imperial castle, of which the Steen is a vestige, and not 1,000 metres to the south on the Scheldt where a fortification (*civitas*) with church had stood until its destruction by the Vikings in 836 (Map 12). The late tenth-century Antwerp castle, whose twelfth/thirteenth-century stone walls are still preserved in fragmentary fashion along with the moat, formed a semicircle on the right bank of the Scheldt.[41] This form and this type of castle are very different from the simple donjon the German emperor built in Ename around the same period and with the same strategic purpose. So it would seem possible that the castle in Antwerp dates back to a semicircular construction which had existed before that and which the emperor simply fortified. This could be the *vicus* referred to in a *c.* 900 text which must have looked very much like the semicircular settlement around the oldest city church on the left bank of the Scheldt in Ghent, which, as we saw in the last chapter, also dates from the late ninth century. However, in Antwerp, unlike in Ghent, its conversion into an imperial castle and the military centre of a

[40] F. L. Ganshof, 'Les origines de la Flandre impériale', *Annales de la Société d'Archéologie de Bruxelles* 46 (1942–3), pp. 99–137; A. C. F. Koch, 'Grenzverhältnisse an der Niederschelde vornehmlich im 10. Jahrhundert', *Rheinische Vierteljahrsblätter* 21 (1956), pp. 182–218; U. Nonn, *Pagus und Comitatus in Niederlotharingien: Untersuchungen zur politischen Raumgliederung im früheren Mittelalter*, Bonn, 1983, pp. 116 and 131; A.-M. Helvétius, *Abbayes, évêques et laïques: une politique du pouvoir en Hainaut au moyen âge (VIIe–XIe siècle)*, Brussels, 1994 (Crédit Communal. Collection Histoire in–8°, no. 92), p. 294.

[41] Verhulst, 'Origins of Antwerp'.

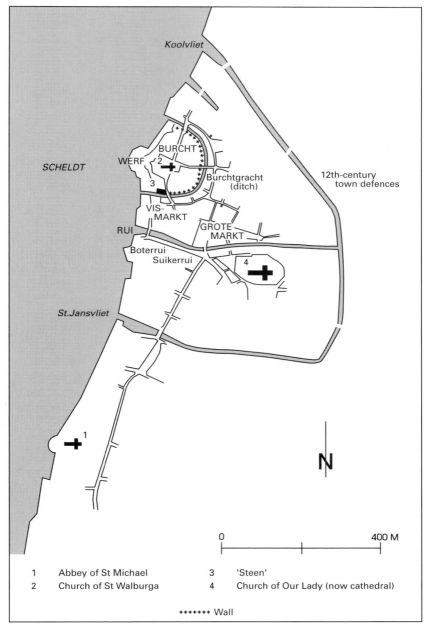

Map 12   Antwerp

Labels within the map:

Koolvliet

SCHELDT

WERF

BURCHT

2

Burchtgracht
(ditch)

12th-century
town defences

3

VIS-
MARKT

RUI

GROTE
MARKT

Boterrui
Suikerrui

4

St.Jansvliet

1

N

0   400 M

1   Abbey of St Michael   3   'Steen'
2   Church of St Walburga   4   Church of Our Lady (now cathedral)

++++++ Wall

margraveship meant that the semicircular *vicus* could not form the basis for its evolution to city. The imperial castle was preserved through later centuries and remained separate from the city even though it had lost its military importance on the former imperial border. In the eleventh century the city developed outside the castle but near its southern wall. The oldest market, called the *Vismarkt* as in so many Flemish cities, was situated at the foot of the extant Steen. The *Vismarkt* continued to serve as a fishmarket until the end of the nineteenth century (now the place where the Flandria boats moor). So in Antwerp, too, the imperial castle played the role that the feudal castles had played elsewhere in the tenth–eleventh centuries in the formation and development of cities, namely that of power centre and economic magnet. Whereas in Ghent the Count's Castle was the reason why the late ninth-century *vicus* on the Scheldt expanded outside its walled moat and towards the castle, in Antwerp the imperial castle probably absorbed the pre-tenth-century *vicus* and in its turn started to act as the magnet for a new urban nucleus outside it, at its feet. We know nothing about the development of this new nucleus, from the *Vismarkt* to the Grote Markt, on whose south-east side Our Lady's Church – the predecessor of the present-day Cathedral – may have been built at the end of the eleventh century (first mention: 1124). By the end of the eleventh century its topographical expansion to the east and south-east had reached a line formed by a number of smaller water-courses known locally as 'ruien' (Suikerrui, Kaasrui, Jezuïetenrui, Min-derbroedersrui). These can be regarded as the city's earliest fortifications. The Church of Our Lady stood outside that line. This topographical expansion is also explained by the intense shipping activity conducted by the people of Antwerp in the second half of the eleventh century, which we shall look at in its general context in the next chapter.[42]

In 1106 the Antwerp margraveship was incorporated into the duchy of Brabant. With the exception of the area around Antwerp, a large part of the two banks of the Scheldt in its course upstream from Antwerp was in the hands of the count of Flanders from the middle of the eleventh century. Indeed, the count had taken possession of the margraveships on the right bank, except for Antwerp: Valenciennes from 1015 until 1047, when it again came under the count of Hainault, and Ename definitively in 1047, after exchanging it for Valenciennes.[43]

Around 974 Emperor Otto II had a fortress built on the right bank of the Scheldt in **Ename**, some 25 km upstream of Ghent. As recent archaeological excavations show, it comprised at least a square stone

---

[42] P. Bonenfant, 'L'origine des villes brabançonnes et la "route" de Bruges à Cologne', in *Revue Belge de Philologie et d'Histoire* 31 (1953), pp. 429–32.
[43] See note 40 above.

donjon and a building containing a hall (*aula*), a living area and a chapel.[44] It became the military and administrative centre of a margraveship whose commander, who was of the house of Verdun, had to defend the Scheldt against the count of Flanders on the left bank of the river. Godfried of Verdun organized a market with toll next to his fortress, and it developed into a trade settlement referred to as *portus* in 1014. The son of the first margrave had two churches built even before 1024–5: one in the trade settlement itself and dedicated to St Salvator and one on its edge near the later agrarian centre of Ename and dedicated to St Laurence. We know neither the exact size nor the structure of the *portus*. However, a large quantity of Pingsdorf earthenware was excavated on its earlier site and traces of artisanal activity were found. The *portus* was first laid waste by the count of Flanders in 1034 and, after the annexation of the margraveship in 1047, it had to make way for a Benedictine abbey which Count Baldwin V of Flanders and his wife Adela founded in 1063. The two churches were all that was spared of the earlier *portus*. After that the abbey collected the toll on the Scheldt and also at the annual fair held on the feast of St Laurence (10 August), which may have been introduced at the time of the *portus*.

It is very probable that the brief presence and the decline of the trade settlement in Ename had to do with the existence, even before 1030, of a stronghold on the opposite, left bank of the Scheldt, in Oudenaarde, a few kilometres upstream from Ename. This fortress was built by Count Baldwin IV of Flanders (988–1035) at the beginning of the eleventh century as the operating base for capturing the margraveship of Ename on the right bank of the Scheldt.[45] The same count may also have founded St Walburga Church, which became the city church of Oudenaarde when a trade settlement grew up there during the second half of the eleventh century. This was called *suburbium* and *oppidum* in 1127, yet its history is a total mystery until 1189 when Count Philip of Alsace bestowed upon it the law of the city of Ghent. As a city of secondary importance, Oudenaarde was to remain a satellite of Ghent in the ensuing centuries.

As the backbone of trade since the early Middle Ages, it seems that the River Scheldt became even more important once it had lost its political and military border function in the middle of the eleventh century and the count of Flanders controlled a large part of its course along both banks. The histories of Antwerp, of Ename and of Oudenaarde show this link in

---

[44] Callebaut, 'Résidences fortifiées', pp. 98–102; G. Berings, *Landschap, geschiedenis en archeologie in het Oudenaardse*, Oudenaarde, 1989, pp. 39–44, 85–98.
[45] Berings, *Landschap in het Oudenaardse*, pp. 99–116; M. Hoebeke, 'Oudenaarde', in *Villes belges en relief*, pp. 263–94.

a positive light, but also in a negative one in the case of Ename after 1047 and Antwerp after 1106.

This also appears to have been the case for **Valenciennes**, which, like Antwerp but unlike Ename, could draw on a tradition that pre-dated the tenth century when, after a silence of almost a hundred years, at the beginning of the eleventh century it again showed signs of urban expansion.[46] Like Antwerp and Ename, Valenciennes became the military and administrative centre of a margraveship on the right bank of the Scheldt before 973. As such it was taken out of the count of Hainault's dominion. A stronghold was built on the site of the earlier Carolingian residence in Valenciennes, which was destroyed by the Vikings in 880–1. That stronghold consisted largely of a donjon, with a motte around it made of earth imported from elsewhere. The Church of the Friars Minor was built on the ruin of this donjon around 1225 (Map 13). Count Arnould of Valenciennes had founded a chapter of canons next to the donjon between 979 and 995, as was quite often the case near comital residences.[47] The fortified area as a whole formed a triangle, completely surrounded by water, on the right bank of the Scheldt. The point of the triangle reached to the bridge over the Scheldt (Pont Néron) near the place called *Rivage*, which even in the ninth century must have been the mooring place for the trade settlement. Adjacent to this point and to the east and south-east of the fortified island, between the Rhônelle and St Catherine rivers, and near the market (the present-day Place d'Armes), there was an urban settlement, called *oppidum* at the beginning of the eleventh century and later *Grand Bourg*. In the course of the eleventh century, the city spread west of this point between the Scheldt, the Rhônelle and the Bruille over an area which was annexed to the city and called *Novus Burgus (Neuf Bourg)*. Here the Church of Notre-Dame-la-Grande was founded by Count Baldwin II of Hainault and his mother Richildis before 1086; as a priory it was assigned to the Abbey of Hasnon. The existence of a merchants' guild in Valenciennes in 1060–70, which was called *karitet* and which we will deal with in the next chapter, is further proof of Valenciennes' great urban expansion in the eleventh century. This began even before Valenciennes came into Flemish hands in 1047 and continued after 1047 when the count of Hainault became master of the city again. In fact it became the most important city in his county, thanks not so much to him, as to the urban network along the Scheldt from Cambrai to Antwerp which economically still belonged to the county of Flanders until into the twelfth century.

---

[46] See chapter 3, note 32.
[47] Helvétius, *Abbayes, évêques et laïques*, pp. 293–5.

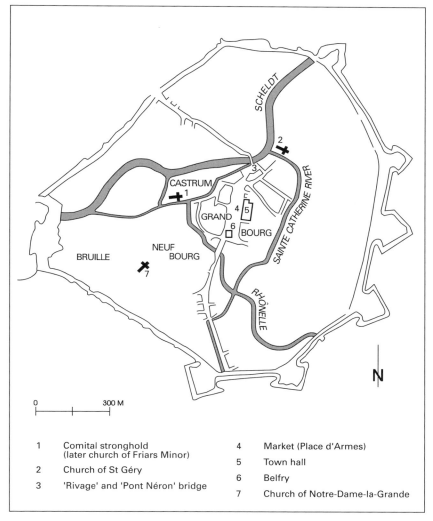

Map 13   Valenciennes

1	Comital stronghold (later church of Friars Minor)	4	Market (Place d'Armes)
2	Church of St Géry	5	Town hall
3	'Rivage' and 'Pont Néron' bridge	6	Belfry
		7	Church of Notre-Dame-la-Grande

New eleventh-century towns: Lille and Ypres

The last of the large Flemish cities to emerge spontaneously, Lille and Ypres, pose great problems as regards their origin, despite the fact that they can be dated as late as the middle of the eleventh century.

For Lille we do have contemporary written data from shortly after the middle of the eleventh century.[48] This is not the case for Ypres, though the two cities date from the same period. In both cases the oldest element, and the starting point and gravitational pole in the city's development, was a castle belonging to the count of Flanders, located near the centre of a large rural manor which he also owned.

In **Lille** the precise location of this manorial centre is not known, though it is sometimes identified with the large farmstead, called *cense du Metz*, situated to the north-west of the count's castle, on the left bank of the Basse Deûle (Map 14). Together with the *Terre de la Vigne* on the other side of the Deûle, to the north-east of the castle, the *cense du Metz* prevented the later city expanding in that direction until the seventeenth century and long preserved the rural character of the surrounding area.

Some historians regard the count's manor in Lille as a former dependence of the large Carolingian manor (*fiscus*) of Annappes, to the south of Lille, described in the famous early ninth-century estate inventory known by the name of *Brevium exempla* and owned in part by the count of Flanders in the twelfth century.[49] This contested identification is based on the name of a dependence of the fisc Annappes named in the *Brevium exempla*, namely *Treola*, a wine-producing manor whose precise location remains a mystery. It is identified as the *Terre de la Vigne* in Lille and linked with the name *La Treille*. This name was given to the Blessed Virgin who was worshipped in the *Chapelle de la Treille* in the castle of Lille, next to the count's residence *La Salle*, until into the thirteenth century and transferred to the modern cathedral of Lille. At the end of the twelfth century the count's manor in Lille still produced a significant quantity of wine.

Whatever the solution to the problem regarding the Carolingian prehistory of Lille, it is certain that the first reference to the count's stronghold in Lille was in 1054, yet it may have existed in 1039 when a castellan of Lille is first mentioned. Something of the early topography of the castle and its surroundings can be deduced from Count Baldwin V of Flanders' famous charter of 1066. It summarizes the effects he gave to the chapter of St Pierre which he had founded in the castle of Lille between 1055 and 1065.[50] The castle occupied some 5 ha to the north of the present Place du Général de Gaulle (formerly *Grand'Place*), between the modern-day Rue Basse to the south and the Rue du Pont Neuf to the north, the

[48] A. Derville, 'Le problème des origines de Lille', in *Mélanges E. Perroy*, Paris, 1973, pp. 65–78; Derville, 'Trois siècles décisifs (XIe–XIIIe siècles)', in L. Trenard (ed.), *Histoire d'une métropole: Lille–Roubaix–Tourcoing*, Toulouse, 1977, pp. 83–131; Derville, 'La genèse et les premiers siècles de Lille', in *La genèse et les premiers siècles*, pp. 247–63.

[49] Derville, 'Trois siècles', pp. 72–4.

[50] F.-L. Ganshof, 'Note sur une charte de Baudouin V, comte de Flandre, pour Saint-Pierre de Lille', in *Mélanges R. Crozet*, Poitiers, 1966, pp. 293–306.

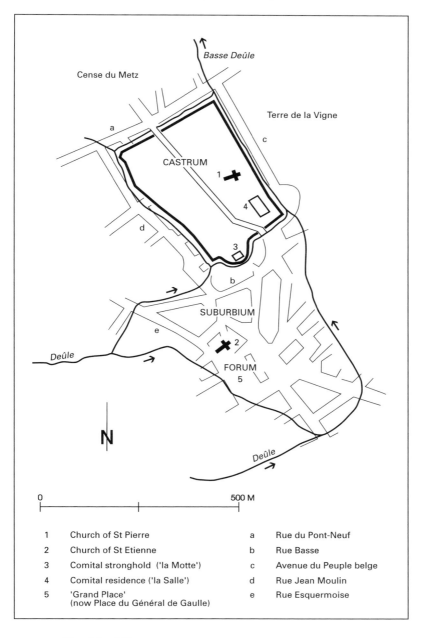

Map 14   Lille

Avenue du Peuple Belge to the east and the Rue Jean Moulin to the west. In 1066 the castle (*castrum*) contained a donjon (*castellum*), possibly the count's original residence but which later belonged to the castellan of Lille and was known as *La Motte*; a later residence of the count (*aula comitis*), later called *La Salle*; the Church of St Pierre and the chapter buildings. A road ran NW–SE through the castle. The complex was surrounded in its entirety by a wall and water. In several respects the castle of Lille resembled that of Bruges in the eleventh century. The site of the castle of Lille is practically the only place above (approximately 20 m) what had once been the marshy area of the *Grand'Place* which was surrounded by two branches of the Deûle. One of them, the Basse Deûle, also bordered the east wall of the castle (mentioned as such in 1066). The branches of the Deûle form at least one island at this point, from which Lille (*L'Isle = Isla = Insulae*) derives its name. What is not clear from the charter of 1066 is whether the name *Isla*, which is older, was originally only that of the castle (*castrum*) – which we believe it was – or also that of the marketplace (*forum*), some 200 m to the south of the castle. This oldest part of the market was located in the north-west corner of the later *Grand'Place* at the beginning of Rue Esquermoise, where the lost church of St Etienne stood which was mentioned in 1066 as being in the middle of the *forum*. People have tried to identify the whole of the very extensive open space of the *Grand'Place* – which, until the Ancienne Bourse was built in the seventeenth century, also comprised the Place du Théâtre on the other (east) side of the Bourse, approximately 3 ha in all – with the eleventh/twelfth-century *forum*. However, whilst it is true that the ar-chaeological excavations were restricted to the southern edge of the *Grand'Place* – so on the very opposite side of this square from where the Church of St Etienne and the *forum* and *castrum* of 1066 were located – they did show that at least this (southern) part of the *Grand'Place* was not drained and laid until the thirteenth century.[51] Before that it was flooded at regular intervals by a branch of the Deûle. So it looks as if the urban settlement with marketplace (*forum*) and church (St Etienne), which is called *oppidum* in a 1060 text and perhaps identifies with the *suburbium castri* from 1066 – though this is only certain in 1127 when the *forum* is sited in the *suburbium*[52] – did not have the later *Grand'Place* as its centre. The greater part of the *Grand'Place* was rather eccentrically sited in relation to the oldest core of the city. This shows once again, as in the case of the Vrijdagmarkt in Ghent, that one should be wary of regarding later

---

[51] G. Blieck, 'Les origines de Lille: bilan et perspectives archéologiques', in *La genèse et les premiers siècles*, pp. 274–9, and the discussion, pp. 281–3.

[52] J. B. Ross (ed.), *Galbert of Bruges, The Murder of Charles the Good, Count of Flanders*, New York, 1967, chapter 93, pp. 265–6.

and still existing market squares as the oldest elements of a city on purely topographical grounds. It would appear from Galbert of Bruges' story dating from 1127–8 about the murder of Count Charles the Good, on the other hand, that at that time the annual fair in Lille on 1 August was held on the marketplace (*forum*) of the *suburbium* at the foot of the castle. This was certainly not the case in all the Flemish cities that hosted an annual fair in the Middle Ages, or at least not before the late twelfth century. In Ypres and in Ghent the annual fair was not held on the city's large, central market square. In the case of Lille, the fair appears to have had close links with the city and may have contributed to its prosperity. But at the same time it was held near the castle, as in Ypres, where the operating centre of the count's manor was also located close to the castle and the annual fair, as in Lille. This may indicate that the count had been responsible for setting up the fair in the first place, and indeed we can assume this was the case for all five of the large Flemish fairs which developed into a cycle in the twelfth–thirteenth centuries: Lille, Messines (Fl. Mesen), Ypres, Torhout, Bruges.[53] So in this way the count of Flanders may have contributed indirectly if not to the very existence of Lille, then at least to its rise as a city.

However, we believe that this rise depended chiefly on Lille's role as a corn market for the north of the county of Flanders. This role can in its turn be explained by Lille's geographical location on the northern edge of the rich corn-producing chalk and loam plateaux of Artois and Mélantois, from the point where the Deûle was navigable and descends into the valley of the Leie. The grain was taken along this river to Ghent, whose growth in the tenth/beginning of the eleventh century and the need of grain for making bread was, we believe, a condition for the emergence of Lille as a city around the middle of the eleventh century.[54] The existence in Lille of an important rural manor belonging to the count, which was still producing large quantities of grain at the end of the twelfth century, was certainly a contributing factor. The rapid growth of Ypres, located only about 30 km to the north of Lille and linked to it by several land routes, may have been another important factor in Lille's rise.[55]

Ypres (Fl. Ieper) also started life as a large manor of the count, though at the end of the twelfth century its production was directed more at cattle breeding and dairy produce than at corn, apart from oats.[56] This can be

[53] M. Yamada, 'Le mouvement des foires en Flandre avant 1200', in Duvosquel and Dierkens (eds.), *Villes et campagnes*, pp. 773–89.

[54] A. Derville, 'Le grenier des Pays-Bas médiévaux', *Revue du Nord* 69 (1987), pp. 267–90.

[55] J.-M. Duvosquel, 'Les routes d'Ypres à Lille et le passage de la Lys au moyen âge ou de l'économie domaniale aux foires de Flandre', in Aerts *et al.* (eds.), *Studia historica oeconomica*, pp. 100–6; Verhulst, 'The Alleged Poverty', in *ibid.*, pp. 379–82.

[56] Verhulst, 'The Alleged Poverty', pp. 374–6.

explained by the many woods and the recent land reclamation all around Ypres until the twelfth century. Consequently, in a sense Ypres and Lille were complementary from the outset as regards the need for and production of food.

However, Ypres' very rapid development from a rural manor to the largest medieval manufacturing city in the county of Flanders can, we believe, only be explained by its location on the River Ieper, called Ieperlee after canalization, more specifically at the point where the river became navigable, albeit as a result of considerable construction work, on the one hand designed to offset the great drop in the river's water level and, on the other, involved in building a parallel canal in the town.[57] The Ieperlee debouches into the River Yser approximately 12 km to the north of Ypres, close to Diksmuide (Fr. Dixmude). The whole of the Yser basin was flooded during the first half of the eleventh century as a result of storm tides in 1014 and 1042 over an even larger expanse between Diksmuide and the sea than was produced by artificial flooding during the First World War. The medieval flooding with salt water created vast salt marshes on which large sheep farms were established as of the middle of the eleventh century. The enormous quantities of wool produced on them could not possibly have been processed locally in the few surrounding villages unaffected by flooding. So it was probably transported along the Yser and the Ieperlee to Ypres, which must have rapidly become an important centre of the textile industry in the second half of the eleventh century.

Be this as it may, the starting point for this development was, as we said, the manor of the Flemish count in Ypres, the centre of which we would expect to find near the fortification which, as the residence of the count in Ypres, was later known by the name of *Zaalhof* (Map 15). However, it lay well to the south and was somewhat eccentrically located in relation to the market (Markt) with the famous cloth hall, the belfry and the main church of Ypres (St Martin's) which are regarded as the centre of the medieval city. Close to the *Zaalhof*, on the other hand, on the other side of the Ieperlee Canal, there stood – and indeed still stands – the Church of St Peter which was first mentioned in 1102 together with St Martin's, on which it depended. Ypres' famous annual fair, which was first mentioned in 1127, was held here every year, beginning on 22 February. Even in those early days it was visited by Italian merchants. The Markt in the medieval centre of Ypres was at that time still a local market selling (among other things) fish. As we were also able to establish was the case in Lille, it did not as yet have the sort of scale it later achieved and still has today.

[57] A. Verhulst, 'Les origines d'Ypres', *Revue du Nord*, 81 (1999), pp. 1–13.

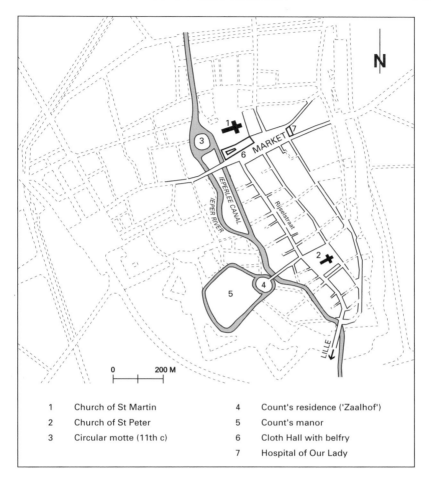

Map 15   Ypres

1	Church of St Martin	4	Count's residence ('Zaalhof')
2	Church of St Peter	5	Count's manor
3	Circular motte (11th c)	6	Cloth Hall with belfry
		7	Hospital of Our Lady

The most difficult problem with regard to the earliest topographical development of Ypres is the fact that the main church there, St Martin's, stood near the market by the year 1102 and also that near the church, on the right bank of the Ieperlee, there was a motte surrounded by a semicircular moat. Though it is difficult to prove beyond doubt the existence of this fortification, it is regarded as the count's eleventh-century fortification whose existence is implied by a text dating from 1066. It must have been abandoned towards the end of that century when the count moved his Ypres residence to the *Zaalhof* which he built between St Peter's

Church and the manorial court annexed to the *Zaalhof*. So in Ypres we find ourselves with two centres from which the city may have developed: first, the late medieval centre of the city around the Markt, with St Martin's Church and a small fortification which was abandoned early on; and second, the area around St Peter's Church where at first the annual fair was held, with the fortified residence of the count – the *Zaalhof* – in the immediate vicinity and a large farmstead which was the operating centre of the count's manor, originally comprising the whole of the territory of the medieval city and even land outside it.

The anteriority of one of the two is difficult to prove. Accordingly we believe that both cores are old and date from the period before the middle of the eleventh century when Ypres was no more than a large but agrarian entity. It is conceivable that this manor consisted partly of a large operating centre, with its own church (in our hypothesis St Peter's) and partly of a peasant community also with a church (in this hypothesis St Martin's). An urban community developed on this manor in the eleventh century as a result of the external factor of a sudden and temporarily enormous wool production in the flooded area north of Ypres. The centre of this community was near St Martin's, possibly because this area was more densely populated. The annual fair, which obviously had a link with the central farmstead of the manor,[58] was initially held outside the urban core, as in Ghent, and near the old, rural Church of St Peter. There the annual fair could enjoy the protection of the fortification which may have been built near the centre of the manor in the second half of the eleventh century, when an older fortification near St Martin's was abandoned.

Urban development in Brabant

So far Brabant has been something of a blind spot in our overview, for there were no perceptible signs of urban life there until the tenth century. The explanation for this may lie partly in the overwhelming importance of the valleys of Meuse and Scheldt, between which the territory of the duchy of Brabant would only begin to form a territorial and political entity at the beginning of the twelfth century. The county of Flanders, with the Scheldt and the North Sea coast as the most important growth points, along with the prince-bishopric of Liège of which one might say that the Meuse forms the backbone, had become important principalities much earlier on, which doubtless affected their urban development. We think of the tenth-century feudal castles in the Flemish cities and of the urban development role of Bishop Notger in Liège at the end of the tenth century.

---

[58] Duvosquel, 'Les routes d'Ypres à Lille', pp. 104–5.

Furthermore, what was missing in Brabant was one large river as a central artery for traffic. The area was crisscrossed from south to north, and in particular from south to north-west, by smaller rivers which were only partly navigable without construction work, like the Zenne from Brussels and the Dijle from Leuven (Fr. Louvain). However, in the traditional historiography dominated by Pirenne, importance was only attached to the location of a number of Brabantine cities on these rivers in relation to their origin in so far as that location coincided with the places where the Cologne–Bruges land route crossed the river. After all Pirenne, and the numerous historians who followed him, regarded this east–west traffic axis as the main factor which led to the creation of the Brabantine cities of Zoutleeuw (Fr. Léau), Tienen (Fr. Tirlemont), Leuven and Brussels from the twelfth century. Pirenne's vision, which in any case fitted in nicely with his explanation of the history of Belgium whereby he believed Brabant formed the binding element between the principalities of Flanders and Liège, was largely refuted by Paul Bonenfant in 1953.[59] Bonenfant showed that the overland link between Bruges and Cologne only began to compete with the importance of the link by water along the estuary area of the large Scheldt, Meuse and Rhine rivers during the last quarter of the twelfth century and – above all – he believed he could prove that a number of Brabantine cities were older in origin. According to him the south–north Brabantine river network played a role in this, at least as far as Brussels, Leuven and Mechelen (Fr. Malines) were concerned.

This was not the case for **Nivelles** and **Gembloux**, where large abbeys were the mainspring of urbanization in the tenth century, thanks to regional trade with their rich agricultural production that was largely directed at the Meuse Valley. Merchants from Nivelles were even sighted in London around the year 1000, together with merchants from Liège and Huy.

Yet, according to Bonenfant, they may have taken a shorter route to London than the Meuse, namely via **Brussels**, located at the point where the Zenne became navigable, some 30 km to the north of Nivelles. The Abbey of Nivelles probably had a mooring place (*stadium*) in Brussels even by 966, though this is not certain.[60] In the second half of the tenth century, the duke of Lower Lotharingia built a fortification (*castrum*) – whose memory lives on in the name *Borchwal* – on one of the islands formed by the branches of the meandering Zenne. It is not certain if an adjoining area, called *Oude Borgh* in the thirteenth century, was part of this for-

---

[59] Bonenfant, 'L'origine des villes brabançonnes'.

[60] G. Despy, 'La genèse d'une ville', in J. Stengers (ed.), *Bruxelles: croissance d'une capitale*, Antwerp, 1979, p. 30; Despy, 'Un dossier mystérieux: les origines de Bruxelles', *Académie royale de Belgique: Bulletin de la Classe des Lettres*, 6th Series, VIII, 1–6 (1997), pp. 241–303.

tification. It is after all possible that the toponym referred to a fortified settlement *next to* the castle but more or less connected to it, as was the case with the Oud(e)burg in Ghent and in Bruges.[61] Neither is it clear if the Church of St Géry, which was founded around the same time as the castle but on another island in the Zenne to the north of the castle, was destined for the latter as the castle church, or if it served as the parish church for an agglomeration which had grown up on the right bank of the Zenne around the year 1000 and was referred to shortly afterwards as *portus*, thereby reflecting its trading character.[62] This agglomeration was to expand to the higher parts of the city in the east in the course of the eleventh century. Around the middle of the eleventh century, the count of Leuven, now also master of the area around Brussels, probably founded the collegiate church of St Michael there, transferring the relics of St Gudele from the Church of St Géry in the lower town to St Michael's. During the second half of the eleventh century he probably built a new residence not far from there, on the Coudenberg, home to the dukes of Brabant and today to the Belgian king. Then in the twelfth century a stone wall must have been built enclosing both the lower town on the Zenne and the upper town, or at least the area around St Michael's and the Coudenberg. The foundation of new parishes inside this enclosed area in the twelfth century and the presence of aldermen as of the second quarter of the twelfth century show that while Brussels' evolution to a city began in the eleventh century, it was largely a twelfth-century phenomenon.[63]

The same can be said of **Leuven**, whose evolution to a city was closely linked to the extension of power of the counts of Leuven, who became dukes of Lower Lotharingia in 1106 and later of Brabant. Their castle originally stood on the site where the Vikings had set up camp between 884 and 892. A new castle was built shortly after the year 1000, downstream on an artificial island in the Dijle, near a river crossing and an older settlement. The settlement's existing St Peter's Church was rebuilt in stone by the count around 1015 and a chapter of canons installed. During the second quarter of the twelfth century, castle, church and settlement were enclosed by a stone wall. The population, which consisted mainly of vassals, servants and semi-free tenants of the duke, was given one aldermen's court around the same time.[64]

Very little is known about the earliest phase in the urban development of **Mechelen** on the River Dijle. A ninth-century abbey, where St Rombout

---

[61] Van Werveke, '*Burgus*', pp. 53–4.
[62] Despy, 'La genèse d'une ville', pp. 28–35.   [63] *Ibid.*
[64] R. Van Uytven (ed.), *Leuven, de beste stad van Brabant*, I, *De geschiedenis van het stadsgewest Leuven tot omstreeks 1600*, Leuven, 1980.

lay buried, together with its manor became the property of the bishop of Liège, who was theoretically also lord of the city in later centuries. Bishop Notger of Liège made the abbey a secular chapter around 992. There had been a settlement of fishermen and perhaps also of merchants since the early Middle Ages, with a church, the Church of Our Lady, some considerable distance to the south of the abbey on the left bank of the Dijle, near an eleventh-century castle of the local advocates of the Liège estate. The two nuclei, St Rombout's and the settlement on the Dijle, began to merge in the twelfth century and before 1200 were incorporated inside one fortification.[65]

Urban development in Brabant, which first began in Nivelles and in Brussels around 1000, but which also underwent a very gradual process of change in the eleventh century in most of the other places that later became cities, shows that the evolution in Brabant lagged behind the principalities of Flanders and Liège by about a century, though they quickly recovered this ground in the twelfth century. The political unification of Brabant and the growing importance of the Cologne–Bruges land route through Brabant were, we believe, important factors in this recuperation. At the same time, there were similarities with urban development in the county of Flanders during the tenth–eleventh centuries: this is the case not only for the feudal castle's role as magnet, but also as regards the manorial origin which still largely determined the evolution during the eleventh century, especially in the case of the youngest group of Flemish cities, namely Lille, Ypres and to a certain extent Douai.

Conclusion

There are two aspects to urbanization in the tenth and eleventh centuries: first, an increase in the number of towns and, second, their growth both in terms of space and population density.

As regards the increase in the number of towns, this was most apparent in the west of the area under consideration here, i.e. chiefly in the county of Flanders. Towns grew up there in the tenth century (Douai, Saint-Omer) and in the eleventh century (Ypres, Lille) which, together with Ghent, Bruges and Arras, were to become the seven largest in the county. In the River Meuse area, which had no more towns older than the tenth century than did the Scheldt Valley, where Cambrai, Valenciennes,

---

[65] P. Bonenfant, 'Aux origines de Malines', in *Dancwerc: opstellen aangeboden aan Prof. Dr. D. Th. Enklaar*, Groningen, 1959, pp. 96–108; R. Van Uytven and H. Installé (eds.), *De Geschiedenis van Mechelen: van Heerlijkheid tot Stadsgewest*, Tielt, 1991; H. Rombaut, 'Mechelen: de vroegste ontwikkeling', in H. Installé (ed.). *Mechelen* (Historische Stedenatlas van België, ed. A. Verhulst), Brussels, 1997, pp. 11–22.

Tournai and Antwerp in addition to Ghent should be mentioned in this respect, there were scarcely any places in the tenth and eleventh centuries which only then became towns. In the duchy of Brabant, which did not exist as such till 1104, we cannot talk about an increase in the number of towns, for they were only just beginning to emerge, and that process was spontaneous rather than the result of a deliberate foundation. Brabant had no towns until around the middle of the tenth century: Gembloux and Nivelles were small towns next to abbeys which originated in the tenth century, while Brussels, Leuven and Mechelen became towns shortly after the year 1000. Thus the ascendancy of the county of Flanders in terms of urban potential dates from an early period, and it rose even further in the twelfth century as new seaports were founded along the coast (Gravelines, Dunkirk, Nieuwpoort, Damme, Biervliet)[66] and as smaller towns inland (Oudenaarde, Aalst (Fr. Alost), Dendermonde (Fr. Termonde), Kortrijk, Geraardsbergen (Fr. Grammont)) and near the coast (Diksmuide, Veurne, Aardenburg, Axel, Hulst)[67] flourished. Economic and political factors aside, there is no doubt that, together with their favourable location near the coast and close to the estuary of the Scheldt and on its tributaries the Leie and the Dender, as well as the Yser and the Aa, the demographic factor was of very great significance in the growth of Flemish towns.

Not only were the towns in the county of Flanders the most numerous and the most densely populated, but the Flemish countryside, too, must have been more densely populated even in the tenth and eleventh centuries than the interior located further to the east, perhaps partly under the stimulus of the towns which created a 'market' for the countryside. This can be deduced retrospectively from the population size and density figures of the late Middle Ages;[68] moreover, it is reflected in the impoldering of land on the coastal plain and in the cultivation of land in the interior which began in the tenth century.[69] The reclamation of land not only was a consequence of the growth in the population, it also stimulated that growth, creating a surplus population that went to live in the towns. Though this immigration is a fact, as the rules of the municipal bye-laws relating to the legal status of the immigrants reveal, account must also be

[66] A. Verhulst, 'Initiative comtale et développement économique en Flandre au XIIe siècle', in *Miscellanea mediaevalia in memoriam J. F. Niermeyer*, Groningen, 1967, pp. 227–40.

[67] W. Prevenier, J. P. Sosson and M. Boone, 'Le réseau urbain en Flandre (XIIIe–XIXe siècle)', in *Le réseau urbain en Belgique dans une perspective historique (1350–1850). 15e Colloque International, Spa, 1990. Actes*, Brussels, 1992 (Crédit Communal, série in–8°, no. 86), pp. 157–200.

[68] W. Prevenier, 'La démographie des villes du comté de Flandre aux XIVe et XVe siècles', *Revue du Nord* 65 (1983), pp. 255–75.

[69] D. Nicholas, 'Structures du peuplement, fonctions urbaines et formation du capital dans la Flandre médiévale', *Annales: Economies–Sociétés–Civilisations* 33 (1978), pp. 501–27.

taken of the strong growth of the original population in the town itself. After all, the town was not uninhabited before the tenth century, as its archaeology (among other things) shows, even though it was probably predominantly agrarian in character.

As a result of the increasing population density, the urban land was quickly – and sometimes very quickly – divided up into small plots just big enough to contain one house. In some cases, like Ghent, this happened very early on, i.e. in the first half of the tenth century. This parcelization is in fact reflected in the evolution of the terminology for plots of land in tenth-century documents from Ghent: from the agrarian *mansus*, through *mansionile* to *mansura*, the typical term for an urban plot, and to *mansio*, which means a house or a piece of land with a house on it. Only the richest inhabitants managed to retain the original size of their agrarian domicile, which they turned into a large patrician residence. This can be seen in the oldest town centre, where the numerous narrow streets, as for example in the so-called *Kuip van Gent*, reflect the density of the habitation.

The spatial expansion of the medieval town is usually determined by the succession of walls that surrounded it.[70] In this respect, too, the county of Flanders and the Meuse Valley led the towns in Brabant as regards the date of the first ramparts. In both the county of Flanders and the Meuse Valley the first ramparts date from before the end of the eleventh century, in Brabant from the twelfth century, as in most north-west European towns with the exception of Cologne where the *Rheinvorstadt* was fortified even in the tenth century. The construction of a wall indicates not only a degree of autonomy and urban consciousness, which in the county of Flanders is also apparent from the role played by the merchants' guilds in the eleventh century.[71] The construction of a wall can perhaps also be regarded as an indication of the fact that people believed the expansion of the town had come to an end, at least temporarily, even though we must bear in mind that in some towns like Ypres, but not Ghent, working-class neighbourhoods were kept outside the wall. In Ghent land, sparsely inhabited and still partly agrarian, had been incorporated inside the first fortification of the town at the end of the eleventh century: as in the case of the Kouter (a typical field name) located against the southern segment of the oldest rampart, and in the case of the marshy area (with the typical names Mere and Paddenhoek) located between the Kouter and the Voldersstraat. The Voldersstraat demarcated the inhabited area of the town until the twelfth century, though the wall lay much further south. And yet certain large market squares, like the Vrijdagmarkt in Ghent, should not be regarded as

---

[70] Ganshof, *Etudes sur le développement des villes*, pp. 35–46.   [71] See chapter 5.

previously having been empty spaces, for in the case of the Vrijdagmarkt in Ghent it has been proved archaeologically that there was habitation there till the end of the twelfth century. Neither is the scale of the walled area a true indication of the size of the population. Indeed, it was as large in Leuven (60 ha) and Brussels (79 ha) as it was in Ghent (80 ha), though Ghent certainly had many more inhabitants.

The creation of urban parishes by splitting up large rural mother-parishes in the area, as in Bruges, or by the division of the one original urban or rural parish, as in Ghent and elsewhere, is another indication of a town's growth. Most important of all, however, is when this happened – usually the late eleventh century. Yet with the spatial expansion of the town or its growing internal population, the link is more difficult to prove and there is a great diversity of local situations.[72]

Topographical development during the tenth and eleventh centuries – which has been described in detail in this chapter for all the large towns between Somme and Meuse – is in most cases dominated by the duality of castle and trade settlement. This duality occurred almost all over north-west Europe: in the area under consideration here, in England, France and West Germany, but also outside the area, more specifically in Central and Eastern Europe.[73] The construction of castles was a general phenomenon in the tenth and eleventh centuries and one that as such was not specific to the development of towns. It was part of the much broader movement known as 'incastellamento', which did not affect only the countryside. Castles were a new phenomenon in the tenth and eleventh centuries in so far as they did not derive from a ninth-century fortification against the Vikings. In the county of Flanders, one of the first principalities to be well organized, both these older and the newer fortifications – the latter dating from the tenth century as in Ghent and Douai – acquired an administrative function as the centre of a castellany and one of the residences of the itinerant count but also as a depot where the products from the count's manors in the castellany were stored.

A number of the fortifications dating from the middle or the second half of the tenth century did not precede the development of a trade settlement, but were constructed after a trade settlement had emerged in their immediate vicinity. Pirenne's generalizing view that castles were the pre-urban nucleus, and that a trade settlement grew up there afterwards because of the so-called military protection provided by the castle, certainly cannot be sustained in all cases.[74] Not only is the priority of the

[72] Ganshof, *Etudes sur le développement des villes*, pp. 47–9.
[73] E. Ennen, *Die Europäische Stadt des Mittelalters*, Göttingen, 4th edn, 1978, pp. 92–100.
[74] H. Pirenne, *Les villes du moyen âge*, Brussels, 1927, reprinted in H. Pirenne, *Les villes et les institutions urbaines*, I , Paris and Brussels, 1939, pp. 342–5, 377–8.

trade settlement proven archaeologically in a number of cases (e.g. Ghent) but, what is more, the feudal castle formed a large complex surrounded by walls and clearly divided from the trade settlement, often by a (possibly artificial) watercourse. Nevertheless, the economic rather than the military factor played a role in the siting of castle and trade settlement in one another's vicinity, especially since the castle functioned as a central depot for the supplies from the manors. This meant there was a surplus of grain and other foodstuffs (meat, dairy produce) stored in these castles that could be sold on the local urban market. Thus a relationship, and particularly an economic relationship, gradually developed between castle and town. For his part, the lord of the castle could purchase from the merchants items that were not produced on his estates, or no longer produced, or perhaps not produced in sufficient quantities, such as metal and leather wares needed for the armour of the castle's military personnel, textiles, the better sort of household effects, etc. Originally and even throughout the tenth century, a number of these items were produced within the castle itself, which, as a manor, was in some respects economically self-sufficient. In some cases (e.g. Douai) the castle, and more specifically its principal element, was in fact originally a large, residential manor court, which at some point – in Douai and in Ghent around the middle of the tenth century – was fortified and/or converted into a keep. In a sort of appendage of the castle – called *(vetus) burgus* or *Oudburg* in various towns in our area (Arras, Ghent, Bruges, Huy, Namur) – specialized craftsmen (in Ghent leather workers) lived and worked for the lord of the castle.[75] They probably did so in a relationship of dependence, for they were not free, either as individuals or economically, and so could not sell their products on the urban market for personal profit. Their situation in north-west Europe is comparable with that of the craftsmen who in the ninth century worked in urban settlements near an abbey as dependants of that abbey, as in Arras.[76] They can be compared to the 'fortified craftsmen's settlements', examined archaeologically in Poland and Russia, which were situated within the fortified enclosure of the 'kremlin'.[77] At some point (in Arras and also in Ghent as early as the second half of the ninth century) a new settlement, very probably inhabited by craftsmen and merchants, emerged not far from the older agglomeration near or within the fortified abbey. This

[75] Van Werveke, '*Burgus*'.
[76] See chapter 3.
[77] Ennen, *Europäische Stadt*, pp. 66–71, 183–90; W. Hensel, 'Untersuchungen über die Anfänge der Städte in Polen', in H. Jankuhn, W. Schlesinger and H. Steuer (eds.), *Vor- und Frühformen der europäischen Stadt im Mittelalter*, 2 vols., Göttingen, 1975, II (Abhandlungen der Akademie der Wissenschaften in Göttingen, Philologisch-Historische Klasse, 3rd Series, nos. 83–4), pp. 176–89.

may explain why this older craftsmen's settlement later came to be called *vetus burgus* or *Oudburg*. In general we can say that, in the course of the eleventh century, these craftsmen's settlements, which had been situated in or as an appendage to a castle or fortified abbey, were freed from their manorial bond, as was also the case on rural manors. This process would have been even quicker in the new urban context than in the countryside. It is doubtful, however, whether this came about much before the eleventh century, given the example of Pavia.[78] Around the years 1010/20 goods had to be supplied to the royal court there, not only by craftsmen organized in *ministeria*, but also by merchants from Venice and Amalfi and even from Europe to the north of the Alps, including England. Though Pavia was already in decline by then, this example shows how strongly regulated and controlled the economy must have been before that, even in a country where the economy of large towns like Venice and Genoa was already experiencing strong growth in a climate of freedom.

[78] Ennen, *Europäische Stadt*, p. 91; D. A. Bullough, 'Urban Change in Early Medieval Italy: The Example of Pavia', in *Papers of the British School Rome* 34 (1966), pp. 82–130; C. Brühl and C. Violante, *Die 'Honorantiae Civitatis Papie': Transkription, Edition, Kommentar*, Cologne, 1983.

5 Industrialization, commercial expansion and emancipation (eleventh–twelfth centuries)

The urbanization process which began to manifest itself in major topographical changes and in the spread of existing cities as well as in the emergence of new cities in the tenth and particularly in the eleventh centuries, as dealt with in the previous chapter, also had important economic, social and institutional aspects which we have scarcely touched upon so far owing to a lack of written sources prior to the eleventh century. Only from the eleventh century onwards is it possible to say something about the inhabitants of these cities: their origin and statutes, their organization and administrative position in the city and *vis-à-vis* the city's original lord and master – bishop or sovereign (prince, territorial monarch) – and their commercial and industrial activities and organization, especially as regards long-distance trade. This chapter deals with all these aspects of the urban community. Chronologically it covers the eleventh and twelfth centuries. Towards the end or sometimes even in the middle of the twelfth century, a development was completed which may have begun in the tenth century but which can only be studied from the beginning of the eleventh century because of a lack of sources. From the middle of the twelfth century and especially at the end of that century, new social, institutional and economic developments began which only had their full impact in the thirteenth century and so fall outside the chronological confines of this book.

The urban community and its organisation, the urban population and its origins

In contrast to earlier beliefs, especially as interpreted by Pirenne and some of his pupils,[1] it is now fairly generally believed that in the eleventh and twelfth centuries the core and perhaps the bulk of the population in

[1] H. Van Werveke, 'De steden. Ontstaan en eerste groei', in J. A. Van Houtte and J. F. Niermeyer *et al.* (eds.), *Algemene Geschiedenis der Nederlanden*, II, Utrecht and Antwerp, 1950, pp. 187–8; Van Werveke, 'The Rise of the Towns', in *The Cambridge Economic History of Europe*, III, Cambridge, 1963, pp. 15–17.

the cities between the Somme and the Meuse were made up of indigenous inhabitants and not of uprooted adventurers with no fixed abode nor of merchants who were constantly travelling. The forefathers of these indigenous inhabitants had usually been dependent in one way or another on the lord who ruled the territory of the later city and who owned the land. In the ninth century they had been inhabitants of a non-agrarian or no longer completely agrarian settlement in the immediate vicinity of an abbey (Arras, Ghent), of the seat of a bishop (Cambrai, Tournai) or of a royal residence (Valenciennes) or fortification. Very often they were skilled manual workers in the service of their lord in a manorial context, for example arms makers, leather or wool workers and the like. Among these inhabitants in the service of a lord there were also those who carried out commercial assignments on behalf of their lord, even travelling by ship. Some also used that opportunity to engage in trade for personal profit.[2] When, as a result of Viking raids and the loss of public power, their lord had to forfeit his authority towards the end of the ninth century, they emerged as independent merchants who worked exclusively on their own account.[3] With the restoration of some abbeys and churches in the tenth century following the Viking raids, or in places where there had been no or scarcely any interruption to their existence at the end of the ninth century, many of them placed themselves under the protection of the relevant abbey or bishop's church in return for payment of a symbolic sum as a sign of their new state of bondage, when they married or died, or simply as a levy on their head as a symbol of their lack of freedom. There were also many others, sometimes of noble birth, who had never had any subordinate connection with a church, who particularly in the tenth century gave themselves up to the saint referred to in the name of the church, after which they belonged to what was called the *familia*. They were then called *homines sancti N.* (e.g., *homines sanctae Mariae, homines sancti Vedasti*), *tributarii, censuales* (Fr. *sainteurs*) and the like.[4] In the eleventh century there were large numbers of them living in several of the cities in the area under study here, though they were not a typicaly urban phenomenon as large numbers of them also lived in the countryside. In addition to the jurisdiction of the church to whose authority they were subjected, being exempted by way of privilege from the normal lay

---

[2] F. Petri, 'Die Anfänge des mittelalterlichen Städtewesens in den Niederlanden und dem angrenzenden Frankreich', in T. Mayer (ed.), *Studien zu den Anfängen des europäischen Städtewesens*, Lindau and Konstanz, 1958 (Vorträge und Forschungen 4), pp. 268–9.

[3] F. Irsigler, 'Grundherrschaft, Handel und Märkte zwischen Maas und Rhein im frühen und hohen Mittelalter', in K. Flink and W. Janssen (eds.), *Grundherrschaft und Stadtentstehung am Niederrhein*, Kleve, 1989, pp. 67–9; B. Diestelkamp, 'Zusammenfassung der Referat- und Diskussionsbeiträge', in *ibid.*, p. 180.

[4] Van Werveke, 'The Rise of the Towns', pp. 18–19.

jurisdiction, in some of these cities they even enjoyed all kinds of privileges and advantages. This was the case in Arras and in Tournai, two cities where the authority and power of the Abbey of St Vaast and of the episcopal chapter respectively were very strong, almost to the exclusion of any other, for example secular, authority, until around the middle of the twelfth century. In Arras these *homines sancti Vedasti* were exempted from the toll, together with another group of the urban population, the *homines de generali placito*, who also belonged to the *familia* of St Vaast.[5] The latter were formerly propertied freemen who in the tenth century placed themselves and their possessions (*allodia*) under the authority of the abbey and had to attend the sitting at its court of law three times a year (*placitum generale*) and pay a small tax on marriage or death, yet not a levy on their person, which meant they were not entirely in bondage, but as semi-freemen were juridically a little higher than the *homines sancti Vedasti*. It was important for the urban development of Arras in the eleventh century that early that century merchants who did not belong to this group tried to acquire this status so as to enjoy toll exemption. This they were granted by the abbot of St Vaast only in the second generation in 1024. Their discontent on this matter was to lead to difficulties a century later on the bench of aldermen to which in the meantime they had been admitted, as we will see shortly. Thus, in the eleventh century Arras was a fine example of the heterogeneous composition of its original population who lived mainly in the immediate vicinity of the abbey. In other cities at an early stage of development the bondsmen or semi-freemen, who worked for their lord in a manorial context, lived with his vassals (often called *ministeriales*) in a fortified dependence of the lord's residence, which we encountered as *Oud(e)burg*, *Vetus Burgus* or simply *burgus* in such places as Ghent, Bruges, Huy and Namur in a previous chapter.

In Tournai the *homines beatae Mariae*, who had placed themselves under the protection of the episcopal cathedral chapter in the course of the tenth century in return for payment of the three taxes, enjoyed exemption from the toll, as in Arras, or at least a more favourable tariff.[6] There were merchants among them even at the beginning of the eleventh century. At the end of the twelfth century they still had the monopoly of one of the seignorial aldermen's benches in the city, with limited authority in civil matters, the *échevinage de Sainte Marie*. A notable and late consequence of the importance of this privilege in Tournai was the gift of the count of Flanders Philip of Alsace of all his serfs within the city (*oppidum*) of Kortrijk to the Church of Notre Dame in Tournai. Like

[5] F. Vercauteren, *Civitates*, pp. 200–2; Kéry, *Errichtung des Bistums Arras*, pp. 280–3.
[6] P. Rolland, 'Les hommes de Sainte-Marie de Tournai', *Revue Belge de Philologie et d'Histoire* 3 (1924), p. 233; Vercauteren, *Civitates*, pp. 250–1.

every serf from outside Kortrijk who came to live in the city with the *burgenses*, they enjoyed the *burgensium libertas* on condition that they paid the three above-mentioned taxes to Notre Dame in Tournai.[7]

Of course, in the eleventh–twelfth centuries and later, all cities grew largely as a result of immigration, perhaps mainly manual workers from the surrounding countryside and to a lesser extent merchants who we believe belonged chiefly to the indigenous population and who had long owned parts of the urban land or held it at quit rent. The rising value of urban land, which they divided up and handed out as free tenure for a higher rent,[8] must have constituted a major part of their starting capital as merchants. The rich Ghent family the Utenhoves (Lat. *de curia*), whose name ('From the manor') recalls the agrarian origin of their residence near St Michael's Church in Ghent and their many other properties spread over the city, is a well-known example of many such Ghent families.[9] Whether these merchants acted as employers and industrial entrepreneurs even in the eleventh–twelfth centuries is a question which cannot be answered on the basis of the available documentation, not even at a later period, for example in the thirteenth century.[10] We will come back up against this problem when we discuss the commercial and industrial activities of the urban bourgeoisie.

In a number of cities under strict ecclesiastical authority, as in Cambrai, but where there were apparently no *sainteurs*, the bishop's vassals constituted an important element of the urban population in the tenth–eleventh centuries. This was also the case in Liège where, as *ministeriales* of the bishop, they played an important military role in the eleventh and twelfth centuries as leaders of the urban militia (*viris militaribus*).[11] In Cambrai, these *ministeriales*, unlike in Liège called burghers (*cives*) of the city in 958 (albeit in a source dating from a century later), led a violent uprising against the bishop which has wrongly been regarded as the oldest manifestation of a civil conscience. This does not alter the fact that there is reference to merchants in this city in the year 1001, a number of whom are known by name to have been involved in long-distance trade in the middle of the eleventh century.[12]

---

[7] N. Maddens (ed.), *De geschiedenis van Kortrijk*, Tielt, 1990, pp. 60–1.

[8] Van Werveke, 'The Rise of the Towns', pp. 19–21.

[9] F. Blockmans, *Het Gentsche Stadspatriciaat tot omstreeks 1302*, Antwerp and The Hague, 1938 (Rijksuniversiteit Gent. Werken uitgegeven door de Faculteit van de Wijsbegeerte en Letteren 85), pp. 79–84.

[10] H. Van Werveke, 'Industrial Growth in the Middle Ages. The Cloth Industry in Flanders', *Economic History Review* 6 (1954), p. 238, reprinted in Van Werveke, *Miscellanea mediaevalia*, Ghent, 1968, p. 382.

[11] Vercauteren, 'De wordingsgeschiedenis der Maassteden', p. 23; Vercauteren, 'Marchands et bourgeois', pp. 212–13; J. Stiennon (ed.), *Histoire de Liège*, Toulouse, 1991, pp. 46–7.

[12] Vercauteren, *Civitates*, pp. 226–8; Trenard (ed.), *Histoire de Cambrai*, pp. 35–6.

Merchants' guilds

We first encounter merchants as a group in the eleventh century in several cities in the south and south-west of our area, largely thanks to the phenomenon of the guilds which brought them together.

Guilds were organizations which existed under that name as of the late eighth century. Their main characteristic at that time was the oath, forbidden by the Carolingian king, whereby members pledged mutual help and financial assistance in the event of shipwreck (*naufragium*), fire and other disasters resulting in sudden impoverishment. Merchants could be members, yet, according to the latest thinking on the subject, the early guilds were not specifically merchants' guilds.[13] The latter did not emerge until the eleventh century, and although the oath and mutual assistance also typified the eleventh-century merchants' guilds, these had additional specific characteristics which do not go back to the Carolingian period. The most remarkable of these characteristics, as exemplified by the well-known case of the merchants' guild of Tiel, are described and abused between 1021 and 1024 by Alpertus of Metz. This monk from the bishopric of Utrecht wrote in Amersfoort. He refers to communal drinking sprees, to the fund into which each member paid his contribution and which financed the drinking sprees and provided assistance for members, and, most importantly of all, to the mutually agreed unwritten law which the members were bound to obey via an internal administration of justice. Among other things, this law made for a much more flexible furnishing of proof in trade disputes than in the customary law.[14]

These characteristic elements of an eleventh-century merchants' guild are to be found in more detail in the statutes of the merchants' guild of Valenciennes and that of Saint-Omer[15] than in Alpertus of Metz's description of the merchants' guild of Tiel. The Valenciennes and Saint-Omer statutes are also the oldest in existence and in fact the only ones we

---

[13] O. G. Oexle, 'Gilden als soziale Gruppen in der Karolingerzeit', in H. Jankuhn, W. Janssen, R. Schmidt-Wiegand and H. Tiefenbach (eds.), *Das Handwerk in vor- und frühgeschichtlicher Zeit*, I, Göttingen, 1981 (Abhandlungen der Akademie der Wissenschaften in Göttingen, Philologisch-Historische Klasse, 3rd Series, no. 122), pp. 284–354.

[14] O. G. Oexle, 'Die Kaufmannsgilde von Tiel', in H. Jankuhn and E. Ebel (eds.), *Untersuchungen zu Handel und Verkehr der vor- und frühgeschichtlichen Zeit in Mittel- und Nordeuropa*, VI, *Organisationsformen der Kaufmannsvereinigungen in der Spätantike und im frühen Mittelalter*, Göttingen, 1989 (Abhandlungen der Akademie der Wissenschaften in Göttingen, Philologisch-Historische Klasse, 3rd Series, no. 183), pp. 173–96.

[15] H. Caffiaux, *Mémoire sur la charte de la frairie de la halle basse de Valenciennes (XIe et XIIe siècles)*, Paris, 1877 (Mémoires de la Société Nationale des Antiquaires de France); reprinted in C. Faider (ed.), *Coutumes du pays et comté de Hainaut*, III, 1878, p. 311–25; G. Espinas and H. Pirenne, 'Les coutumes de la gilde marchande de Saint-Omer', *Le Moyen Age* 14 (1901), pp. 189–96; E. Coornaert, 'Les ghildes médiévales', *Revue Historique* 199 (1948), pp. 22–55 and 208–43, esp. p. 48; A. Derville, *Saint-Omer*, pp. 95–8; Platelle (ed.), *Histoire de Valenciennes*, pp. 26–7.

know of in Western Europe dating from the eleventh century: those of the *Caritet* of Valenciennes dating from the last third of the eleventh century (*c.* 1067?) and preserved in the later *Charte de la Halle Basse* or *de la Halle aux Draps* and those of the guild of Saint-Omer, later also called *Caritet* and handed down in a later version, but known to date from around the same time as the statutes of the *Caritet* of Valenciennes because an article of the statutes refers to an oral agreement from the years 1072–83.

A first constituent element of the guild was the obligation to provide mutual protection and mutual assistance, first and foremost in a foreign country (Valenciennes § 10). Moreover, this assistance had to be rendered on the loss of merchandise while travelling as a result of confiscation, looting or accident (Valenciennes §§ 43–5; Saint-Omer § 1). Assistance also had to be offered when a member of the guild was obliged to appear before a foreign court of law (Saint-Omer § 1). Guild members also enjoyed rights and privileges on the home market (Saint-Omer §§ 2 and 3).

The regulations with regard to life within the guild constitute a second group. They relate to admission as a member, the admission fee, reading out the statutes, attending the meetings, the drinking sprees (Lat. *potaciones*) and feasts, the religious ceremonies and the commemoration of the dead. Special attention was paid to the guild members' pledge of brotherhood and the renouncement of violence which included a ban on bringing weapons into the guildhall (*gildhalla*: Saint-Omer §§ 7 and 10; Valenciennes § 4), though they were obliged to carry arms (bow and arrow, javelin) and wear chain mail on their travels (Valenciennes §§ 8 and 9). If it did come to abuse and brawls between members of the guild then the guild's internal tribunal was authorized to administer punishments which were enumerated in the statutes.

A third group of rules in the statutes of Valenciennes and Saint-Omer regulated the guild's relations with the outside world. These included the obligation to provide non-members with poor relief and above all to participate in the provision of community services (Lat. *communis utilitas*), such as maintaining the streets and the city walls (Saint-Omer § 27). This last item in the statutes proves that even by the end of the eleventh century the guilds had begun to play a role in running the city. This role was confirmed a few decades later in Arras, where in 1111 the chief alderman was called *Hugo maior de gilda eorum* and had to be distinguished from the *villicus* or *maior* of St Vaast Abbey.[16] This Hugo

[16] F. Vercauteren (ed.), *Actes des comtes de Flandre 1071–1128*, Brussels, 1938, no. 52, p. 132; A. C. F. Koch, *De rechterlijke organisatie van het Graafschap Vlaanderen tot in de 13e eeuw*, Antwerp and Amsterdam, 1951, pp. 66–7.

can be compared to the head of the sworn commune (*maior communionis*) in Saint-Omer. The *communio*, together with the count's aldermen, ran the city, a development to which we will return in just a moment. In Tournai, too, the *charité St Christophe* was to become part of the city administration in 1188 and took charge of the city lime kilns and the export of the famous Tournai stone. And later on this guild was granted the right to control the city finances.[17]

Sworn communes

This was the end of a development which probably began early in the twelfth century and whereby the guild served as the model for the formation of the *commune jurée* or 'sworn commune' which ran many a Flemish city together with the aldermen during the twelfth century.[18] It can be no coincidence that in cities where merchants' guilds existed in the eleventh–twelfth centuries (Valenciennes, Saint-Omer, Tournai and perhaps others as well), sworn communes emerged around the same time or a little later. This is particularly, if not exclusively, the case in cities in the west and south of the area under consideration here, and to a lesser extent much later or not at all in cities in the Meuse Valley where there is nothing to suggest the existence of guilds and where the sworn commune was a late twelfth-century phenomenon. An explanation for this difference probably lies in the great power and importance of the merchants in the cities of the county of Flanders, which we will try to account for further on in this chapter in connection with the great boom in trade and industry there. Other explanations are however not excluded, such as the great power, still in the eleventh and twelfth centuries, wielded by the bishop of Liège in most of the cities along the Meuse, by comparison with the real autonomy which a number of Flemish cities and especially their citizens managed to acquire on different occasions in the tenth–eleventh centuries. The curtailment in the count's authority in Flanders during the second half of the tenth century, the power struggle between Flanders and Hainault under Robrecht the Frisian (1067–71) or the location of certain cities (Arras, Saint-Omer, Tournai) on the periphery of the count's sphere of influence, are all possible explanations. These circumstances would then be examples of the weakening of authority and the

[17] L. Verriest, 'La Charité Saint Christophe et ses comptes au XIIIe siècle', *Bulletin de la Commission Royale d'Histoire* 73 (1904), pp. 143–268; P. Rolland, *Les origines de la commune de Tournai*, Brussels, 1931, pp. 171–3, 255–7.
[18] Van Werveke, 'The Rise of the Towns', pp. 26–9; Petri, 'Anfänge', pp. 287–90; A. Vermeesch, *Essai sur les origines et la signification de la commune dans le Nord de la France (XIe et XIIe siècles)*, Heule, 1966.

resultant disintegration in which some historians have sought a general explanation for the phenomenon of the guilds.[19]

Explanations such as these do not entirely account for the emergence of the sworn communes, even though the guilds very probably served as a model for this form of participation by the citizenry, that is to say the well-to-do traders, who were involved in the running of many cities from around the year 1100. However, in contrast to earlier views such as those of Planitz,[20] the sworn communes were not a direct extension of the merchants' guilds and they alone do not explain the emergence of the communes. It is nevertheless true to say that, with the emergence of the communes, the real *raison d'être* for the merchants' guilds – namely the commitment made under oath to ensure protection, surety and equality in law – was passed on to the urban commune, where the oath was also the essential characteristic.[21] The subject of this oath was, as with the guilds, internal peace, flexible laws of their own and subjection to an internal tribunal. The difference was that under the regime of the commune this applied to all the inhabitants of the city who enjoyed civil rights. Not all the guilds disappeared: some retained certain administrative duties, as in Tournai; others took on economic functions, as in Valenciennes where the *caritet* came to resemble a Hanse, which did not exist here as a separate institution; and elsewhere, such as in Saint-Omer, the guild retained only its religious function with related festivities.

The oldest and best-known sworn communes appeared at the end of the eleventh and at the beginning of the twelfth centuries in a few cities in the south-west of the area between the Somme and the Meuse, namely in Cambrai (1077), Valenciennes (1114), Saint-Omer (1127), Aire (1093–1111) and Tournai (1147). They may also have existed in Ghent and in Bruges, where, as in Saint-Omer, they disappeared between 1168 and 1177 as a result of intervention on the part of the count of Flanders Philip of Alsace, as we will see further on. In Arras, where a merchants' guild must still have existed in 1111, all traces of a commune have been erased, perhaps again because of intervention by the count. As we have already said and as will be explained further on, in Liège and in Huy jurors were only introduced later and their presence cannot be proved before 1230.

The oldest commune within the area under consideration here was created in Cambrai in 1077, in response to an uprising against the

---

[19] Oexle, 'Die Kaufmannsgilde von Tiel', pp. 187–8.
[20] H. Planitz, 'Kaufmannsgilde und städtische Eidgenossenschaft in niederfränkischen Städten im 11. u. 12. Jh.', *Zeitschrift für Rechtsgeschichte, Germanistische Abteilung* 60 (1940), pp. 1–116; Petri, 'Anfänge', p. 291.
[21] Oexle, 'Die Kaufmannsgilde von Tiel', pp. 194–5.

castellan.[22] It was later recognized by the bishop and by the emperor and instituted. The name *communio* was then replaced by the more peaceful word *paix* (Lat. *pax*) which supplanted the name *communio* in Valenciennes as well. The *jurati pacis* (jurors of the peace) in Cambrai were responsible for criminal matters while the aldermen who were dependent on the bishop were now only responsible for civil matters. We encounter a similar curtailment of the powers of the aldermen in Tournai where *jurati* were first mentioned in 1147, and also and above all in Valenciennes where the earliest detailed information about the sworn commune is provided by the elaborate charter in which Baldwin III count of Hainault granted the city the *Pax* in 1114 and defined the organization of the commune.[23] These stipulations, though of great importance for the administrative and judicial organization of the city as a whole, chiefly concerned those who had become men or jurors of the peace (*viri pacis*, *iurati pacis*) through an oath. They were mainly punishments laid down for all kinds of criminal acts and for which only the communal court of law was competent. As we have said, by 1114 the jurisdiction of the aldermen, who were appointed by the count of Hainault for the city of Valenciennes, was reduced to purely civil matters. Both courts of law continued to exist side by side until the thirteenth century, though the bench of aldermen was gradually incorporated into the commune.

From sworn commune to aldermen's rule

This merging of the two courts of law is a process that took place in the course of the twelfth century in all the cities where they had existed side by side. It was first and foremost the result of changes in the relationship between the original lord of the city, count or bishop, and the aldermen who governed on his behalf and administered justice. It began with the appointment of separate aldermen for the city. With a clearly defined border (sometimes limited to the twelfth-century walls of the city, sometimes to a few kilometres beyond them), the city became a jurisdiction in its own right and quite separate from the surrounding countryside; in some respects justice was administered according to different rules adapted to city life. A well-known example of this is Ypres where in 1116 the count of Flanders replaced the duel and the trial by ordeal as a means of proof by the testimony of a witness within the jurisdiction of the city

---

[22] Trenard (ed.), *Histoire de Cambrai*, pp. 45–52; E. M. Meyers, *Le droit coutumier de Cambrai*, 3 vols., Haarlem, 1955, esp. vol. II, pp. xvii–xviii.

[23] P. Godding and J. Pycke, 'La paix de Valenciennes de 1114. Commentaire et édition critique', *Bulletin de la Commission pour la Publication des Anciennes Lois et Ordonnances de Belgique* 29 (1971) [1981], pp. 1–142; Platelle (ed.), *Histoire de Valenciennes*, pp. 28–9.

which was then referred to as the *Jus Iprense*.[24] There is some uncertainty about the exact dates on which the lord of a city appointed separate aldermen for the city as his representatives, even though the possible dates for the various cities fall predominantly at the beginning of the twelfth century:[25] Aire 1096–1111, Tournai 1098, Arras 1111–12, Douai 1112–17, Valenciennes 1114, Ypres 1116, Saint-Omer 1127, Bruges 1127 and Ghent 1127. At that time sworn communes still existed in most of these cities as a rival court of law, even if this is so difficult to prove in some of these cities that Pirenne simply denied their existence there, regarding the aldermen as representatives, no longer of the lord but of the burghers.[26] Yet the existence of a *communio* in Ghent in 1128 is an established fact, even if nothing more is known about it and even if, as in Bruges, leaders other than the aldermen – perhaps also jurors, though not called this but referred to vaguely as *meliores* or *sapientiores* – had a voice in the city administration as representatives of the people.

There they were probably charged with providing general political leadership and with administering the city, while the administration of justice was still the responsibility of the aldermen. In other cities, such as Valenciennes, Cambrai and Tournai, it was just the opposite, as we mentioned above. In large cities like Ghent and Bruges the aldermen were to obtain general administrative powers when their law was brought into line by Count Philip of Alsace between 1168 and 1177, at which the jurors disappeared as administrators. But before that could happen, the aldermen had to be seen as the representatives not of the lord any more, but of the people. This was another aspect of the *rapprochement* between the two administrative bodies and their eventual amalgamation. This was usually the result of the fact that the aldermen were increasingly elected by the lord of the city from among its burghers.[27] We can follow this evolution in Arras, for instance, where in 1111 the chief alderman Hugo, who bore the title *maior* (reeve), was elected from the merchants' guild. This meant that the person responsible for summoning the aldermen of St Vaast, who was also called *maior* or *villicus*, was forced to take a back seat. Moreover, some of the city aldermen of Arras did not belong to the *familia* of St Vaast Abbey and so were not exempt from the tolls. They were newcomers, strangers who were regarded as freemen. It was they who made difficulties about their lack of exemption from the toll and sought the mediation of the count of Flanders who may have become

[24] Vercauteren, *Actes*, no. 79, pp. 177–8.   [25] Van Werveke, 'De steden', p. 385.
[26] H. Pirenne, 'La question des jurés dans les villes flamandes', *Revue Belge de Philologie et d'Histoire* 5 (1926), pp. 401–21, reprinted in Pirenne, *Les villes et les institutions urbaines*, II, Paris-Brussels, 1939, pp. 201–18.   [27] Van Werveke, 'De steden', pp. 383–6.

involved in the religious immunity of St Vaast on the basis of the count's right over strangers.[28]

The appointment by the lord of separate aldermen for the city, moreover chosen by him with increasing frequency from among the city's leading burghers, often went hand in hand with the granting of a charter or statute (Flem. *keure*) to the city. In addition to domestic, customary law, such charters contain a number of regulations with regard to the autonomy of the aldermen, their powers in criminal matters and above all a number of penalty clauses alongside certain privileges.[29] The problem is that the only extant count's charter of this sort dating from the time that separate aldermen for the city were first appointed, i.e. the first third of the twelfth century, is that of Saint-Omer, for the charter of Count Baldwin III of Hainault for Valenciennes dating from 1114 relates to the sworn commune. For the other large Flemish cities, Ghent, Bruges, Ypres, Lille and Douai, such charters (*keuren*) date only from 1168–77 when Philip of Alsace brought the law and the administration of the large Flemish cities into line with the *keure* or statute which he had imposed on Arras in 1157–63. This has been called a 'monarchical reaction' because it substantially extended the count's power in the cities, especially with regard to penal law, and reduced their autonomy. As a result, earlier charters lost their significance, which explains why they have not been preserved. In most of these cities the sworn communes also disappeared as an important administrative institution. This was not the case in Saint-Omer prior to 1168–77.[30] Here city charters dating from 1127, 1128 and 1164 have been preserved and they contain substantial concessions from the count to the city, especially to the commune. However the charter which was imposed on Saint-Omer as on the other large cities in the county of Flanders between 1168 and 1177, and whereby the achievements of the charters of previous years perished, has not been preserved. These idiosyncrasies of the written tradition are not accidental. The exceptional position of Saint-Omer in this respect until 1168–77, though difficult to explain, may be connected with the strength of its sworn commune.

In any case the twelfth-century charters for Saint-Omer show that the relationship between the authority of the count and the cities, notably through the parallel existence of a bench of aldermen and a commune, was more complicated than Pirenne and others after him claimed purely on the basis of Philip of Alsace's city charters dating from 1168–77. Saint-Omer was probably no exception and so the development that occurred there in terms of a strengthening of the municipal autonomy can

[28] Koch, *Rechterlijke organisatie*, pp. 65–70.
[29] Van Werveke, 'De Steden', pp. 390–2.   [30] Derville, *Saint-Omer*, pp. 105–9.

be considered to have applied to the other large cities in the county of Flanders as well. So it is wrong to speak of a *type flamand* as Pirenne does, according to which the bench of aldermen, which was originally that of the count, would have become the city's only administrative body very early on and moreover would have served from the outset and with the count's approval as the citizens' only representative. In this respect Pirenne wrongly interpreted Philip of Alsace's city charters of 1168–77 and mistakenly denied the existence of communes in the Flemish cities up until that time. Moreover, with this simplification and reduction of the urban institutional development in the county of Flanders to one *type flamand*, based on the role of the count's bench of aldermen as the citizens' only representative with the approval of the count, a simplification which takes little or no account of the development before the great charters of 1168–77, Pirenne wanted to establish a contrast with a *type liégeois* which would have characterized the cities along the River Meuse.[31]

In Pirenne's mind the latter type would have been the exact opposite of the situation in the Flemish cities and consisted of *two* administrative bodies for the city: the episcopal bench of aldermen, made up of the *ministeriales* or semi-free knights dependent on the bishop and, as a twelfth-century reaction against it, a sworn association of jurors, with which the citizens, who were less well-organized than in Flanders, would have reacted against the already excessive power of the bishop. As we have contended, recent historical research has found insufficient proof of the existence of jurors in Liège before 1230.[32] That same year also provides the first firm mention of jurors in Huy. In Dinant their emergence dates from under the episcopacy of Albert of Cuyck in 1196, a period which probably also applies to Liège and Huy. Even then the jurors in Dinant had no judicial power and as 'counsel' they were only responsible for urban regulations and the police.[33]

On the other hand it would be quite untrue to suggest that there was no bourgeoisie of any significance in the cities mentioned along the Meuse. It was rather that its political power was limited compared to that of the bishop of Liège. Yet the merchants who largely made up this bourgeoisie managed to exact certain privileges fairly early on. The best known of these is the charter that the burghers of Huy succeeded in obtaining from Bishop Theoduin of Liège in 1066, albeit in return for remuneration,

---

[31] H. Pirenne, *Les anciennes démocraties des Pays-Bas*, Paris, 1910, reprinted in *Les villes et les institutions urbaines*, I, pp. 183–93.

[32] J. L. Kupper 'Le village était devenu une cité' in J. Stiennon (ed.), *Histoire de Liège*, Toulouse, 1991, pp. 46–8.

[33] H. Pirenne, *Histoire de la constitution de la ville de Dinant au moyen âge*, Ghent, 1889, reprinted in Pirenne, *Les villes et les institutions urbaines*, II, pp. 21–2.

because the bishop was pressed for cash.[34] In exchange for one third, after that even half of their moveables, they obtained a freedom charter (*libertas*) in which the rights of the bishop were considerably curtailed, not least with respect to the unfree in the city and concerning the citizens' military service. Above all, however, it simplified the proof procedure regarding debts and suchlike, also for strangers, partly by the procedure of oath helping. We have already encountered a similar sort of innovation with regard to the trading bourgeoisie in Ypres in 1116 and in the statutes of the guild of Saint-Omer. However, there was no guild in Huy, and according to Joris, in contradiction of Planitz, the charter of 1066 was not granted to an *organized* bourgeoisie. In Liège, the merchants accounted for a smaller proportion of the population of the city than in Huy (Liège had a large number of clerics), but they nevertheless succeeded early on (1107) in gaining the recognition of a *judicium forense* or *civile*, the right to hold a market though confined to 'known' merchants.[35]

Manual workers' organisation

There is little or no mention in the preceding pages of the skilled manual workers who must have populated the cities in growing numbers from the tenth–eleventh centuries onwards. This is because we know nothing about them before the thirteenth century owing to a lack of written sources, and in particular we know nothing about their relationship with the merchants in so far as the latter must have acted as their employers. Neither do we know anything about how they were organized. Only in this last respect do we suspect that in the twelfth century the skilled manual workers were grouped according to occupation in religious brotherhoods, in some ways comparable with the merchants' guilds which were in fact also brotherhoods and frequently called that (Lat. *caritates*, *confraternitates*) but from which the skilled manual workers were excluded. In Arras there is proof of such brotherhoods from the twelfth century.[36] It is assumed that the organization into professional groups was encouraged by the city authorities, for military reasons – the formation of city militias – and with a view to bringing work regulations into force. These groups were not, however, recognized by the city authorities until the thirteenth century.

Hanses

A remarkable twelfth-century organization in which merchants from

---

[34] Joris, *Huy*, pp. 107–27.   [35] Vercauteren, 'Marchands et bourgeois', pp. 666–8.
[36] Van Werveke, 'De steden', p. 411.

more than one city were grouped for the purpose of long-distance trade was the so-called 'hanses'.[37] What we know about hanses allows us to make the transition to the last part of this chapter where we will look at trade in and from the cities between Somme and Meuse. Indeed, hanses emerged around the middle of the twelfth century, when most of the merchants' guilds, with Valenciennes as the main exception, saw their economic function as regards the provision of aid to member merchants abroad pass to the hanses. There must have been a link between the two phenomena, the emergence of hanses and the disappearance – sometimes only of their economic function – of merchants' guilds, at least in those Flemish cities where a hanse emerged in addition to the merchants' guild, as in Ghent and Saint-Omer, and in the cities which were affiliated with the Flemish Hanse of London in the thirteenth century (Bruges, Ypres, Lille, Tournai, Diksmuide, etc.) yet which had probably had their own autonomous hanses before that. In Valenciennes, on the other hand, as well as in a few other cities in areas on the periphery of the county of Flanders (Antwerp, Mechelen, Middelburg), there was no hanse in addition to the merchants' guild. Here the latter performed the functions which were carried out by hanses elsewhere. In the cities of the Meuse Valley there were neither guilds nor hanses.

The main tasks of a hanse were: the provision of mutual assistance abroad between merchants of one city or of various cities affiliated with the hanse, for example when they were taken prisoner, were summoned before a foreign court of law or had their goods confiscated. This assistance was ensured financially by a communal fund which was fed by a very high membership fee. The membership fee was originally called *hansa* and its collection is reflected in the verb *hansare*. At the same time, this high membership fee was a means of restricting admission to the hanse to the richest burghers and their sons and of keeping out newcomers or impecunious adventurers.

This restriction was essentially intended to guarantee this privileged group the large profits which they could still make in the twelfth century by controlling and even monopolizing trade in a specific market or in a specific region abroad. Because this was more difficult when a hanse was restricted to one city, the merchants of large cities endeavoured either to have those merchants from other cities who conducted trade in the same region or market join their hanse in return for payment of a high membership fee (thus Ghent with regard to trade in the Rhineland), or to federate small, local hanses all operating in the same market (e.g. London) under the leadership of the most powerful of them (namely Bruges and Ypres,

[37] H. Van Werveke, 'Das Wesen der flandrischen Hansen', *Hansische Geschichtsblätter* 76 (1958), pp. 7–20, reprinted in Van Werveke, *Miscellanea mediaevalia*, pp. 88–103.

which thus gave rise to the Flemish Hanse of London between 1212 and 1241). Saint-Omer, which also occupied an important place on the London market, retained an independent hanse of its own, perhaps for this very reason. The situation in Ghent and Douai with regard to trade with England, which was important in their case too, is unclear.

Urban industry and commercial expansion

The area between the Somme and the Meuse lies between England and the Rhineland and so it is hardly surprising that the oldest traces of long-distance trade by merchants from the cities between the two rivers point in these two directions. Indeed, these merchants may well have provided the link between England and the Rhineland. It so happens that a toll tariff has been preserved for each of these areas. These contain the oldest evidence of trade activity by merchants from the southern Low Countries: a toll tariff for trade in London, collected at Billingsgate, traditionally believed to date from *c.* 991–*c.* 1002 though possibly two to three decades later,[38] and a toll tariff for trade on the Rhine in Koblenz. Conflicting opinions have been expressed about the date of the latter in recent years, but its content is now considered to relate to the years before 1070.[39] In both tariffs we once again encounter merchants from the two areas for which we furnished proof, in a previous chapter, of internal urbanization in the tenth–eleventh centuries on the basis of other data. On the one hand, these were merchants from the county of Flanders in London (*Flandrenses*) and in Koblenz ('men from the county of [Count] Baldwin [V of Flanders]'), and merchants from Antwerp in Koblenz; on the other hand, these were merchants from cities along the River Meuse, namely Huy and Liège, in both London and Koblenz, while merchants of Nivelles in Walloon Brabant are mentioned in the London tariff and of Namur and Dinant in the Koblenz tariff. With the exception of Nivelles, neither of the two tariffs mentions people from Brabant or Brabantine cities, which also accords with what we already know from other sources about the retardation of urban development in Brabant compared to the county of Flanders and the prince-bishopric of Liège.

[38] H. R. Loyn, *Anglo-Saxon England and the Norman Conquest*, London, 1962, pp. 93–4; D. Keene, 'London in the Early Middle Ages', *London Journal* 20–2 (1995), p. 11; edition of the toll tariff by Lebecq, *Marchands et navigateurs*, II, pp. 442–4 after F. Liebermann, *Die Gesetze der Angelsachsen*, I, Halle, 1903, pp. 232–4.

[39] W. Hess, 'Zoll, Markt und Münze im 11. Jh. Der älteste Koblenzer Zolltarif im Lichte numismatischer Quellen', in H. Beumann (ed.), *Historische Forschungen für W. Schlesinger*, Cologne, 1974, pp. 170–93; B. Tissen, 'Het oudste toltarief van Koblenz', in P. Bange and P. M. J. C. de Kort (eds.), *Mélanges Prof. dr. A. Weiler*, Nijmegen, 1989, pp. 180–222; T. Kölzer, 'Nochmals zum ältesten Koblenzer Zolltarif', in H. Mordek (ed.), *Festschrift für R. Kottje*, Frankfurt, 1992, pp. 291–310.

The metal industry in the Meuse Valley

According to a toll tariff from Cologne which, despite discussion, would seem to date from 1103,[40] merchants from cities along the Meuse – firstly from Huy and Liège, a little later also from Dinant – purchased copper which may have originated from the Harz. Red copper and yellow copper (brass) were made respectively in an alloy of copper and tin which was brought from England and also from Cologne, or of copper and zinc which was obtained from zinc spar from the region to the east of Liège (Moresnet) or from sphalerite from the area between Liège and Namur. Production took place until the middle of the twelfth century in Huy, Dinant and Liège, but later only in Dinant, which was famed for its copper industry in the centuries that followed. Huy switched over to textiles which were also made in Maastricht, where no metal industry of any significance had existed. Cloth from Maastricht and Huy was exported further east than Cologne or Koblenz towards the end of the twelfth century, more specifically to Austria (Enns and Vienna). Liège had started to specialize in money dealing a century earlier and continued to be held in esteem internationally in the sector.[41]

The early burgeoning of the metal industry in the cities along the Meuse which, with the exception of Dinant, were no longer of international importance in this respect after the middle of the twelfth century, mainly because of competition from Cologne, can probably be ascribed to tradition and technical know-how dating back to the early Middle Ages. At that time iron production and metal processing were carried out on several rural manors in the Ardennes where iron ore was found. As in large parts of Western Europe, this rural production was probably eclipsed by production in the cities once the manorial organization with its concentration of (compulsory) work had died out in the late ninth and in the course of the tenth–eleventh centuries. At the same time freer and larger population groups, partly from the defunct manors, began to form in places where rudimentary urban development can be identified even in the ninth century and which had become regional market centres. The rural metal industry moved there with its know-how so that by the end of the tenth century the merchants who were based there had an industrial product to export. They switched from regional to international trade and imported raw materials such as copper, lead and tin from Germany and England. The fact that this came to an end, except in Dinant, around the middle of the twelfth century, can perhaps be explained by nearby

---

[40] Joris, *Huy*, p. 235; G. Despy and C. Billen, 'Les marchands mosans aux foires de Cologne pendant le XIIe siècle', *Acta Historica Bruxellensia* 3 (1974), pp. 31–61.

[41] H. P. H. Janssen, 'Handel en Nijverheid 1000–1300', in D. P. Blok and W. Prevenier *et al.* (eds.), *Algemene Geschiedenis der Nederlanden*, II, Haarlem, 1982, pp. 152–6.

Cologne's dramatic burgeoning, particularly in the field of metal processing, in the course of the twelfth century.

The cloth industry in Flanders

In contrast to the cities in the valley of the Meuse, the toll tariffs of London and Koblenz name no individual cities in the county of Flanders except for Antwerp which was part of the county economically but not politically. This can perhaps be explained by the fact that the number of Flemish cities from where merchants conducted trade in London and Koblenz were more numerous than the four to five cities in the area of the Meuse. However, we must not lose sight of the fact that around the year 1000 – date of the toll tariff of London – Ypres, Lille and perhaps also Douai and even Saint-Omer were not yet fully fledged cities and were certainly not important in terms of international commerce, so that only Ghent, Bruges, Tournai, Cambrai and Arras might have merited a separate mention in *c.* 1000.

The information about trade activity originating from these cities in the eleventh–twelfth centuries is scarce, fragmentary and not very explicit. This applies even more to the merchandise and products which were exported, although as far as the county of Flanders is concerned, cloth occupied the number-one position. But we know practically nothing about how the cloth was manufactured or by whom. Neither do we know exactly when the cloth industry became an urban industry. It was probably the result of a relatively long evolution, which may even have begun in the tenth century in Ghent and Arras and in the eleventh century in the other cities. The eleventh century still mentions, in a seignorial context, a *gynaeceum* (i.e. a workshop where women carried out collectively all the processes including the finishing of the cloth) in places such as Ename on the River Scheldt to the south of Ghent. At the end of the eleventh century, the case is mentioned even in Tournai of a woman who was skilled in every stage of wool processing. After 1100 the whole process, with the exception of the initial processing of raw wool and the spinning, was carried out exclusively by men in the cities. Even later on, the spinning was usually done by women, often in the countryside not far from the city and by order of employers from the city.

The explanation for this shift – which was never total – of a rural industry to the city has been the subject of many a hypothesis.[42] In our opinion the decline and ousting of the classical manor during the tenth–eleventh centuries, which also enabled the mass immigration from the

---

[42] Van Werveke, 'Industrial Growth', pp. 238–9 (p. 383 of the reprint).

surrounding countryside to the city, was one of the main reasons for this shift. It brought an end to the production of the sometimes very numerous textile items made out of wool and out of flax, finished shirts, underclothes, etc., which mainly female inhabitants of the manor had to make at home as compulsory service and deliver up to the lord of the manor. This evolution, accidentally or otherwise, may have coincided with an important change in the weaving technique which some historians regard as the main reason for the phenomenon outlined here. According to an unproven hypothesis, the vertical loom, on which only small and narrow pieces could be woven, may have been replaced in the city by the much wider horizontal loom with treadles and two wooden cylinders. Much longer pieces of cloth could be wound round the rear cylinder, the so-called cloth beam. This instrument also speeded up production, while the division of labour, which was possible because of the concentration of people in the cities, made for improvements in quality.[43]

Throughout the eleventh century the wool which was used came from the flocks of sheep on the marshes and pastures which were still very numerous along the Flemish and Zealand coasts in the tenth–eleventh centuries. Many marshes (Lat. *marisci*) had formed there back in the eighth–ninth centuries as a result of flooding in the early Middle Ages and could be used only as grazing for sheep because of the salty vegetation.[44]

The wool from the flocks of sheep which were kept on these pastures was then worked on the spot and the textile products delivered up to the owners, usually large abbeys, as rent in kind. Yet even early on, perhaps in the ninth century and certainly in the tenth, when the manorial organization in Flanders was on the decline, much of this wool production may have been taken as raw wool to the very seat of abbeys such as St Vaast in Arras and St Bavo and St Peter in Ghent, possibly even in return for payment. Then it was probably processed in the urban settlements which grew up next to these abbeys in the ninth century, as we saw in chapter 3.

Again there was severe flooding during the first half of the eleventh century (in 1014 and 1042) and very large areas of marshland formed in

[43] Jansen, 'Handel en Nijverheid', pp. 157–8, following W. Endrei, *L'évolution du filage et du tissage du moyen âge à la révolution industrielle*, Paris and The Hague, 1968. See also C. Verlinden, 'Marchands ou tisserands? A propos des origines urbaines', *Annales: Economies–Sociétés–Civilisations* 27 (1972), pp. 396–406; D. Keene, *Survey of Medieval Winchester*, Oxford, 1985, pp. 295–321 and Keene, 'The Textile Industry', in M. Biddle (ed.), *Object and Economy in Medieval Winchester*, Oxford, 1990, pp. 200–14.

[44] A. Verhulst, 'Sheep Breeding and Wool Production in pre-13th Century Flanders and their Contribution to the Rise of Ypres, Ghent and Bruges as Centres of the Textile Industry', *Archeologie in Vlaanderen* (forthcoming).

the Yser Valley some 12 km to the north of Ypres. Shortly after the middle of the eleventh century numerous sheep farms (Lat. *bercariae*) were set up on them. The bulk of their wool production was probably transported to Ypres via the Ieperlee, a tributary of the Yser. This must have accounted for Ypres' rapid rise as a city in the second half of the eleventh century, as was explained in chapter 4. In the tenth–eleventh centuries, numerous flocks of sheep were also kept near Ostend, on the accretions around the island of Testerep beyond what was then the coast, as well as to the north-east of Bruges along the banks of the inlet of the sea which was called *Sincfal* and, as of the twelfth century, *Zwin*. At the beginning of the twelfth century, around 1120, St Peter's Abbey in Ghent leased about 200 ha of grazing for sheep, located along the frequently flooded bank of the Western Scheldt some 20 km to the north of Ghent, to a rich inhabitant of Ghent.

Until then Flemish cloth must have been made chiefly from domestic wool. Indeed, the earliest evidence of wool imported from England dates from 1113/26.[45] By February 1128 the citizens of some large Flemish cities were complaining that the appointment of the pro-French and anti-English Guillaume Clito as count had adversely affected profits from their trade with England which very probably derived from imports of English wool.[46] This change in the origin of the raw material can perhaps be explained by the technical progress made in wool processing during the eleventh century. It probably brought about a need for quality improvement, which could be achieved through the better quality of the English wool. Yet the drop in Flanders' own wool production certainly played a role as well. Indeed, in the course of the twelfth century the marshes disappeared as a result of natural drainage and desalination, as well as of land reclamation. From then on domestic wool played only a subordinate role, certainly in the large Flemish textile cities with their production of luxury goods.

Flemish foreign trade

It was this luxury production on an industrial scale that must have stimulated Flemish exports. The earliest references to these exports all date from the twelfth century and this cannot have been purely coincidental. One of the earliest references is the information about cloth from Ypres in Novgorod between 1130 and 1136; there it was given as a present by the merchants of that city to the head of the militia and to the bishop. According to a theory held by Pirenne, who drew attention to this

[45] Jansen, 'Handel en Nijverheid', note 35 (on page 511).
[46] Ross (ed.), *Galbert of Bruges*, § 95, pp. 270–1.

information, the cloth from Ypres could have been taken to Novgorod by Scandinavian merchants.[47] The fame and the high quality of this cloth in that far corner of Europe led Pirenne to assume not only that the export of cloth from Ypres had reached this distant market even before 1100, but consequently also that the export of Flemish cloth to less distant parts, such as Italy, had been prevalent even by around the year 1100. Yet the first mention of cloth from Arras in Genoa is in 1179. In the case of Italy, the importation of Flemish cloth, especially from the cities in the south of the county, may indeed be older, though Pirenne's dating of around 1100 does seem to us to be rather early.[48] Yet it is not impossible, since even in 1127 merchants from Italy visited the annual fair in Ypres, possibly to buy cloth.[49] This last fact urges caution if, as per the classic view,[50] exports and sales by Flemish merchants abroad – the so-called 'active' Flemish trade – is held to be older than the presence of foreign merchants in Flanders, which should suggest a 'passive' Flemish trade thereafter. It is true that the above-mentioned toll tariffs of London and of Koblenz prove the presence of Flemish merchants abroad even at the beginning and in the middle of the eleventh century, but at the same time evidence has been found recently of the presence of Cologne merchants in Flanders around 1166, i.e. about the time they were importing wine to London.[51] Now it is in Cologne that the dynamism and the combativeness, particularly on the part of the merchants of Ghent, is demonstrated. Shortly after the middle of the twelfth century they did not want to make Cologne the end point of their active trade with the Rhineland.[52] Despite growing resistance from the Cologne merchants, they wanted to go and buy Rhine wine upstream from Cologne, as they may have done since the end of the tenth century, thereby making use of privileges extended to St Bavo's Abbey in Ghent.

[47]   H. Pirenne, 'Draps d'Ypres à Novgorod au commencement du XIIe siècle', *Revue Belge de Philologie et d'Histoire* 9 (1930), pp. 563–7, reprinted in Pirenne, *Histoire économique de l'Occident médiéval*, [Bruges], 1951, pp. 571–4.

[48]   R. L. Reynolds, 'The Market for Northern Textiles in Genoa 1179–1200', *Revue Belge de Philologie et d'Histoire* 8 (1929), pp. 831–51, esp. p. 849; Reynolds, 'Merchants of Arras and the Overland Trade with Genoa', *Revue Belge de Philologie et d'Histoire* 9 (1930), pp. 495–533.   [49] Ross (ed.), *Galbert of Bruges*, § 16, pp. 123–4.

[50]   H. Van Werveke, 'Essor et déclin de la Flandre', in *Studi in onore di Gino Luzatto*, Milan, 1949, pp. 152–60, reprinted in Van Werveke, *Miscellanea mediaevalia*, pp. 3–11, esp. p. 7; Van Werveke, 'Der flandrische Eigenhandel im Mittelalter', *Hansische Geschichtsblätter* 6 (1936), pp. 7–24, reprinted in Van Werveke, *Miscellanea mediaevalia*, pp. 45–59.

[51]   A. Verhulst, 'Keulse handelaars in het Zwin tijdens de twaalfde eeuw en de vroegste ontwikkeling van de Vlaamse zeehavens', *Bijdragen tot de geschiedenis* (*Liber amicorum Raymond Van Uytven*) 81 (1998) pp. 351–8; A. Verhulst, T. de Hemptinne and L. De Mey, 'Un tarif de tonlieu inconnu, institué par le comte de Flandre Thierry d'Alsace (1128–1168), pour le port de "Littersuerua", précurseur du port de Damme', *Bulletin de la Commission Royale d'Histoire* 164 (1998), pp. 143–72.

[52]   Blockmans, *Stadspatriciaat*, pp. 175–8.

When this became increasingly difficult and the import of wine from the Rhine region by people from Ghent was restricted by the archbishop of Cologne under pressure from his subjects, in 1173 Emperor Frederick Barbarossa set up two annual fairs in Aachen and two more in Duisburg at the request of the count of Flanders, Philip of Alsace.[53] But the Ghent merchants' hopes of thus sidestepping resistance from Cologne in the Rhineland were dashed. However, on that occasion we expressly learn that the people of Ghent sold cloth in the Rhineland. Towards the end of the twelfth century they also sold cloth to northern Germany.

Flemish exports to England, again mainly of cloth, with English wool as the return merchandise, were largely in the hands of Saint-Omer and to a lesser extent of Bruges and Ghent. In 1155–8 the merchants from Saint-Omer were the first Flemings to obtain the right to own places in London where they were even allowed to sell their cloth retail. The most famous of these merchants, Willem Cade, was King Stephen's financier around 1150.[54] On Cade's death in 1166, the English king laid claim to the recovery of his debts, half of which related to merchants from Saint-Omer to whom he had lent money for the advance payment to English abbeys and lords of future deliveries of wool. Even at that early stage a number of them may have taken wine to England from Gascony, a trade that was stimulated by the accession of the Plantagenets to the throne.

Flemish trade with France was the county's most recent trade link with abroad.[55] It consisted largely of imports, mainly of Bordeaux wine, for which Damme, founded shortly before 1180 as the outport of Bruges, was to become the great depot, and of salt from the Bay of Bourgneuf to the south of Brittany. Flemish exports to France were less significant and were less concerned with France itself than with the annual fairs in Champagne. In the second half of the twelfth century these fairs were visited mainly by merchants from Arras, Douai, Lille and Saint-Omer, who were particularly keen to export their cloth to Italy. In Champagne they could meet their Italian counterparts who in exchange brought spices.

The Italians, who were the first foreigners at the annual fair in Ypres in 1127, were, in fact, to become the Flemings' number-one competitors in the county itself, along with the merchants from Cologne. Before the early thirteenth century when foreign merchants began to converge on Bruges,[56] which did not obtain the right to hold an annual fair until 1200,

[53] *Ibid.*, p. 243.
[54] Derville, *Saint-Omer*, pp. 73–5; A. Derville, 'De Godric de Finchale à Guillaume Cade, l'espace d'une révolution', in *Le marchand au moyen âge*, Reims, 1992 (Société des historiens médiévistes de l'enseignement supérieur public), pp. 35–47.
[55] H. Van Werveke, 'Der flandrische Eigenhandel', pp. 18–21 (pp. 53–5 of the reprint).
[56] *Ibid.*, pp. 13–14 (pp. 49–50 of the reprint).

they were seen mainly at the Flemish annual fairs, which by the end of the twelfth century had formed a cycle of four and, with Bruges, of five as of 1200:[57] Ypres (28 February to 29 March); Bruges (23 April to 22 May); Torhout (24 June to 24 July); Lille (15 August to 14 September) and Messines (1 October to 1 November).

Of these the annual fairs at Torhout and Messines existed even before the end of the eleventh century, Ypres as of 1127 and perhaps earlier, like Lille. By the later years of the twelfth century, their chain through western Flanders, from Lille to Bruges, gradually caused the importance of other, no less significant annual fairs, such as that of Ghent (mentioned from *c.* 1000 to 1199), Saint-Omer, Douai and Kortrijk, to dwindle and eventually they disappeared.

Conclusion

In concluding this overview we can say that there was an unmistakable connection between the political power of the bourgeoisie in the cities and their economic activity, first and foremost as merchants. The high point of this power, which was reflected in merchants' guilds, in sworn communes, in city aldermen elected from among the middle classes and in hanses, clearly came in the last quarter of the eleventh and the first half of the twelfth centuries. During the same period international trade also peaked with the export of industrially manufactured and high-quality luxury products, such as costly cloth and machined copper. This applies to the cities in the Meuse Valley as well, even if their economic burgeoning was less pronounced and the political power of the bourgeoisie more limited, as for example is apparent from the absence of sworn communes there before the end of the twelfth century and from the nonexistence of guilds and hanses at any stage. The economic burgeoning of these cities, with the exception of Dinant, came to a standstill in the middle of the twelfth century, not least because of growing competition from Cologne as a metalworking centre. The merchants from Flanders also felt the effect of competition, particularly at the commercial level, not only from Cologne but also and above all from the Italians. However, because the Flemish cities were in a strong position economically and especially industrially and were also much larger, the recession made little or no impact on Flanders compared with the cities of the Meuse Valley during the second half of the twelfth century. In the third quarter of the twelfth century, however, Count Philip of Alsace brought the large Flemish cities more firmly under the authority of the count, who was then

[57] Yamada, 'Le mouvement des foires en Flandre', pp. 773–89.

at the height of his power, imposing on them new, strict and fairly uniform *keuren* or statutes. The power and the political autonomy of the middle classes in the large cities, which in 1127/8 had even enabled them to remove the count who had been imposed on them and to appoint one of their own choice, had apparently become too great for Philip of Alsace's liking. His 'monarchical' reaction against the large cities mainly served to benefit a few smaller port towns along the coast which he himself had founded. After his death (1191) the Flemish bourgeoisie took revenge and was able to recover its political power in the cities. The growing enmity between France and England in the thirteenth century would, however, be detrimental to Flemish trade, for while politically dependent on France, Flanders was economically dependent on England.

The internal social, economic and politico-institutional development of the large towns between Somme and Meuse during the eleventh and twelfth centuries, which was closely linked to their commercial expansion over much of Europe, as this chapter describes, must in conclusion be examined in a broader comparative context so as to be able to show their specificity, individual or collective, in these areas compared to the other large towns in western and southern Europe. The rise of the cities in the eleventh and twelfth centuries may have been a general European phenomenon, yet the chronology and the forms of the social, economic and political organization within these towns give evidence of differences as well as similarities, and these differences sometimes bring to light more than a nuance and a specificity which can have deeper-lying causes.

One of the major causes was the historical background of the towns, their past and the effect of the past on tradition. Thus in most large Italian towns, bar Venice, continuity with the Roman past was highly significant because of the strong urban tradition which continued throughout the early Middle Ages. It not only explains the very large populations of the major Italian towns (data are only available for the late Middle Ages), which in a number of cities like Venice and Milan may even have surpassed that of the largest cities in Western Europe such as London, Ghent and perhaps even Paris,[58] but may also explain the considerable degree of personal freedom enjoyed by Italy's urban population, without its excluding social and class distinctions or certain obligations to the ruler of the city, initially very often a bishop. This urban tradition may also explain the fact that in Italy the aristocracy lived in the towns and, except

[58] Van Werveke, 'The Rise of the Towns', pp. 38–9; C. T. Smith, *An Historical Geography of Western Europe before 1800*, London, 1967, pp. 303–4. The figures in P. M. Hohenberg and L. H. Lees, *The Making of Urban Europe*, Cambridge, Mass. and London, 1995, p. 10, cannot be trusted.

in Venice, conducted trade there for which it raised the capital.[59] This was in sharp contrast to the towns in north-west Europe, where only the episcopal cities (which were mostly Roman in origin) had a tradition. Here clerics as well as *ministeriales* of the bishop lived, leading an aristocratic life but with no involvement in trade.[60] This they left to merchants, who in that capacity were perhaps originally also in the bishop's service and dependent on him. In these towns, however, they were fewer in number in the eleventh and twelfth centuries and less dynamic than the merchants in the towns that did not have this tradition and only later, at the end of the twelfth and in the early thirteenth centuries, did they manage to acquire the autonomy and freedom which the Flemish towns, for example, had obtained at the beginning of the twelfth century. In terms of content, the famous freedom charter which the merchants of Huy obtained from the bishop of Liège in 1066 is one of the very few exceptions to this.

The first merchants in the towns under consideration here were not, however, the constantly travelling adventurers with no fixed abode that Pirenne took them for; rather they were part of the original population of the settlement from which the town developed. The land they owned outright, or held at a fixed rent, had soared in value and, after parcelization and sub-letting, provided them with the capital they needed for trade. Only after the middle of the thirteenth century did they buy up land outside the town with the profit they had made from trade;[61] only then did they start to strive for the domination by the town of the surrounding countryside, the *contado* which the Italian aristocratic merchants had long controlled through the ownership of land there.

Another difference that existed from a social viewpoint between the towns of north-west Europe and southern Europe in the eleventh and twelfth centuries, and which we believe also had its roots in the weakness or even absence of a Roman tradition in the former group and the survival of that tradition in Italy and the southern half of France, has to do with the role of the oath in all kinds of urban social organizations in the northern towns and with the role of writing in the social and commercial life of the southern towns.

In the eleventh and twelfth centuries there were various sorts of merchant organizations in the towns in the western half of the area between Somme and Meuse, namely in the towns of the Scheldt Valley and along the North Sea coast in the county of Flanders. These organizations – guilds, hanses and communes – were more numerous and older than

[59] R. S. Lopez, 'Italien. Die Stadtwirtschaft vom 11. bis 14. Jh.', in H. Kellenbenz (ed.), *Handbuch der europäischen Wirtschafts- und Sozialgeschichte*, II, Stuttgart, 1980, pp. 453–5.
[60] Van Werveke, 'The Rise of the Towns', p. 19.   [61] *Ibid.*, pp. 21, 32.

those in the towns along the Meuse and they were characterized by the formal oath taken by their members. In the large Italian cities, on the other hand, where the word 'guild' and its concept were unknown, even early on there were forms of cooperation and of solidarity among merchants, less collective in orientation and based more on individual and written agreements, such as the 'commenda', apparent in Venice in the eleventh century and in the other large seaports in the twelfth century.[62] In the twelfth century there existed some organization of merchants from various Italian towns visiting the annual fairs in Champagne (*Universitas mercatorum Italiae nundinas Campaniae ac regni Franciae frequentantium*). This was not a hanse in the true sense, however, but rather a loose association comparable with the merely nominal 'Hanse of the XVII Towns' in our region and northern France, as discussed above.[63]

We know that in Italy many merchants were literate even before the year 1000, while in the towns of north-west Europe special instruction for laymen, and especially merchants, was not introduced until towards the end of the twelfth century.[64] Considering the important role played by the oath in social life in these northerly areas, it is, we believe, reasonable to suppose that this difference in the commercial sector resulted in forms of cooperation and solidarity based on the written word in Italy and on the oath in north-west Europe.

At first glance the existence of 'communes' both in Italy and in numerous towns between the Seine and the Rhine would seem to fit less well into this comparison than the existence and/or non-existence, on the one hand, of guilds and hanses and, on the other, of 'commenda' and related forms of commercial cooperation and solidarity in these areas. If one shares Susan Reynolds' view, there is scarcely any difference with regard to communes between the towns in Italy and the towns in the region between the Seine and the Rhine. In her opinion, the word 'commune' had no specific significance in Italy and was simply the standard word for any collective unit of local government that enjoyed a measure of autonomy[65] In Genoa in the early twelfth century, the word *compagna* was used to mean more or less the same thing. On the other hand, Reynolds[66] regarded it as misleading to use the words 'commune' and *conjuratio* interchangeably and to regard sworn associations as the basis on which the towns in the north

[62] Lopez, 'Italien. Die Stadtwirtschaft', pp. 456–7, 464–5.

[63] H. Pirenne, *Histoire économique et sociale du moyen âge* (1933), ed. H. Van Werveke, Paris, 1969, p. 82.

[64] H. Pirenne, 'L'instruction des marchands au moyen âge', *Annales d'Histoire Economique et Sociale* I (1929), pp. 13–28, reprinted in Pirenne, *Histoire économique de l'Occident médiéval*, pp. 551–70; Pirenne, *Histoire économique et sociale*, pp. 105–6.

[65] S. Reynolds, *Kingdoms and Communities in Western Europe 900–1300*, 2nd edn, Oxford, 1997, p. 170.   [66] *Ibid.*, p. 173.

established their collective liberties. Yet she cannot ignore explicit texts from northern France (Le Mans 1070, Cambrai 1077, Saint-Quentin 1081, Beauvais 1099, Noyon 1108)[67] and from the county of Flanders (Saint-Omer 1127) (to which we might also add the texts for other Flemish towns referred to in this chapter but which Reynolds does not cite) from which it is clear that these communes were sworn associations. We can agree with Reynolds that, except in a few of these towns, the communes were not the result of violent or revolutionary plots. Where they were, the communes had, she believed, been a 'small and temporary feature of the urban scene'.[68] Though this does in our view seem rather exaggerated, it is true to say, as this chapter has illustrated, that the communes in Flanders were not blessed with a long life. Apart from the commune in Saint-Omer which held out longest, Count Philip of Alsace did such a thorough job of abolishing them in all the large Flemish towns between 1168 and 1177 that Pirenne thought they had never existed there.

This action on the part of the count of Flanders brings us on to another specific characteristic of the Flemish towns. The liberties they had managed to secure up until then have often been compared to the freedom of the large Italian cities. In the fourteenth century in particular, when the Flemish towns, especially Ghent, took advantage of the weakness of the count to extend their powers – frequently using violence – over a large part of the countryside, they did at times resemble the urban republics in Italy.[69] But whereas the latter had established their authority over the *contado*, usually without violence, very early on and with lasting effect thanks to the urban aristocracy's ownership of land outside the town, for the Flemish towns this was a late phenomenon. Moreover, the freedom and political power which the Flemish towns enjoyed in certain periods and for some time were never as absolute as in the large Italian towns. After the Flemish towns had succeeded in ousting the anti-English count forced upon them by the French king and in imposing upon the king a count of their own choice (1128), they experienced great prosperity for about forty years and displayed considerable political power, not least through the communes.[70] Count Philip of Alsace curtailed this power very substantially between 1168 and 1177, but after his death (1191) the towns succeeded in regaining much of their autonomy. As the count's authority was now frail, the towns were able to retain that autonomy throughout the thirteenth century, till their temporary alliance with the count, after an initial victory over the French king in 1302, was defeated by the latter in 1305.[71]

[67] Van Werveke, 'The Rise of the Towns', p. 28.   [68] Reynolds, *Kingdoms*, p. 177.
[69] D. Nicholas, *Medieval Flanders*, London and New York, 1992, pp. 211–31.
[70] *Ibid.*, pp. 62–6, 119–23.   [71] *Ibid.*, pp. 132–5, 180–97.

On the other hand, our exposition in this chapter has shown that the autonomy of cathedral towns like Liège and Tournai (the latter under the direct authority of the French king from 1180), or of towns like Huy and Dinant, which were under the authority of the prince-bishopric of Liège, was never as great as that of the Flemish towns and only became so much later, from the end of the twelfth century onwards. This also applies to the cathedral towns along the Rhine, like Cologne, and to most of the towns in northern France.[72] Despite the survival of communes in the latter area, they were brought into the royal tax system under the firm rule of Philip II August, and the king maintained his influence in the city law courts through a representative. In England, finally, only London enjoyed autonomy comparable with that of the large towns in the north-west of the European continent from an early date (beginning of the twelfth century).[73]

There is no doubt that political factors such as those discussed briefly above were responsible for the degree of autonomy which the large towns managed to acquire in the eleventh and twelfth centuries. This even applies to Italy, where the struggle between the frequently absent emperor and the pope, who left some allied towns to their own devices, was largely responsible for the far-reaching autonomy or even independence the large towns to the north of Rome were able to acquire.[74] This, however, would not have been possible without economic power, which we will turn our attention to now.

Pirenne explained the early and numerous signs of an economic revival in the Italian towns, and Venice in particular, by the recovery of trade in the Mediterranean area during the tenth/early eleventh centuries, when Arab supremacy at sea came to an end. This explanation was of course based on Pirenne's 'Mahomet et Charlemagne' theory according to which the conquest of Spain by the Arabs at the beginning of the eighth century had made the Mediterranean Sea a 'lac musulman' from which all Western shipping traffic and trade were excluded. Apart from the fact that this latter statement was far too absolute, as Amalfi's trade with Byzantium, Antioch, Egypt and even Spain as early as the ninth century and through the tenth and eleventh centuries shows, according to Pirenne Venice's trade links with Byzantium from the middle of the tenth century, their trade colonies on the Dalmatian coast from around the year 1000, and the presence of merchants from Genoa on the Syrian coast as rivals of the already present Venetians *c.* 1065, immediately served as an 'excitation extérieure' for trade in north-west Europe. Because of that – and

---

[72] Van Werveke, 'The Rise of the Towns', pp. 22–4; Ennen, *Europäische Stadt*, pp. 122–31.
[73] Van Werveke, 'The Rise of the Towns', pp. 28–9; Reynolds, *Kingdoms*, pp. 180–1.
[74] G. Chittolini, 'Cities, "City-States", and Regional States in North-Central Italy', in Tilly and Blockmans (eds.), *Cities and the Rise of States*, pp. 29–36.

according to Pirenne only because of that – this trade was revived as international trade in the course of the eleventh century and for the first time since the end of the seventh century ('la renaissance du commerce').[75] As criticism of his proposition has since shown, Pirenne overlooked the internal dynamic of the agrarian society which had given new impetus to trade since Carolingian times at local and regional level, and also at interregional and even international level, if one takes into consideration the trade with Scandinavia.[76] Pirenne is, moreover, not very explicit or specific with regard to the route and the predominant direction the trade flow between Italy and north-west Europe followed initially, or about the merchants who conducted that trade. Were the Italians the first to visit north-west Europe and were they here before the Flemings, for example, were in Italy? Or did they meet from the outset, i.e. during the eleventh century – as must regularly have been the case in the twelfth century – in Champagne where, however, there were as yet no annual fairs of international significance? These are questions which must be asked, even though, because of the dearth of texts on the subject, we have no answers. There are two isolated facts dating from the beginning of the eleventh century which prove first the presence of transalpine and more specifically English merchants *c.* 1010/20 in Pavia,[77] and second of a *Robertus negociator* in Barcelona in 1009, whom some have wanted to believe was a Flemish cloth merchant from Saint-Omer, though this would have been very early.[78] Although the first explicit proof of regular trade traffic in cloth from north-west Europe to Italy, namely Genoa, in particular by merchants from Arras, dates from the end of the twelfth century, merchants 'from over the mountains' were selling cloth even in 1128, also in Genoa. Quite correctly, they were taken for Flemings.[79] A year earlier, in the spring of 1127, Italian merchants from Lombardy attended the fair in Ypres, and as that was an annual event their visit was probably not a one-off. The Flemish count bought a silver jug of particularly fine workmanship from them at that fair.[80] On the basis of this scanty information, it is difficult to speak of a priority as regards the presence of merchants of one of the two nationalities in the other country. Other information, too, like the presence of merchants from Cologne in

[75] Pirenne, *Villes du moyen âge*, pp. 303–431, esp. pp. 348, 360 of the reprint.
[76] Pirenne, *Histoire économique et sociale*, pp. 197–200 (critical note and bibliography by H. Van Werveke on the Mahomet-et-Charlemagne theory); Toubert, 'La part du grand domaine', pp. 82–6; Devroey, 'Courants et réseaux d'échange'; Verhulst, 'Grundherrschaftliche Aspekte'.   [77] See chapter 4, note 78.
[78] P. Wolff, 'Quidam homo nomine Roberto negociatore', *Le Moyen Age* 69 (1963), pp. 123–39; Ennen, *Europäische Stadt*, p. 89; Derville, *Saint-Omer*, pp. 62, 74–5, 117.
[79] R. Doehaerd, *Les relations commerciales entre Gênes, la Belgique et l'Outremont*, I, Brussels and Rome, 1941, pp. 82, 89.   [80] Ross (ed.), *Galbert of Bruges*, p. 124 and note 20.

Flanders shortly after the middle of the twelfth century,[81] while around the same period Ghent merchants sailed up the Rhine past Cologne to buy wine,[82] refutes a long-accepted proposition put forward by Van Werveke, one of Pirenne's foremost pupils, that till the end of the twelfth century trade from and to Flanders was conducted mainly, though not exclusively, by Flemish merchants.[83] The so-called 'active' Flemish trade, a concept introduced by Van Werveke with the connotation of a degree of exclusivity, probably does not mean that the Flemish towns had a real commercial advantage, certainly not over the Italians. Rather, the Flemish towns' great advantage and specificity in Europe before the thirteenth century consisted in the fact that they – and to a lesser extent also some towns on the Meuse, like Huy and Dinant, or on the Rhine, like Cologne – were industrial centres geared to export. This was what gave them their originality till the end of the twelfth century compared to the towns of northern Italy.[84] With the industrial silk centre of Lucca as the main exception, before the thirteenth century Italian towns were largely trading towns.[85] Their merchants brought with them to north-west Europe costly Eastern wares that were small in size and weight but of great value, such as spices and on some occasions also silk, silverware and gold. As return merchandise they probably took with them Flemish cloth, which had been made from English wool since the beginning of the twelfth century and was some of the finest in north-west Europe, and which made a useful return cargo in terms of weight and volume. Indeed, we should not lose sight of the fact that, till well into the thirteenth century, north-west Europe's trade with Italy was conducted over land using wagons and carts whose carrying capacity was 2 to 2.5 tons and 1 to 2 tons respectively.[86] This was much more expensive than transport by sea whereby bulk goods such as alum, cotton, plants for dyes, etc. could be brought in from the Mediterranean area from the late thirteenth century. Here, too, the Italians had the ascendancy over north-west Europe and it was not broken until the late Middle Ages.[87]

The advantages of the Italian towns, referred to by way of comparison in concluding our study about the social, political and economic charac-

---

[81] A. Verhulst, T. de Hemptinne and L. De Mey, 'Un tarif de tonlieu inconnu', pp. 160–1, 165–6.

[82] F. Irsigler, 'Köln und die Staufer im letzten Drittel des 12. Jahrhunderts', in W. Hartmann (ed.), *Europas Städte zwischen Zwang und Freiheit*, Regensburg, 1995, pp. 83–96.   [83] Van Werveke, ' Eigenhandel', pp. 45–9 of the reprint.

[84] Ennen, *Europäische Stadt*, p. 89.

[85] Lopez, 'Italien. Die Stadtwirtschaft', pp. 461–7; Ennen, *Europäische Stadt*, p. 88.

[86] R. Van Uytven, 'Landtransport durch Brabant im Mittelalter und im 16. Jahrhundert', in F. Burgard and A. Haverkamp (eds.), *Auf den Römerstrassen ins Mittelalter: Beiträge zur Verkehrsgeschichte zwischen Maas und Rhein*, Mainz, 1997, pp. 479–82.

[87] Lopez, 'Italien. Die Stadtwirtschaft', p. 462.

teristics of the towns between Somme and Meuse during the eleventh and twelfth centuries, were in the end outweighed, despite their larger populations, by the industrial capacity of the towns in the north-west of the European continent. It was really this capacity and the export trade that went hand-in-hand with it, that was able to generate the capital which, in the hands of Italian financiers operating in Flemish towns and in Flemish government service in the late Middle Ages,[88] made the great revolutions of the early modern period possible.

[88] Nicholas, *Medieval Flanders*, p. 300 (referring to the studies of R. De Roover).

6   Conclusion

As this book is made up of chapters which examine chronologically in detail the topographical, economic and social development of every town between Somme and Meuse which was important before the thirteenth century, it would seem appropriate as a general conclusion first to draw comparisons with eligible towns in other parts of Europe during the same period and to do so within a chronological overview of the broad outlines of this development as a whole. Hopefully this will make the specific characteristics of urbanization between Somme and Meuse during the early and high Middle Ages clearer than does the monographic treatment which has often had to be used in the different chapters. Secondly, by taking a long-term approach to the fundamental factors which determined the urban phenomenon in our region, we shall try to show why north-west Europe and more specifically the Low Countries as a whole continued to be one of the most urbanized areas in the world even after the Middle Ages.

As regards the late Roman period (fourth–fifth centuries) and the transition to the sixth–seventh centuries, the development between the Somme and the Meuse is not so very different from the development that took place along the Mosel and the Rhine or to the south of the Somme. The continuity between the places with more or less urban characteristics in the fourth–fifth centuries and the same places in the sixth–seventh centuries is weaker only between the Somme and the Meuse than in the other Romanized areas. In most cases this continuity was geographical at most and not functional at all, unless from an administrative and ecclesiastical viewpoint. The role of the bishops as administrators of an urban settlement, which was emphasized by Edith Ennen for the Rhineland among other places,[1] was a significant factor in providing a degree of continuity in Maastricht and in Huy on the River Meuse and in Tournai and Cambrai on the River Scheldt. This does not alter the fact that there was a shift or fragmentation in these centres of habitation and buildings,

---

[1] Ennen, *Europäische Stadt*, pp. 41–3.

as Maastricht clearly exemplifies and as there was in London, York, Tours, Metz, etc. It was the result of, or at least linked to, a certain ruralization of the city, as a fairly in-depth study of places like Metz has shown,[2] and which led to polyfocal settlement in the larger centres between Somme and Meuse such as Maastricht.

The new beginning of urban life that manifested itself in the course of and especially towards the end of the seventh century in some of the places dating from the Roman period under consideration here is not chiefly and directly attributable to economic factors, but rather to the rise of new political forces and to their territorial base in the vicinity of earlier administrative and religious centres. This is probably the explanation for the leading edge that Maastricht and Huy had over the centres in the west of the area under consideration here, which is proven partly by the monetary activity there. This advantage was very probably linked to the territorial power base of the forefathers of the Carolingians, the Pippinids, along this part of the River Meuse. An analogous development had started in Metz back at the end of the sixth century, when, in addition to the Church which had provided the continuity, the Merovingian king chose Metz as the regional capital and thus helped bring about a revival of urban life.[3] In this respect, even centres like Quentovic, Domburg (*Walichrum*) and Dorestat, on the maritime periphery of the kingdom, though undoubtedly of economic significance, nevertheless owed their importance as of the end of the seventh to into the ninth century to their special protection by royal power. This was also the case for some similar trading places in England (Hamwic) and in Scandinavia (Ribe, Haithabu, Birka, etc.).[4] With the exception perhaps of Maastricht and Huy, they were of limited importance to trade in the urban centres along the Meuse and the Scheldt.

In the ninth century the growing importance, not least economically, of a number of places along the Meuse – such as Maastricht and soon afterwards Liège too, and then also in the west of the area under consideration here, along the Scheldt (Ghent and Tournai) and more to the south (Arras) – is largely to be attributed to the burgeoning and wealth of abbeys and churches: St Servaas in Maastricht, St Bavo in Ghent, St Vaast in Arras and the cathedral chapter in Tournai, or the church on the grave of St Lambert in Liège. Even royal residences, such as Valenciennes, played that role. Small urban settlements emerged in their vicinity and, though they existed in a manorial context and were hierarchically

---

[2] G. Hallsall, 'Towns, Societies and Ideas: The Not-so-strange Case of Late Roman and Early Merovingian Metz', in N. Christie and S. T. Loseby (eds.), *Towns in Transition: Urban Evolution in Late Antiquity and the Early Middle Ages*, Aldershot, 1996, pp. 235–61.
[3] *Ibid.*   [4] Clarke and Ambrosiani, *Towns in the Viking Age*, pp. 11–23, esp. p. 23.

subordinate to the abbey or church, they nevertheless show evidence of commercial and industrial importance, as is clearly the case in Ghent and in Arras. What is more, in both these places there was also the beginning of autonomous urban life a short, yet significant, distance from the abbey. This happened a little earlier than along the Rhine, while there is some discussion as to whether a similar development in the south and south-east of England was or was not checked by militarization, as reflected in the construction of fortifications against the Danes, known as *burhs*, by King Alfred the Great at the end of the ninth century.[5]

And in the west of the area under consideration here, fortifications were erected (Bruges, Saint-Omer), abbeys fortified (Arras) and late-Roman walls repaired (Tournai) as defence against the Vikings – also chiefly Danes. The degree of destruction by the Vikings varied according to time and place, but, apart from exceptions such as Valenciennes, it did not interrupt the urban development that was under way to any great extent or for any length of time. Ghent is a case in point. This continuity gave the area between the Somme and the Meuse an advantage in terms of urban development over adjacent areas such as the Rhineland and England.

Two factors served to strengthen this advantage still further in the tenth century, especially in the western part of our area: the erection or ac-quisition of feudal castles by the count of Flanders, one of the earliest and strongest successors of the weak Carolingian dynasty, and the rapid disappearance of the Carolingian manorial system.

The feudal castle concentrated within its walls power, wealth and revenue in kind from the district for which it was the administrative and manorial centre, thereby serving as a magnet for the existing, small and non-agrarian communities in its neighbourhood which expanded topog-raphically in the direction of the castle (e.g. Ghent). Another small, non-agrarian community was often based in a fortified appendage of the castle, called *(Oud)burg(us)* and consisted of skilled manual workers (leather workers, arms makers, etc.) in the service of the lord of the castle. In a few cases (Bruges), it seems that this community served as the cradle of the city. In some respects this situation is comparable to the evolution of *burhs* to *boroughs* in England during the same tenth century,[6] to the *bourgs castraux* in France[7] and to the *Doppelburgen* to the east of the Rhine.[8] The difference, however, is that the latter did not become large cities, while in the cases we have studied, the city centre actually develop-ed *outside* the castle.

[5] S. Reynolds, *An Introduction to the History of English Medieval Towns*, Oxford, 1977, pp. 30–4.   [6] *Ibid.*
[7] G. Duby (ed.), *Histoire de la France urbaine*, II, *La ville médievale*, Paris, 1980, pp. 59–87.
[8] Ennen, *Europäische Stadt*, pp. 58–9.

This was possible partly because of mass immigration from the countryside which was hastened by the early disintegration (tenth century) of the manorial system in Flanders. In the eastern parts of the area we are concerned with here and to the east of the Rhine, this disintegration was a later phenomenon. Moreover, the power structures in the German Empire, including the system of bishops with secular power (Liège, Cologne, Mainz, etc.), were better preserved and for longer. Consequently, the creation of cities was also less spontaneous and it was led by kings and emperors who granted them market, toll and mintage rights.[9] Broadly speaking this situation can be compared to the *burhs* in England, to which the all-powerful king granted mintage and market rights, as a result of which they evolved into *boroughs*, i.e into actual (though usually small) towns.[10]

In our large Flemish cities, on the other hand, markets were established without the mediation of the count. They were, however, usually located at the foot of or directly opposite the castle, though outside it. Their location as well as their name (often *vismarkt* or fish market) still refer to their local and regional function at that time, which consisted partly of the sale of considerable quantities of supplies stored in the castle.

Later on, in the eleventh century, international trade was grafted onto these tenth-century, regional market functions. International trade became possible just as soon as these cities began to produce luxury products suitable for export (cloth, metal) on an industrial scale. So it is incorrect to say that the large cities with long-distance trade were the result of a 'revival of trade', as Pirenne believed. In fact, the reverse was true. The industrialization process in the cities was complete towards the end of the eleventh century. It had come about partly because of the transfer of age-old artisanal activities from the rural manors to the city following the disintegration of the manorial system and because of the application of new techniques in the city. Trade and industry were in the hands of the bourgeoisie, largely indigenous in origin, whose wealth enabled them to acquire great autonomy in Flanders. In the second half of the eleventh century, it was a *factual* autonomy, partly because of the formation of the guilds, which soon took on certain responsibilities in the city administration. Then, in most of the Flemish cities, this factual autonomy was embodied by the sworn communes in the first half of the twelfth century. In addition to the aldermen specially appointed for the city by the count, these sworn communes were initially recognized by him as city administrators. After the middle of the twelfth century, the communes were absorbed by the aldermen, who as a rule were

---

[9] *Ibid.*, pp. 65–6.   [10] Reynolds, *Introduction*, pp. 34–6; Ennen, *Europäische Stadt*, p. 74.

now chosen by the count from among the leading burghers of the city.

In terms of scale, the autonomy of the large Flemish cities – which Count Philip of Alsace clamped down on in the third quarter of the twelfth century by the imposition of *keuren* or statutes – is comparable only to the development that began in the large cities of northern Italy at the end of the eleventh century.[11] The Italians, who had appeared in Flanders as early as 1127, had in fact become the Flemish merchants' main rivals in the twelfth century. The merchants of Cologne succeeded in securing an important position in their city and in the foreign markets only after the middle of the twelfth century, the English, under Richard I and John Lackland, only at the end of the twelfth century[12] and similarly the French only under Philippe August and Louis VIII.[13]

We hope it is clear from the first part of this conclusion that the foundations of the medieval town as we know them in north-west Europe in the late Middle Ages, with their geographical, economic, social and political characteristics, were laid during the three crucial centuries which in other respects too (e.g. the rural landscape, the agricultural technique, the political structure, etc.) determined the face of late medieval and early modern Europe, namely the tenth, eleventh and twelfth centuries. Here we can go along with Pirenne, as in his proposition that it was the bourgeoisie that was responsible for this realization, for this creation of something totally new, mainly because wealth was concentrated in its hands. It is our belief that the concentration of wealth in the hands of certain social groups or classes was indeed – and this does not make us Marxist! – a fundamental factor in the historical development.

Until approximately the tenth century, wealth was concentrated in the hands of aristocracy and church. We must, we believe, look to the seventh and eighth centuries for the origin of this concentration, which came about not only through gifts of land made by the Merovingian kings and mayors of the palace to churches and abbeys or by granting *beneficia* to members of the aristocracy, but just as much – if not more – by increasing the total available wealth in the hands of Carolingian mayors of the palace and kings and of the church through the reorganization of their rural estates according to the new model of the classic bipartite manor. There is no doubt that the income from land ownership and the purchasing power of the upper classes rose as a result, albeit at the expense of the unfree and semi-free population of these manors.[14] Perhaps this increase explains the – usually commercial – circulation of rare and luxury products from the

---

[11] Ennen, *Europäische Stadt*, p. 140.   [12] Reynolds, *Introduction*, pp. 107–8.
[13] Van Werveke, 'The Rise of the Towns', pp. 24–30.
[14] C. Wickham, *Land and Power*, London, 1994, pp. 222–5.

end of the seventh century and during the eighth and the first quarter of the ninth centuries. This traffic and trade flow largely passed through trading places, the so-called 'emporia', situated along the continental coasts of the southern North Sea and the coasts of eastern and southern England, and which were under the protection and control of the king or were located in the vicinity of large abbeys or royal residences. They cannot be called towns as yet because of their ephemeral character, and in any case no important towns developed from them. Yet they provided the initial impetus for the development of real towns because, after their disappearance around the middle of the ninth century, new trading places emerged in other places nearby and these did continue to develop and become towns.

The conditions that enabled this to happen during the late ninth and the tenth centuries are linked, we believe, to the decline of the manorial economy in that period. Agents who had previously conducted trade on behalf of a king, bishop or abbey, but who were now free of personal ties, could capitalize on the know-how they had acquired and conduct trade for their own account.[15] To this end they settled in places favourably located along waterways and coasts, often not far from where they had previously operated. At the same time, the decline of the classic manorial system in the tenth and eleventh centuries loosened the tie with the manor of those who had lived and worked as unfree or semi-free peasants or craftsmen within this system. In particular, those who had worked as artisans on the manors could now emigrate to the town, where technical improvements in wool processing (horizontal handlooms, etc.) enabled production on an industrial scale through the division of labour. In our opinion it was largely thanks to this creation of an urban industry that the most dynamic towns in the eleventh and twelfth centuries, which were mostly located in Flanders, remained important in the late Middle Ages. This did not prevent the tertiary sector gradually growing in importance, as in Bruges, which reached the height of its prosperity and fame in the fourteenth century as the financial centre for world trade.[16] This trend was to continue all over the Low Countries with the rapid burgeoning of Antwerp in the late fifteenth and the sixteenth centuries as the successor of Bruges, followed by the urbanization of Holland, first with industrial centres such as Leiden, Haarlem, Gouda, etc., and later, especially after the fall of Antwerp, with the financial centre Amsterdam which, like Holland in general, owed its prosperity in the seventeenth century to the mass influx of hundreds of thousands of immigrants from the southern

[15] Toubert, 'La part du grand domaine', pp. 82–6; Irsigler, 'Grundherrschaft, Handel und Märkte', pp. 68–71; Verhulst, 'Grundherrschaftliche Aspekte', p. 164.
[16] Nicholas, Medieval Flanders, pp. 295–305, 384–91.

Netherlands when the territory was retaken by Spain.[17] These immigrants were mainly literate and skilled craftsmen from the large but also from the smaller Flemish and Brabantine towns. As a result, urbanization in Holland, where 44 percent of the population lived in mostly smaller towns at the beginning of the sixteenth century, exceeded the level that urbanization in Flanders had reached back at the beginning of the fourteenth century (36 percent). Once again the urban vocation of the area around the delta of the large rivers, the Scheldt, Meuse and Rhine, was strengthened. A concentration of this sort, unique in Europe outside northern Italy, with roots going back to the tenth and eleventh centuries, calls for an explanation.

The most obvious explanation is of a geographical nature. The favourable geographical location of the areas around a delta in which three large rivers discharge via various branches and tributaries into the south of the North Sea, opposite the coasts of England and with a link to Scandinavia via inland waters and coastal navigation, is indeed notable and exceptional. Nowhere were communications so easy, thanks to navigable rivers and sandy coasts. Perhaps partly attracted by these factors, the population there had been particularly dense ever since the migration of the Germanic peoples and the constant flow of migrations from the Germanic areas during the subsequent centuries.[18] In terms of technique, the agriculture here had been one step ahead of the rest of Europe since the eighth/ninth centuries and exceptionally intensive since the twelfth century, so that, initially, large towns could be supplied. Indeed, it was not necessary to import grain from more distant areas until the late Middle Ages (except in the case of famine, as in 1316).[19]

It goes without saying, however, that so many large cities would not have grown had the political circumstances not been right. The most striking characteristic of the Low Countries in this respect during the growth period of the towns, from the tenth to the thirteenth centuries, was political fragmentation in a number of territorial principalities. In the strongest of these principalities, namely in the county of Flanders, the substantial power of the count could prevent the intrusion of noble or ecclesiastical feudal lords into the towns. Only with the Burgundian

[17] J. De Vries, *European Urbanization 1500–1800*, Cambridge, Mass., 1984, p. 81; W. Prevenier and W. Blockmans, *The Burgundian Netherlands*, Cambridge, Mass., 1986, p. 29; W. Blockmans, 'The Economic Expansion of Holland and Zeeland in the 14th–16th Centuries', in Aerts *et al.* (eds.), *Studia historica oeconomica*, pp. 43–4.

[18] Nicholas, 'Structures du peuplement'.

[19] A. Verhulst, *Précis d'histoire rurale de la Belgique*, Brussels, 1990, pp. 64–72; E. Thoen, 'The Count, the Countryside and the Economic Development of the Towns in Flanders from the 11th to the 13th Century', in Aerts *et al.* (eds.), *Studia historica oeconomica*, pp. 259–78; W. C. Jordan, *The Great Famine*, Princeton, 1996, pp. 158–62.

unification of the principalities in the Low Countries in the first half of the fifteenth century did a less favourable political and economic climate come about, especially in Flanders, as a result of the centralization and taxation that came with a unified state apparatus, exercising closer political control and imposing a heavier financial burden on the towns. In fact, from the late fifteenth century the Brabantine towns, first and foremost Antwerp, but also Mechelen and finally Brussels, were to enjoy the support of the Burgundian dukes, often at the expense of the older Flemish towns.[20] Antwerp's prosperity as the centre of world trade during the first half of the sixteenth century is well known. With it there dawned a new era in the urban history of the Low Countries.

[20] W. Blockmans, 'Voracious States and Obstructing Cities: An Aspect of State Formation in Preindustrial Europe', in Tilly and Blockmans (eds.), *Cities and the Rise of States*, pp. 218–50.

Bibliography

Aerts, E., B. Henau, P. Janssens and R. Van Uytven (eds.), *Studia historica oeconomica: liber amicorum Herman Van der Wee*, Leuven, 1993.

Amand, M., 'Les origines de Tournai. Le point de vue de l'archéologue', in *La genèse et les premiers siècles des villes médiévales dans les Pays-Bas méridionaux*, Brussels, 1990 (Crédit Communal, Collection Histoire in-8°, no. 83), pp. 169–202.

Berghaus, P., 'Wirtschaft, Handel und Verkehr der Merowingerzeit im Licht numismatischer Quellen', in K. Düwel, H. Jankuhn, H. Siems and D. Timpe (eds.), *Untersuchungen zu Handel und Verkehr der vor- und frühgeschichtlichen Zeit in Mittel- und Nordeuropa*, III, *Der Handel des frühen Mittelalters*, Göttingen, 1985 (Abhandlungen der Akademie der Wissenschaften in Göttingen, Philologisch-Historische Klasse, 3rd Series, no. 150), pp. 193–213.

Berings, G., *Landschap, geschiedenis en archeologie in het Oudenaardse*, Oudenaarde, 1989.

Besteman, J. C., J. M. Bos and H. A. Heidinga, *Mediaeval Archaeology in the Netherlands: Studies presented to H. H. van Regteren Altena*, Assen and Maastricht, 1990.

Blackburn, M., 'Money and Coinage', in R. McKitterick (ed.), *The New Cambridge Medieval History*, II, *c. 700–c. 900*, Cambridge, 1995, pp. 538–59.

Blieck, G., 'Les origines de Lille: bilan et perspectives archéologiques', in *La genèse et les premiers siècles des villes médiévales dans les Pays-Bas méridionaux*, Brussels, 1990 (Crédit Communal, Collection Histoire in-8°, no. 83), pp. 265–79.

Blockmans, F., *Het Gentsche Stadspatriciaat tot omstreeks 1302*, Antwerp and The Hague, 1938 (Rijksuniversiteit Gent. Werken uitgegeven door de Faculteit van de Wijsbegeerte en de Letteren 85).

Blockmans, W., 'The Economic Expansion of Holland and Zeeland in the 14th–16th Centuries', in E. Aerts *et al.* (eds.), *Studia historica oeconomica: liber amicorum Herman Van der Wee*, Leuven, 1993, pp. 41–58.

'Voracious States and Obstructing Cities: An Aspect of State Formation in Preindustrial Europe', in C. Tilly and W. Blockmans (eds.), *Cities and the Rise of States in Europe A.D. 1000 to 1800*, Boulder, Co. and Oxford, 1994, pp. 218–50.

Bonenfant, P., 'L'origine des villes brabançonnes et la "route" de Bruges à Cologne', *Revue Belge de Philologie et d'Histoire* 31 (1953), pp. 399–447.

'Aux origines de Malines', in *Dancwerc: Opstellen aangeboden aan Prof. Dr. D. Th. Enklaar*, Groningen, 1959, pp. 96–108.

Brühl, C., *Palatium und Civitas*, I, *Gallien*, Cologne and Vienna, 1975.

Brühl, C., and C. Violante, *Die 'Honorantie Civitatis Papie': Transkription, Edition, Kommentar*, Cologne, 1983.

Brulet, R., 'Le Litus Saxonicum continental', in V. A. Maxfield and M. J. Dobson (eds.), *Roman Frontier Studies 1989*, Exeter 1991, pp. 155–69.

'Réflexions sur la recherche archéologique à Tournai', in *La genèse et les premiers siècles des villes médiévales dans les Pays-Bas méridionaux*, Brussels, 1990 (Crédit Communal, Collection Histoire in−8°, no. 83), pp. 203–10.

Bullough, D. A., 'Urban Change in Early Medieval Italy: The Example of Pavia', *Papers of the British School Rome* 34 (1966), pp. 82–130.

Caffiaux, H., *Mémoire sur la charte de la frairie de la halle basse de Valenciennes (XIe et XIIe siècles)*, Paris, 1877 (Mémoires de la Société Nationale d'Antiquaires de France 38), reprinted in C. Faider (ed.), *Coutumes du pays et comté de Hainaut*, III, Brussels, 1878, pp. 311–25.

Callebaut, D., 'Résidences fortifiées et centres administratifs dans la vallée de l'Escaut', in P. Demolon, H. Galinié and F. Verhaeghe (eds.), *Archéologie des villes dans le Nord-Ouest de l'Europe (VIIe-XIIIe siècle)*, Douai, 1994, pp. 93–112.

Chittolini, G., 'Cities, "City-States" and Regional States in North-Central Italy', in C. Tilly and W. Blockmans, *Cities and the Rise of States in Europe A.D. 1000 to 1800*, Boulder, Co. and Oxford, 1994, pp. 28–43.

Clarke, H. and B. Ambrosiani, *Towns in the Viking Age*, revised edn, London, 1995.

Claude, D., *Untersuchungen zu Handel und Verkehr der vor- und frühgeschichtlichen Zeit in Mittel- und Nordeuropa*, II, *Der Handel im westlichen Mittelmeer während des Frühmittelalters*, Göttingen, 1985 (Abhandlungen der Akademie der Wissenschaften in Göttingen, Philologisch-historische Klasse, 3rd Series, no. 144).

Coornaert, E., 'Les ghildes médiévales', *Revue Historique* 199 (1948), pp. 22–55 and 208–43.

Dasnoy, A., 'Les origines romaines et mérovingiennes', in A. Dasnoy, A. Dierkens and G. Despy et al. (eds.), *Namur: le site, les hommes, de l'époque romaine au XVIIIe siècle*, Brussels, 1988 (Crédit Communal, Collection Histoire in −4°, no. 15), pp. 9–32.

Dasnoy, A., A. Dierkens, G. Despy et al. (eds.), *Namur: le site, les hommes, de l'époque romaine au XVIIIe siècle*, Brussels, 1988 (Crédit Communal, Collection Histoire in−4°, no. 15).

Decavele, J. (ed.), *Ghent: In Defence of a Rebellious City*, Antwerp, 1989.

Declercq, G., 'Oorsprong en vroegste ontwikkeling van de burcht van Brugge (9e–12e eeuw)' (with a summary in English), in H. De Witte (ed.), *De Brugse Burg*, Bruges, 1991, pp. 15–45.

Deisser-Nagels, F., 'Valenciennes. Ville carolingienne', *Le Moyen Age* 68 (1962), pp. 51–90.

Delmaire, B., *Le diocèse d'Arras de 1093 au milieu du XIVe siècle*, 2 vols. Arras, 1994.

Demolon, P., H. Galinié and F. Verhaeghe (eds.), *Archéologie des villes dans le Nord-Ouest de l' Europe (VIIe–XIIIe siècle)*, Douai, 1994.

Demolon, P. and E. Louis, 'Naissance d'une cité médiévale flamande. L'exemple de Douai', in P. Demolon, H. Galinié and F. Verhaeghe (eds.), *Archéologie des villes dans le Nord-Ouest de l'Europe (VIIe–XIIIe siècle)*, Douai, 1994, pp. 47–58.

Derville, A., 'Le problème des origines de Lille', in *Economies et sociétés au moyen âge: mélanges E. Perroy*, Paris, 1972, pp. 65–78.

'Trois siècles décisifs (XIe–XIIIe siècles)', in L. Trenard (ed.), *Histoire d'une métropole: Lille–Roubaix–Tourcoing*, Toulouse, 1977, pp. 83–131.

'Le grenier des Pays-Bas médiévaux', *Revue du Nord* 69 (1987), pp. 267–90.

'La genèse et les premiers siècles de Lille', in *La genèse et les premiers siècles des villes médiévales dans les Pays-Bas méridionaux*, Brussels, 1990 (Crédit Communal, Collection Histoire in–8°, no. 83), pp. 247–63.

'De Godric de Finchale à Guillaume Cade, l'espace d'une révolution', in *Le marchand au moyen âge*, Reims (Société des historiens médiévistes de l'enseignement supérieur public), 1992, pp. 35–47.

Saint-Omer des origines au début du XIVe siècle, Lille, 1995.

Despriet, P., *2000 jaar Kortrijk*, Kortrijk, 1990.

Despy, G., 'Note sur le "portus" de Dinant au IXe et Xe siècles', in *Miscellanea mediaevalia in memoriam J. F. Niermeyer*, Groningen, 1967, pp. 61–9.

'Villes et campagnes aux IXe et Xe siècles: l'exemple du pays mosan', *Revue du Nord* 50 (1968), pp. 145–68.

'La genèse d'une ville', in J. Stengers (ed.), *Bruxelles: croissance d'une capitale*, Antwerp, 1979, pp. 28–37.

'L'agglomération urbaine pendant le haut moyen âge', in A. Dasnoy, A. Dierkens and G. Despy *et al.* (eds.), *Namur: le site, les hommes, de l'époque romaine au XVIIIe siècle*, Brussels, 1988 (Crédit Communal, Collection Histoire in –4°, no. 15), pp. 63–78.

'Un dossier mystérieux: les origines de Bruxelles', *Académie Royale de Belgique: Bulletin de la Classe des Lettres*, 6th Series, VIII, 1–6 (1997), pp. 241–303.

Despy, G. and C. Billen, 'Les marchands mosans aux foires de Cologne pendant le XIIe siècle', *Acta Historica Bruxellensia* 3 (1974), pp. 31–61.

De Vries, D., 'The Early History of Aardenburg to 1200', *Berichten van de Rijksdienst voor het Oudheidkundig Bodemonderzoek*, Amersfoort, 18 (1968), pp. 227–60.

De Vries, J., *European Urbanization 1500–1800*, Cambridge, Mass., 1984.

Devroey, J. P., *Le polyptyque et les listes de biens de l'abbaye Saint-Pierre de Lobbes (IXe–XIe siècles)*, Brussels, 1986.

'Courants et réseaux d'échange dans l'économie franque entre Loire et Rhin', in *Mercati e mercanti nell'alto medioevo*, Spoleto, 1993 (Settimane di studio del Centro italiano di studi sull'alto medioevo 40), pp. 327–89.

Devroey, J. P. and C. Zoller, 'Villes, campagnes, croissance agraire dans le pays mosan avant l'an mil', in J.-M. Duvosquel and A. Dierkens (eds.), *Villes et campagnes au moyen âge: mélanges Georges Despy*, Liège, 1991, pp. 223–60.

De Witte, H., 'La fortification de Bruges. Les fouilles de 1987–1989 au "Burg" de Bruges', in P. Demolon, H. Galinié and F. Verhaeghe (eds.), *Archéologie des villes dans le Nord-Ouest de l'Europe (VIIe–XIIIe siècle)*, Douai, 1994, pp. 83–91.

De Witte, H. (ed.), *De Brugse Burg*, Bruges, 1991.

D'Haenens, A., *Les invasions normandes en Belgique au IXe siècle*, Leuven, 1967.

Dhondt, J., 'L'essor urbain entre Meuse et Mer du Nord à l'époque mérovin-gienne', in *Studi in onore di A. Sapori*, Milan, 1957, pp. 57–78.

'Les problèmes de Quentovic', in *Studi in onore di Amintore Fanfani*, I, Milan, 1962, pp. 181–248.

Dierkens, A., 'La ville de Huy avant l'an mil', in *La genèse et les premiers siècles des villes médiévales dans les Pays-Bas méridionaux*, Brussels, 1990 (Crédit Communal, Collection Histoire in−8°, no. 83), pp. 391–409.

Diestelkamp, B., 'Zusammenfassung der Referat- und Diskussionsbeiträge', in K. Flink and W. Janssen (eds.), *Grundherrschaft und Stadtentstehung am Niederrhein*, Kleve, 1989, pp. 176–83.

Doehaerd, R., *Les relations commerciales entre Gênes, la Belgique et l'Outremont*, 3 vols., Brussels and Rome, 1941–52.

Duby, G. (ed.), *Histoire de la France urbaine*, II, *La ville médievale*, Paris, 1980.

Dury, C., 'Les ponts de Tournai des origines à la fin du XVIIe siècle', in F. Thomas and J. Nazet (eds.), *Tournai: une ville, un fleuve (XVIe–XVIIe siècle)*, Brussels, 1995, pp. 117–41.

Duvosquel, J.-M., 'Les routes d'Ypres à Lille et le passage de la Lys au moyen âge ou de l'économie domaniale aux foires de Flandre', in E. Aerts *et al.* (eds.), *Studia historica oeconomica: liber amicorum Herman Van der Wee*, Leuven, 1993, pp. 100–6.

Endrei, W., *L'évolution du filage et du tissage du moyen âge à la révolution industrielle*, Paris and The Hague, 1968.

Ennen, E., *Die europäische Stadt des Mittelalters*, Göttingen, 4th edn, 1987.

Espinas, G. and H. Pirenne, 'Les coutumes de la gilde marchande de Saint-Omer', *Le Moyen Age* 14 (1901), pp. 189–96.

Fanchamps, M.-L., 'Etude sur les tonlieux de la Meuse Moyenne du VIIe au milieu du XIVe siècle', *Le Moyen Age* 70 (1964), pp. 205–64.

Gaier-Lhoest, J., *L'évolution topographique de la ville de Dinant au moyen âge*, Brussels, 1964 (Crédit Communal, Collection Histoire, in−8°, no. 4).

Ganshof, F. L., 'Les origines de la Flandre Impériale', *Annales de la Société d'Archéologie de Bruxelles* 46 (1942–3), pp. 99–137.

Etudes sur le développement des villes entre Loire et Rhin au moyen âge, Paris, 1943.

'Note sur le "Praeceptum Negotiatorum" de Louis le Pieux', in *Studi in onore di Armando Sapori*, I, Milan, 1956, pp. 92–112.

'A propos du tonlieu à l'époque carolingienne', in *La citta nell'alto medioevo*, Spoleto, 1959 (Settimane di studio del Centro italiano di studi sull'alto medioevo, 6), pp. 485–508; extended version in Dutch: *Het tolwezen in het Frankisch rijk onder de Karolingen*, Brussels, 1959 (Mededelingen van de Koninklijke Vlaamse Academie voor Wetenschappen. Klasse der Letteren 21 (1959), no. 1).

'A propos du tonlieu sous les Mérovingiens', in *Studi in onore di Amintore Fanfani*, I, Milan, 1962, pp. 293–315.

'Note sur une charte de Thierry d'Alsace, comte de Flandre, intéressant la propriété foncière à Saint-Omer', in H. Aubin, E. Ennen, H. Kellenbenz *et al.*, *Beiträge zur Wirtschafts- und Stadtgeschichte: Festschrift für Hektor Ammann*, Wiesbaden, 1965, pp. 84–96.

'Note sur une charte de Baudouin V, comte de Flandre, pour Saint-Pierre de Lille', in *Mélanges offerts à René Crozet à l'occasion de son soixante-dixième anniversaire*, Poitiers, 1966, pp. 293–306.

Godding, P. and J. Pycke, 'La paix de Valenciennes de 1114. Commentaire et édition critique', *Bulletin de la Commission pour la Publication des Anciennes Lois et Ordonnances de Belgique* 29 (1971), pp. 1–142.

Grierson, P., 'Commerce in the Dark Ages: A Critique of the Evidence', *Transactions of the Royal Historical Society*, 5th Series, 9 (1959), pp. 123–40.

Grierson, P. and M. Blackburn, *Medieval European Coinage*, I. *The Early Middle Ages, 5th–10th Centuries*, Cambridge, 1986.

Hallsall, G., 'Towns, Societies and Ideas: The Not-so-strange Case of Late Roman and Early Merovingian Metz', in N. Christie and S. T. Loseby (eds.), *Towns in Transition: Urban Evolution in Late Antiquity and the Early Middle Ages*, Aldershot, 1996, pp. 235–61.

Helvétius, A.-M., *Abbayes, évêques et laïques: une politique du pouvoir en Hainaut au moyen âge (VIIe–XIe siècle)*, Brussels, 1994 (Crédit Communal. Collection Histoire in−8°, no. 92).

Henderikx, P. A., 'The Lower Delta of the Rhine and the Maas: Landscape and Habitation from the Roman Period to c. 1000', *Berichten van de Rijksdienst voor het Oudheidkundig Bodemonderzoek*, Amersfoort, 36 (1986), pp. 445–599.

'Walcheren van de 6e tot de 12e eeuw', in *Archief van het Koninklijk Zeeuws Genootschap der Wetenschappen*, Middelburg, 1993, pp. 113–56.

Hensel, W., 'Untersuchungen über die Anfänge der Städte in Polen', in H. Jankuhn, W. Schlesinger and H. Steuer (eds.), *Vor- und Frühformen der europäischen Stadt im Mittelalter*, 2 vols., Göttingen, 1975, II (Abhandlungen der Akademie der Wissenschaften in Göttingen, Philologisch-Historische Klasse, 3rd Series, no. 83–4), pp. 176–89.

Hess, W., 'Zoll, Markt und Münze im 11. Jh. Der älteste Koblenzer Zolltarif im Lichte numismatischer Quellen', in H. Beumann (ed.), *Historische Forschungen für W. Schlesinger*, Cologne, 1974, pp. 170–93.

Hill, D. 'The Siting of the Early Medieval Port of Quentovic', in *Rotterdam Papers* 7, Rotterdam, 1992, pp. 17–23.

Hill, D., D. Barrett, K. Maude *et al.*, 'Quentovic defined', *Antiquity* 64 (1990), pp. 51–8.

Hodges, R., *Dark Age Economics: The Origins of Towns and Trade AD 600–1000*, London, 1982.

'North Sea Trade before the Vikings', in K. Biddick (ed.), *Archaeological Approaches to Medieval Europe*, Kalamazoo, 1984 (Studies in Medieval Culture 18, Western Michigan University), pp. 192–201.

Hoebeke, M., 'Oudenaarde', in *Villes belges en relief*, Brussels, 1965 (Crédit Communal, Collection Histoire in−4°, no. 1), pp. 263–94.

Hohenberg, P. M. and L. H. Lees, *The Making of Urban Europe 1000–1994*, Cambridge, Mass. and London, 1995.

Installé, H., *Mechelen* (Historische Stedenatlas van België, ed. A. Verhulst), Brussels, 1997.

Irsigler, F., 'Grundherrschaft, Handel und Märkte zwischen Maas und Rhein im frühen und hohen Mittelalter', in K. Flink and W. Janssen (eds.), *Grundherrschaft und Stadtentstehung am Niederrhein*, Kleve, 1989, pp. 52–78.

'Köln und die Staufer im letzten Drittel des 12. Jahrhunderts', in W. Hartmann (ed.), *Europas Städte zwischen Zwang und Freiheit*, Regensburg, 1995, pp. 83–96.

Jankuhn, H., 'Die frühmittelalterlichen Seehandelsplätze im Nord- und Ostseeraum', in T. Mayer (ed.), *Studien zu den Anfängen des europäischen Städtewesens*, Lindau and Konstanz, 1958 (Vorträge und Forschungen 4), pp. 451–98.

Jankuhn, H., W. Schlesinger and H. Steuer (eds.), *Vor- und Frühformen der europäischen Stadt im Mittelalter*, 2 vols., Göttingen, 1975 (Abhandlungen der Akademie der Wissenschaften in Göttingen, Philologisch-Historische Klasse, 3rd Series, nos. 83–4).

Janssen, H. P. H., 'Handel en Nijverheid 1000–1300', in D. P. Blok, W. Prevenier *et al.* (eds.), *Algemene Geschiedenis der Nederlanden*, II, Haarlem, 1982, pp. 148–86.

Johanek, P., 'Der "Aussenhandel" des Frankenreiches der Merowingerzeit nach Norden und Osten im Spiegel der Schriftquellen', in K. Düwel, H. Jankuhn, H. Siems and D. Timpe (eds.), *Untersuchungen zu Handel und Verkehr der vor- und frühgeschichtlichen Zeit in Mittel- und Nordeuropa*, III, *Der Handel des frühen Mittelalters*, Göttingen, 1985 (Abhandlungen der Akademie der Wissenschaften in Göttingen, Philologisch-Historische Klasse, 3rd Series, no. 150), pp. 214–54.

'Der fränkische Handel der Karolingerzeit im Spiegel der Schriftquellen', in K. Düwel, H. Jankuhn, H. Siems and D. Timpe (eds.), *Untersuchungen zu Handel und Verkehr der vor- und frühgeschichtlichen Zeit in Mittel- und Nordeuropa*, IV, *Der Handel der Karolinger und Wikingerzeit*, Göttingen, 1987 (Abhandlungen der Akademie der Wissenschaften in Göttingen, Philologisch-Historische Klasse, 3rd Series, no. 156), pp. 7–68.

Jordan, W. C., *The Great Famine*, Princeton, 1996.

Joris, A., *La ville de Huy au moyen âge*, Paris, 1959.

'A propos de "burgus" à Huy et à Namur', in *Die Stadt in der europäischen geschichte: Festschrift Edith Ennen*, Bonn, 1972, pp. 192–9.

Keene, D., *Survey of Medieval Winchester*, Oxford, 1985.

'The Textile Industry', in M. Biddle (ed.), *Object and Economy in Medieval Winchester*, Oxford, 1990, pp. 200–14.

'London in the Early Middle Ages 600–1300', *London Journal* 20–2 (1995), pp. 9–21.

Kellenbenz, H., *Handbuch der europäischen Wirtschafts- und Sozialgeschichte*, II, Stuttgart, 1980.

Kéry, L., *Die Errichtung des Bistums Arras 1093/1094*, Sigmaringen, 1994.

Koch, A. C. F., *De rechterlijke organisatie van het graafschap Vlaanderen tot in de 13e eeuw*, Antwerp and Amsterdam, 1951.

'Grenzverhältnisse an der Niederschelde vornehmlich im 10. Jahrhundert',

Rheinische Vierteljahrsblätter 21 (1956), pp. 182–218.

'Phasen in der Entstehung von Kaufmannsniederlassungen zwischen Maas und Nordsee in der Karolingerzeit', in G. Droege (ed.), *Landschaft und Geschichte: Festschrift für Franz Petri*, Bonn, 1970, pp. 312–24.

Kölzer, T., 'Nochmals zum ältesten Koblenzer Zolltarif', in H. Mordek (ed.), *Festschrift für R. Kottje*, Frankfurt, 1992, pp. 291–310.

Kupper, J.-L., *Liège et l'église impériale, XIe–XIIe siècles*, Paris, 1981.

'Archéologie et histoire: aux origines de la cité de Liège (VIIIe–XIe siècle)', in *La genèse et les premiers siècles des villes médiévales dans les Pays-Bas méridionaux*, Brussels, 1990 (Crédit Communal, Collection Histoire in−8°, no. 83), pp. 377–89.

'Le village était devenu une cité', in J. Stiennon (ed.), *Histoire de Liège*, Toulouse, 1991, pp. 34–73.

'Notger de Liège revisité', *Cahiers de Clio* 124 (1995), pp. 5–16.

Lafaurie, J., 'Les monnaies émises à Cambrai aux VIe–IXe siècles', *Revue du Nord* 69 (1986), pp. 393–404.

Lebecq, S., *Marchands et navigateurs frisons du haut moyen âge*, 2 vols., Lille, 1983.

'La Neustrie et la mer', in H. Atsma (ed.), *La Neustrie: les pays au nord de la Loire de 650 à 850*, I, Sigmaringen, 1989 (Beihefte der Francia 16/1), pp. 405–40.

'Entre les invasions et le grand essor du XIe siècle: vrai ou faux départ de la croissance urbaine dans l'espace rhéno-mosan', in *Les petites villes en Lotharingie. Actes des 6e journées lotharingiennes*, Luxembourg, 1992 (Publications de la Section Historique de l'Institut G.-D. de Luxembourg 108), pp. 21–40.

'Quentovic: un état de la question', *Studien zur Sachsenforschung* 8 (1993), pp. 73–82.

'L'emporium proto-médiéval de Walcheren-Domburg: une mise en perspective', in J.-M. Duvosquel and E. Thoen (eds.), *Peasants and Townsmen in Medieval Europe: Studia in honorem Adriaan Verhulst*, Ghent, 1995, pp. 73–89.

Levison, W., 'Das Testament des Diakens Adalgisel-Grimo (634)', *Trierer Zeitschrift*, 7 (1932), pp. 69–85.

Liebermann, F., *Die Gesetze der Angelsachsen*, 3 vols., Halle, 1903–16.

Lohrmann, D., 'Entre Arras et Douai, les moulins de la Scarpe au XIe siècle et les détournements de la Satis', *Revue du Nord* 66 (1984), pp. 1023–50.

Lopez, R. S., 'Italien. Die Stadtwirtschaft vom 11. bis 14. Jh.', in H. Kellenbenz, *Handbuch der europäischen Wirtschafts- und Sozialgeschichte*, II, Stuttgart, 1980, pp. 451–70.

Lot, F. (ed.), *Hariulf: Chronique de l'abbaye de Saint-Riquier*, Paris, 1894.

Lottin, A. (ed.), *Histoire de Boulogne-sur-Mer*, Lille, 1983.

Loyn, H. R., *Anglo-Saxon England and the Norman Conquest*, London, 1962.

Maddens, N. (ed.), *De geschiedenis van Kortrijk*, Tielt, 1990.

Mertens, J., 'Oudenburg and the Northern Sector of the Continental Litus Saxonicum', in D. E. Johnston (ed.), *The Saxon Shore*, London, 1977 (CBA Report 18), pp. 51–62.

'La destinée des centres urbains gallo-romains à la lumière de l'archéologie et des textes', in *La genèse et les premiers siècles des villes médiévales dans les*

Pays-Bas méridionaux, Brussels, 1990 (Crédit Communal, Collection Histoire in−8°, no. 83), pp. 61–74.

Meyers, E. M., *Le droit coutumier de Cambrai*, 3 vols., Haarlem, 1955.

Milis, L., 'The Medieval City' in J. Decavele (ed.), *Ghent: In Defence of a Rebellious City*, Antwerp, 1989, pp. 61–79.

Muehlbacher, E. (ed.), *Diplomata Karolinorum*, I, MGH in−4°, Hannover, 1906.

Nicholas, D., 'Structures du peuplement, fonctions urbaines et formation du capital dans la Flandre médiévale', *Annales: Economies–Sociétés–Civilisations* 33 (1978), pp. 501–27.

Medieval Flanders, London and New York, 1992.

Niermeyer, J. F., *Mediae Latinitatis Lexicon Minus*, Leiden, 1976.

Nonn, U., *Pagus und Comitatus in Niederlotharingien: Untersuchungen zur politischen Raumgliederung im früheren Mittelalter*, Bonn, 1983.

Oexle, O. G., 'Gilden als soziale Gruppen in der Karolingerzeit', in H. Jankuhn, W. Janssen, R. Schmidt-Wiegand and H. Tiefenbach (eds.), *Das Handwerk in vor- und frühgeschichtlicher Zeit*, I, Göttingen, 1981 (Abhandlungen der Akademie der Wissenschaften in Göttingen, Philologisch-Historische Klasse, 3rd Series, no. 122), pp. 284–354.

'Die Kaufmannsgilde von Tiel', in H. Jankuhn and E. Ebel (eds.), *Untersuchungen zu Handel und Verkehr der vor- und frühgeschichtlichen Zeit in Mittel- und Nordeuropa*, VI, *Organisationsformen der Kaufmannsvereinigungen in der Spätantike und im frühen Mittelalter*, Göttingen, 1989 (Abhandlungen der Akademie der Wissenschaften in Göttingen, Philologisch-Historische Klasse, 3rd Series, no. 183), pp. 173–96.

Oost, T. and R. Van Uytven, 'Een historisch-archeologisch overzicht van het vroegste Antwerpen', in *La genèse et les premiers siècles des villes médiévales dans les Pays-Bas méridionaux*, Brussels, 1990 (Crédit Communal, Collection Histoire in−8°, no. 83), pp. 331–45.

Panhuysen, T., 'Wat weten we over de continuïteit van Maastricht?', in C. G. De Dijn (ed.), *Sint-Servatius, Bisschop van Tongeren-Maastricht: het vroegste christendom in het Maasland*, Borgloon and Rijkel, 1986, pp. 125–46.

Panhuysen, T. and P. H. Leupen, 'Maastricht in het eerste millennium', in *La genèse et les premiers siècles des villes médiévales dans les Pays-Bas méridionaux*, Brussels, 1990 (Crédit Communal, Collection Histoire in−8°, no. 83), pp. 411–49.

Patze, H. (ed.), *Die Burgen im deutschen Sprachraum: ihre rechts- und verfassungsgeschichtliche Bedeutung*, 2 vols., Sigmaringen, 1976 (Vorträge und Forschungen 19).

Petri, F., 'Die Anfänge des mittelalterlichen Städtewesens in den Niederlanden und dem angrenzenden Frankreich', in T. Mayer (ed.), *Studien zu den Anfängen des europäischen Städtewesens*, Lindau and Konstanz, 1958 (Vorträge und Forschungen 4), pp. 227–95.

'Merowingerzeitliche Voraussetzungen für die Entwicklung des Städtewesens zwischen Maas und Nordsee', *Bonner Jahrbücher* 158 (1958), pp. 233–45.

Pirenne, H., *Histoire de la constitution de la ville de Dinant au Moyen âge*, Ghent, 1889 (reprinted in H. Pirenne, *Les Villes et les institutions urbaines*, II, Paris and Brussels, 1939, pp. 1–94).

Les anciennes démocraties des Pays-Bas, Paris, 1910 (reprinted in H. Pirenne, *Les villes et les institutions urbaines*, I, Paris and Brussels, 1939, pp. 143–301).

'Le fisc royal de Tournai', in *Mélanges d'histoire offerts à Ferdinand Lot*, Paris, 1925, pp. 641–98 (reprinted in H. Pirenne, *Histoire économique de l'Occident médiéval*, [Bruges], 1951, pp. 83–9).

'La question des jurés dans les villes flamandes', *Revue Belge de Philologie et d'Histoire* 5 (1926), pp. 401–21 (reprinted in H. Pirenne, *Les villes et les institutions urbaines*, II, Paris and Brussels, 1939, pp. 201–18).

Medieval Cities: Their Origins and the Revival of Trade, Princeton, 1925 = *Les villes du moyen âge*, Brussels, 1927 (reprinted in H. Pirenne, *Les villes et les institutions urbaines*, I, Paris and Brussels, 1939, pp. 303–431).

'Le commerce du papyrus dans la Gaule mérovingienne', in *Comptes-rendus de l'Académie des Inscriptions et Belles-Lettres*, Paris, 1928 (reprinted in H. Pirenne, *Histoire économique de l'Occident médiéval*, [Bruges], 1951, pp. 90–100).

'L'instruction des marchands au moyen âge', *Annales d'Histoire Economique et Sociale*, 1 (1929), pp. 13–28 (reprinted in H. Pirenne, *Histoire économique de l'Occident médiéval*, [Bruges], 1951, pp. 551–70).

'Draps d'Ypres à Novgorod au commencement du XIIe siècle', *Revue Belge de Philologie et d'Histoire* 9 (1930), pp. 563–7 (reprinted in H. Pirenne, *Histoire économique de l'Occident médiéval*, [Bruges], 1951, pp. 571–4).

Histoire économique et sociale du moyen âge (1933), ed. H. Van Werveke, Paris, 1969.

Planitz, H., 'Kaufmannsgilde und städtische Eidgenossenschaft in niederfränkischen Städten im 11. u. 12. Jh.', *Zeitschrift für Rechtsgeschichte, Germanistische Abteilung* 60 (1940), pp. 1–116.

Platelle, H., 'Du "domaine de Valentinus" au comté de Valenciennes (début du XIe siècle)', in *La genèse et les premiers siècles des villes médiévales dans les Pays-Bas méridionaux*, Brussels, 1990 (Crédit Communal, Collection Histoire in−8°, no. 83), pp. 159–68.

Platelle, H. (ed.), *Histoire de Valenciennes*, Lille, 1982.

Pol, A., 'Les monétaires à Huy et Maastricht. Production et distribution des monnaies mérovingiennes mosanes', *Bulletin de l'Institut Archéologique Liégeois* 107 (1995), pp. 185–200.

Polyptyque de l'abbé Irminon de Saint-Germain-des-Prés ou dénombrement des manses, des serfs et des revenus de l'abbaye de Saint-Germain-des-Prés sous le règne de Charlemagne, publié avec des Prolégomènes, ed. B. Guérard, 3 vols., Paris, 1844.

Prevenier, W., 'La démographie des villes du comté de Flandre aux XIVe et XVe siècles', *Revue du Nord* 65 (1983), pp. 255–75.

Prevenier, W. and W. Blockmans, *The Burgundian Netherlands*, Cambridge, Mass., 1986.

Prevenier, W., J.-P. Sosson and M. Boone, 'Le réseau urbain en Flandre (XIIIe–XIXe siècle)', in *Le réseau urbain en Belgique dans une perspective historique (1350–1850). 15e Colloque international, Spa, 1990. Actes*, Brussels, 1992 (Crédit Communal, Collection Histoire in−8°, no. 86), pp. 157–200.

Pycke, J., 'Urbs fuerat quondam quod adhuc vestigia monstrant. Réflexions sur l'histoire de Tournai pendant le haut moyen âge (Ve–Xe siècle)', in *La genèse et les premiers siècles des villes médiévales dans les Pays-Bas méridionaux*, Brussels, 1990 (Crédit Communal, Collection Histoire in−8°, no. 83), pp. 211–33.

Reynolds, R. L., 'The Market for Northern Textiles in Genoa 1179–1200', *Revue Belge de Philologie et d'Histoire* 8 (1929), pp. 831–51.

'Merchants of Arras and the Overland Trade with Genoa', *Revue Belge de Philologie et d'Histoire* 9 (1930), pp. 495–533.

Reynolds, S., *An Introduction to the History of English Medieval Towns*, Oxford, 1977.

Kingdoms and Communities in Western Europe, 900–1300, 2d edn, Oxford, 1997.

Rolland, P., 'Les hommes de Sainte-Marie de Tournai', *Revue Belge de Philologie et d'Histoire* 3 (1924), pp. 233–50.

Les origines de la commune de Tournai, Brussels, 1931.

Rombaut, H., 'Mechelen: de vroegste ontwikkeling', in H. Installé (ed.), *Mechelen* (Historische Stedenatlas van België, ed. A. Verhulst), Brussels, 1997, pp. 11–22.

Ross, J. B. (ed.), *Galbert of Bruges, the Murder of Charles the Good, Count of Flanders*, New York, 1967.

Rouche, M., 'Topographie historique de Cambrai durant le haut moyen âge', *Revue du Nord* 58 (1976), pp. 339–47.

Rouche, M. (ed.), *Histoire de Douai*, Dunkirk, 1985.

Rousseau, F., *La Meuse et le pays mosan en Belgique: leur importance historique avant le XIIIe siècle*, Namur, 1930 (Annales de la Société archéologique de Namur 39).

Ryckaert, M., 'Les origines et l'histoire ancienne de Bruges: l'état de la question et quelques données nouvelles', in J.-M. Duvosquel and E. Thoen (eds.), *Peasants and Townsmen in Medieval Europe: studia in honorem Adriaan Verhulst*, Ghent, 1995, pp. 117–34.

Smith, C. T., *An Historical Geography of Western Europe before 1800*, London, 1967.

Steuer, H., 'Die Handelsstätten des frühen Mittelalters im Nord- und Ostsee-Raum', in *La genèse et les premiers siècles des villes médiévales dans les Pays-Bas méridionaux*, Brussels, 1990 (Crédit Communal, Collection Histoire in−8°, no. 83), pp. 75–116.

Stiennon, J. (ed.), *Histoire de Liège*, Toulouse, 1991.

Streich, G., *Burg und Kirche während des deutschen Mittelalters: Untersuchungen zur Sakraltopographie von Pfalzen, Burgen und Herrensitzen*, 2 vols., Sigmaringen, 1984 (Vorträge und Forschungen 29).

Termote, J. (ed.), *Tussen Land en Zee: Het duingebied van Nieuwpoort tot De Panne*, Tielt, 1992.

Tessier, G., *Recueil des actes de Charles II le Chauve, roi de France*, 2 vols., Paris, 1955.

Theuws, F. C. W. J., 'Centre and Periphery in Northern Austrasia (6th–8th Centuries)', in J. C. Besteman, J. M. Bos and H. A. Heidinga (eds.), *Medieval Archaeology in the Netherlands: Studies presented to H. H. van Regteren Altena*, Assen and Maastricht, 1990, pp. 41–69.

Thoen, E., 'The Count, the Countryside and the Economic Development of the Towns in Flanders from the 11th to the 13th Century', in E. Aerts *et al.* (eds.), *Studia historica oeconomica: liber amicorum Herman Van der Wee*, Leuven, 1993, pp. 259–78.

Thoen, H., *De Belgische kustvlakte in de romeinse tijd*, Brussels, 1978.

Tilly, C. and W. Blockmans (eds.), *Cities and the Rise of States in Europe A.D. 1000 to 1800*, Boulder, Co. and Oxford, 1994.

Tissen, B., 'Het oudste toltarief van Koblenz', in P. Bange and P. M. J. C. de Kort (eds.), *Mélanges Prof. dr. A. Weiler*, Nijmegen, 1989, pp. 180–222.

Toubert, P. 'La part du grand domaine dans le décollage économique de l'Occident (VIIIe–Xe siècles)', in *La croissance agricole du haut moyen âge*, Auch, 1990, pp. 53–86 (Flaran 10, 1988).

Trenard, L. (ed.), *Histoire de Cambrai*, Lille, 1982.

Van Bostraeten, H. C., *De nederzetting Sloten en de merovingische begraafplaats te Gent–Port Arthur*, Brussels, 1972 (Crédit Communal, Collection Histoire, in −8°, no. 25) (with a summary in French).

van Es, W. A., 'Dorestad centred', in J. C. Besteman, J. M. Bos and H. A. Heidinga (eds.), *Medieval Archaeology in the Netherlands*, Assen and Maastricht, 1990, pp. 151–82.

van Heeringen, R. M., P. Henderikx and A. Mars, *Vroeg-Middeleeuwse ringwalburgen in Zeeland*, Goes and Amersfoort, 1995.

Van Ommeren, H. R., 'Bronnen voor de geschiedenis van Maastricht (359–1204)', part I, *Publications de la Société Historique et Archéologique dans le Limbourg* 127 (1991), pp. 5–48.

Van Uytven, R., 'Landtransport durch Brabant im Mittelalter und im 16. Jahrhundert', in F. Burgard and A. Haverkamp (eds.), *Auf den Römerstrassen ins Mittelalter: Beiträge zur Verkehrgeschichte zwischen Maas und Rhein*, Mainz, 1997, pp. 471–99.

'Flämische Belfriede und südniederländische städtische Bauwerke im Mittelalter: Symbol und Mythos', in A. Haverkamp (ed.), *Information, Kommunikation und Selbstdarstellung in mittelalterlichen Gemeinden*, Munich, 1998, pp. 125–59.

Van Uytven, R. (ed.), *Leuven, de beste stad van Brabant*, I, *De geschiedenis van het stadsgewest Leuven tot omstreeks 1600*, Leuven, 1980.

Van Uytven, R. and H. Installé (eds.), *De Geschiedenis van Mechelen: Van Heerlijkheid tot Stadsgewest*, Tielt, 1991.

Van Werveke, H., 'Der flandrische Eigenhandel im Mittelalter', *Hansische Geschichtsblätter* 6 (1936), pp. 7–24 (reprinted in H. Van Werveke, *Miscellanea mediaevalia: Verspreide opstellen over economische en sociale geschiedenis van de Middeleeuwen*, Ghent, 1968, pp. 45–59).

'Essor et déclin de la Flandre', in *Studi in onore di Gino Luzatto*, Milan, 1949, pp. 152–60 (reprinted in H. Van Werveke, *Miscellanea mediaevalia*, Ghent, 1968, pp. 3–11).

'De steden. Ontstaan en eerste groei', in J. A. Van Houtte and J. F. Niermeyer *et al.* (eds.), *Algemene Geschiedenis der Nederlanden*, II, Utrecht and Antwerp, 1950, pp. 180–202.

'Industrial Growth in the Middle Ages. The Cloth Industry in Flanders',

Economic History Review 6 (1954), pp. 237–45 (reprinted in H. Van Werveke, *Miscellanea mediaevalia*, Ghent, 1968, pp. 381–91).

'Das Wesen der flandrischen Hansen', *Hansische Geschichtsblätter* 76 (1958), pp. 7–20 (reprinted in H. Van Werveke, *Miscellanea mediaevalia*, Ghent, 1968, pp. 88–103).

'The Rise of the Towns', in *The Cambridge Economic History of Europe*, III, Cambridge, 1963, pp. 3–41.

'Burgus': versterking of nederzetting?, Brussels, 1965 (with a summary in French) (Verhandelingen van de Koninklijke Vlaamse Academie voor Wetenschappen van België, Klasse der Letteren, XXVII, no. 59).

F. Vercauteren, *Etude sur les civitates de la Belgique Seconde*, Brussels, 1934.

'De wordingsgeschiedenis der Maassteden in de hoge Middeleeuwen', *Bijdragen en Mededelingen van het Historisch Genootschap te Utrecht* 71 (1957), pp. 12–28.

'Marchands et bourgeois dans le pays mosan aux XIe et XIIe siècles', in *Mélanges Felix Rousseau*, Brussels, 1958, pp. 655–72.

'La vie urbaine entre Meuse et Loire du VIe au IXe siècle', in *La città nell'alto medioevo*, Spoleto, 1959, pp. 453–84 (Settimane di studio del Centro italiano di studi sull'alto medioevo, 6).

'Tournai', in *Villes belges en reliëf*, Brussels, 1965, pp. 185–93.

'Un exemple de peuplement urbain au XIIe siècle. Le cas d'Arras', *Annales de la Faculté des Lettres et Sciences Humaines de Nice*, 9–10 (1969), pp. 15–27.

Vercauteren, F. (ed.), *Actes des comtes de Flandre 1071–1128*, Brussels, 1938.

Verhaeghe, F., 'Continuity and Change: Links between Medieval Towns and the Roman Substratum in Belgium', *Studia Varia Bruxellensia* 2 (1990), pp. 229–53.

Verhulst, A., 'Over de stichting en vroegste geschiedenis van de Sint-Pieters- en Sint-Baafs-abdijen te Gent', *Handelingen van de Maatschappij voor Geschiedenis en Oudheidkunde te Gent*, new series, 7 (1953), pp. 1–51.

'Les origines et l'histoire ancienne de la ville de Bruges (IXe–XIIe siècle)', *Le Moyen Age* 66 (1960), pp. 37–63 (reprinted in A. Verhulst, *Rural and Urban Aspects of Early Medieval Northwest Europe*, Aldershot, 1992, XIII).

'Initiative comtale et développement économique en Flandre au XIIe siècle', in *Miscellanea mediaevalia in memoriam J. F. Niermeyer*, Groningen, 1967, pp. 227–40.

'Die gräfliche Burgenverfassung in Flandern im Hochmittelalter', in H. Patze (ed.), *Die Burgen im deutschen Sprachraum: ihre rechts- und verfassungsgeschichtliche Bedeutung*, Sigmaringen, 1976 (Vorträge und Forschungen 19), pp. 267–82.

'An Aspect of the Question of Continuity between Antiquity and Middle Ages: The Origin of the Flemish Cities between the North Sea and the Scheldt', *Journal of Medieval History* 3 (1977), pp. 175–206 (reprinted in A. Verhulst, *Rural and Urban Aspects of Early Medieval Northwest Europe*, Aldershot, 1992, IX).

'The Origins of Towns in the Low Countries and the Pirenne Thesis', *Past and Present* 122 (1989), pp. 1–35 (reprinted in A. Verhulst, *Rural and Urban Aspects of Early Medieval Northwest Europe*, Aldershot, 1992, X).

Précis d'histoire rurale de la Belgique, Brussels, 1990.

'The Decline of Slavery and the Economic Expansion of the Early Middle Ages', *Past and Present* 133 (1991), pp. 195–203.

'The Origins and Early History of Antwerp', in A. Verhulst, *Rural and Urban Aspects of Early Medieval Northwest Europe*, Aldershot, 1992, XIV, pp. 1–33.

'The Alleged Poverty of the Flemish Rural Economy as Reflected in the Oldest Account of the Comital Domain, known as "Gros Brief" (A.D. 1187)', in E. Aerts *et al. Studia historica oeconomica: liber amicorum Herman Van der Wee*, Leuven, 1993, pp. 369–82.

'Grundherrschaftliche Aspekte bei der Entstehung der Städte Flanderns', in A. Verhulst and Y. Morimoto (eds.), *Economie rurale et économie urbaine au moyen âge*, Ghent and Fukuoka, 1994, pp. 157–64 (Centre belge d'histoire rurale, publication no. 108).

'The Origins and Early Development of Medieval Towns in Northern Europe (Bibliography and Criticism)', *Economic History Review* 47 (1994), pp. 362–73.

'Keulse handelaars in het Zwin tijdens de twaalfde eeuw en de vroegste ontwikkeling van de Vlaamse zeehavens', *Bijdragen tot de geschiedenis*, 81 (1998), pp. 351–8 (with a summary in English).

'Les origines de la ville d'Ypres', *Revue du Nord* 81 (1999), pp. 1–13.

'Sheep Breeding and Wool Production in pre-13th-Century Flanders and their Contribution to the Rise of Ypres, Ghent and Bruges as Centres of the Textile Industry', *Archeologie in Vlaanderen* (forthcoming).

Verhulst, A. (ed.), *Anfänge des Städtewesens an Schelde, Maas und Rhein bis zum Jahre 1000*, Cologne, Weimar and Vienna, 1996 (Städteforschung. Veröffentlichungen des Instituts für vergleichende Städtegeschichte in Münster, A/40).

Verhulst, A. and G. Declercq, 'Early Medieval Ghent between Two Abbeys and the Count's Castle', in J. Decavele (ed.), *Ghent: In Defence of a Rebellious City*, Antwerp, 1989, pp. 37–59 (reprinted in A. Verhulst, *Rural and Urban Aspects of Early Medieval Northwest Europe*, Aldershot, 1992, XII, pp. 1–50).

Verhulst, A., T. de Hemptinne and G. De Mey, 'Un tarif de tonlieu inconnu, institué par le comte de Flandre Thierry d'Alsace (1128–1168), pour le port de "Littersuerua", précurseur du port de Damme', *Bulletin de la Commission Royale d'Histoire* 164 (1998), pp. 143–72.

Verhulst, A. and Y. Morimoto (eds.), *Economie rurale et économie urbaine au moyen âge*, Ghent and Fukuoka, 1994 (Centre belge d'histoire rurale. Publication no. 108).

Verhulst, A. and J. Semmler, 'Les statuts d'Adalhard de Corbie de l'an 822', *Le Moyen Age* 68 (1962), pp. 91–123, 233–69.

Verlinden, C., 'Marchands ou tisserands? A propos des origines urbaines', *Annales: Economies–Sociétés–Civilisations* 27 (1972), pp. 396–406.

Vermeesch, A., *Essai sur les origines et la signification de la commune dans le Nord de la France (XIe et XIIe siècles)*, Heule, 1966.

Verriest, L., 'La Charité Saint Christophe et ses comptes au XIIIe siècle', *Bulletin de la Commission Royale d'Histoire* 73 (1904), pp. 143–268.

Wickham, C., *Land and Power*, London, 1994.

Wightman, E. M., *Gallia Belgica*, London, 1985.

Wolff, P., 'Quidam homo nomine Roberto negociatore', *Le Moyen Age* 69 (1963), pp. 123–39.

Wood, I., *The Merovingian North Sea*, Alingsås, 1983.

'Teutsind, Witlaic and the History of Merovingian *Precaria*', in W. Davies and P. Fouracre (eds.), *Property and Power in the Early Middle Ages*, Cambridge, 1995, pp. 31–4.

Yamada, M., 'Le mouvement des foires en Flandre avant 1200', in J.-M. Duvosquel and A. Dierkens (eds.), *Villes et campagnes au moyen âge: mélanges Georges Despy*, Liège, 1991, pp. 773–89.

Index of cities and towns

General index

Adalhard, abbot of Corbie Abbey 34,
  58
Alpertus of Metz, author 123
Amand, saint, missionary, bishop of
  Tongeren-Maastricht, 12, 24, 33,
  38–9, 57
  and Antwerp 39, 40
  and Ghent 12, 38
  and Tongeren-Maastricht 38
Arnulf I, Count of Flanders 88, 95, 97
Aubert, saint, bishop of Cambrai 35
aula, hall 101, 106
  and Ename 101
  and Lille (*aula comitis*) 106

Baldwin III, Count of Hainault
  and Valenciennes 127, 129
Baldwin V, Count of Flanders 101, 104,
  133
  and Lille 104
burgenses
  and Huy 73
  and Kortrijk 122
burg (us), Oud(e)burg, bourc(q), bourg
  and Arras (*vetus burgus, novus burgus*)
    54, 73, 77, 82–3, 117
  and Bruges (*Oudeburg*) 64–5,67, 73,
    77, 83, 91–2, 97, 112, 117, 121
  and Brussels (*Oude Borgh, Borchwal*)
    111
  and Ghent (*Oudburg*) 62, 64–5, 67, 73,
    77, 79, 83, 90–2, 97, 112, 117, 121
  and Huy (*bourc*) 73, 75, 77, 117, 121
  and Namur 73–5, 77, 117, 121
  and Saint-Omer (*bourc*) 83, 94
  and Tournai (*bourcq*) 86
  and Valenciennes (*novus burgus, Grand
    Bourg*) 102

caritas, caritet, charité, karitet, merchants'
  guild
  and Saint-Omer 124

and Tournai 125
and Valenciennes 102, 123, 126
castellum 3, 8, 26–7, 32
  and Bruges 91
  and Douai 95
  and Ghent (*vetus castellum, novum
    castellum*) 62, 65, 77
  and Namur 32
  and Saint-Omer 64, 94
  and Bourbourg, Burgh, Middelburg,
    Sint-Winoksbergen, Souburg, Veurne
    (*castella recens facta*) 63
castrum 3, 12, **48**
  and Antwerp 14, 39, 40
  and Arras (*castrum sive monasterium*: St
    Vaast Abbey) 9, 10, 60
  and Brussels 111
  and Dinant 7, 48–9
  and Ghent (*castrum Gandavum*: St
    Bavo's Abbey) 12, 61, 65, 77
  and Huy 6, 29, 30, 48, 72
  and Liège 48
  and Lille 106
  and Maastricht 48, 51
  and Namur 7, 31, 48
  and Tongeren 48
censuales 120; *see also homines sancti N.*
Charlemagne 19, 45–6, 61
Charles the Bald 53–4, 57–8
cives 72, 94, 122
civitas 10, 23, 45, 59
  and Antwerp 14, 39, 52, 98
  and Arras 10, 35, 58–9, 60, 82–3
  and Cambrai 58–9, 86
  and Dinant 32
  and Liège 51
  and Maastricht 48
  and Namur 31
  and Tournai 37, 57, 59, 84, 86

Domitian, saint, bishop of
  Tongeren-Maastricht 5, 29, 30